PRAISE FOR *THE SOCIAL CUSTOMER*

"There are plenty of good social media books out there that help you understand how to use Twitter and Facebook. This is not one of them. This is a business book which goes beyond tools, fans, and followers and really helps organizations understand the business impact of the social customer. If your organization has customers, then you need to read this book."

—JACOB MORGAN, PRINCIPAL, CHESS MEDIA GROUP

"Now more than ever, customers are empowered when they conduct business online. *The Social Customer* clearly educates today's business leaders on how to create mature, effective and dynamic processes to leverage social business properly."

—CLATE MASK, COFOUNDER AND CEO, INFUSIONSOFT

"Social Media is no longer just a buzzword—it's a means of doing business with your brand's community. Never in history has it been so simple, and so affordable, to turn regular ol' customers into powerful evangelists. Adam Metz meets the challenge of delivering a definitive guidebook on Social CRM."

—CHRIS PIRILLO, BUSINESS STRATEGIST, PIRILLO.COM

"Adam Metz is a social CRM pioneer, consultant, and practitioner. His book is well-written and engaging, offering practical guidance to anyone interested in this important topic. In a field dominated by self-proclaimed gurus, it's nice to find someone doing solid work. This book is worth an investment of your time!"

—MICHAEL KRIGSMAN, CEO OF ASURET INC.,
AND RESPECTED BLOGGER AT ZDNET

"With breathtakingly rapid influence in the hand of every customer, brands clearly must join the conversation to survive and thrive. Adam Metz clearly lays out the case—and plan—for large-scale social CRM strategy."

—DAVID WEEKLY, FOUNDER, CHAIRMAN, AND CHIEF PRODUCT OFFICER OF PBWORKS

"The new 'breed' of customer wants to deal with brands that offer a positive experience and they want to have that interaction 'when, where and how' they choose. This new customer, the 'social customer', is a reality that businesses must learn to deal with and engage."

—MIKE FAUSCETTE, GVP, SOFTWARE BUSINESS SOLUTIONS, IDC

"A valuable and information read for any business executive looking to drive results and revenue by leveraging social media and social CRM tools. Adam's done a great job of making sure that *The Social Customer* provides tangible strategies to help businesses ensure ROI from these initiatives."

—LARISSA GSCHWANDTNER, VICE PRESIDENT AT SELLING POWER

"Whether you are looking at Social Customer Management for the first time or are a savvy user/believer, Adam Metz's *The Social Customer* is a must-read. Not only is it informative and educational, but it is overwhelmingly entertaining! The background, tools, and resources to make it happen are in the book ... a great roadmap! Adam avoids enterprise marketing vernacular and writes for every audience."

—OWEN HARTMAN, PRINCIPAL, BADGER REAL ESTATE INVESTMENTS

"Metz really gets it——he combines respect, even reverence, for the social customer with deep subject knowledge and a salesperson's zeal. And I hear he's good to his parents."

—MARSHALL LAGER, PRINCIPAL, THIRD IDEA CONSULTING AND A CRM MAGAZINE COLUMNIST

THE SOCIAL CUSTOMER

HOW BRANDS CAN USE SOCIAL CRM TO ACQUIRE, MONETIZE, AND RETAIN FANS, FRIENDS, AND FOLLOWERS

WITHDRAWN

ADAM METZ

NEW YORK   CHICAGO   SAN FRANCISCO
LISBON   LONDON   MADRID   MEXICO CITY   MILAN
NEW DELHI   SAN JUAN   SEOUL   SINGAPORE
SYDNEY   TORONTO

1 2 3 4 5 6 7 8 9 10 DOC/DOC 1 9 8 7 6 5 4 3 2 1

ISBN: 978-0-07-175918-2
MHID: 0-07-175918-2

e-ISBN: 978-0-07-176214-4
e-MHID: 0-07-176214-0

This publication is designed to provide accurate and authoritative information in regard to the subject matter covered. It is sold with the understanding that neither the author nor the publisher is engaged in rendering legal, accounting, securities trading, or other professional services. If legal advice or other expert assistance is required, the services of a competent professional person should be sought.
—From a Declaration of Principles Jointly Adopted
by a Committee of the American Bar Association
and a Committee of Publishers and Associations

McGraw-Hill books are available at special quantity discounts to use as premiums and sales promotions or for use in corporate training programs. To contact a representative, please e-mail us at bulksales@mcgraw-hill.com.

This book is printed on acid-free paper.

To Susie,
my partner in crime,
and Teddy,
my best friend

CONTENTS

FOREWORD

Paul Greenberg

author of CRM at the Speed of Light

I've been around the world of Customer Relationship Management (CRM) for a long time—far more years than any modest person would be willing to admit—though that might be a cover for me saying I'm kind of old and don't want to tell you that.

But I am a veteran in the world of CRM, which, while not having much cachet in the game of life, has a lot in the world of customer strategy.

One thing that's changed in the last seven years in particular is that we now "face" a different kind of customer than we've ever faced before—what Chris Carfi originally labeled "a social customer."

Don't look puzzled. If you use a social network to communicate with your friends, or you text regularly on a mobile device, or recommend something to someone you kind of know but not well that they pay attention to—and you do it via a consumer review site—you're a social customer. Ever gone to complain about a company on a Web site that isn't owned by the company? You're a social customer. Even if you've used your mobile device to order something after reading the reviews on the Web that you simply Googled (how quaint is that?)—you're a social customer.

The thing is, the social customer, who trusts differently and predominates on the social Web, is now the most powerful customer that a business has to deal with. They number probably in the hundreds of millions, which in the grand scheme is a small percentage of customers. However, they have two things that businesses can either fear or see as a lip-smacking opportunity. First, social customers have a lot of influence with their peers. As the Edelman Trust Barometer points out, since 2003, the most trusted source for anyone is a "person like them." Not necessarily someone who you know, but someone instead who has the same interests, the same likes and dislikes, and maybe even the same politics. Second, social customers have a *huge* amount of buying power. For example, according to a 2009 Forrester Research study, 74 percent of all those who can afford to use broadband Internet connectivity are members of social networks, regardless of age. I would guess this high percentage is largely due to Facebook, and stretching it a little, Twitter. This means that those social customers with the loot can also communicate and influence their peers with the dough.

That's the nature of a social customer. And their numbers and power are continually increasing.

Hence the value of Social CRM.

Let me clarify a few things before we go on to why I think Adam's book is something that should be read by everyone out there.

Social CRM is an extension of CRM—it recognizes that not only do strategies and programs for customer engagement have to be formulated, but the processes needed to operationally handle the business on behalf of those engagement programs must be created and they have to be run. The culture that accepts that the social customer now actually can control the conversation has to be in place while businesses...Wait a minute, Greenberg, you're probably thinking. What do you mean, controls the conversation? How do customers do that? That makes no sense, Greenberg, you lunatic.

Don't get twisted up too much here. It's not that complicated. What I mean is that customers have the wherewithal to damage or support your business, without your permission. It also means they can do this in channels your business doesn't own. Simple. No more nor less than that.

Okay, back to what I was saying. The culture that accepts that the social customer actually can now control the conversation must be in place even as businesses continue to set their own specific goals on how they will run and what they want to achieve—with the customers in mind, but not acquiescing to everything the customer wants. If businesses did acquiesce to everything, we'd all be flying for free. Social CRM is a response to this social customer.

Which brings me to this book and Adam Metz.

Adam is a bright, dynamic guy and he knows from where he speaks. What makes this book as good as it is—and me even willing to write the foreword to it, not something I do every day—is that Adam did something here that few others have done. He's been able to apply Social CRM principles to thinking about a brand.

He manages to mix concepts, frameworks, and practical advice into a heady and rich brew that pretty much lets readers—especially those in marketing and sales—know what they need to do when it comes to dealing with this new breed of customer. What makes these concepts particularly important at this juncture is that marketing is changing dramatically. No longer can marketers push messages at potential customers. Instead, they now have to be the first line of engagement with the customer. That's not an easy transition when it comes to figuring out not just how your brand will engage, but even what your brand now represents. Adam Metz provides you with a way to actually begin to untangle this morass—simply, with some humor, and even links to pop culture.

Adam's book is a welcome addition to the industry's literature and to a library of business books that are likely to be used enough to be dog-eared quickly. I would not only highly recommend that you read the book and figure out how to use it as a guidepost for your approach to your brand via the social customer, but then I'd read it again, because the likelihood is that you missed something else you can use. Since you own it, a second time around is easy. But I will also guarantee you'll be coming back to it more than a few times—because the information on using Social CRM for your brand efforts is going to be valuable to you for years to come.

PREFACE

Brian Solis

author of *The End of Business as Usual* and *Engage!*

Social media represents an important shift in the evolution of CRM.

Social networks such as Twitter, Facebook, Google+, LinkedIn, et al, empower consumers to connect with one another, with the brands they value and to also share their experiences with friends, fans and followers. In a traditional CRM model, businesses would recognize this new activity and attempt to introduce it into an existing framework of methodologies, software, and processes.

To effectively manage customer relationships, we must assume that the individual is open to engagement. However, the shift that social media presents is *profound* and forces businesses to rethink the idea of management and engagement.

The social customer as you'll soon learn, isn't amenable to existing infrastructures that define "customer relationship management." In fact, that's part of the reason they're in social networks in the first place. They seek to *distance* themselves from the rigmarole of messaging, sales, advertising, spam, and cold calling.

In social media, consumers are in control of their own experiences. As such, relationships are not something that can be easily managed, especially within the dated frameworks and philosophies that govern today's businesses. Just because we add the word "social" in front of CRM or even customer doesn't mean that businesses understand the dynamics of what it means to be social.

As my good friend Paul Greenberg states in his foreword, businesses are introduced to a new kind of customer. They're important to the future of business not because of how, when or where they connect with one another but instead, *why*. Sure they're influential. Yes they're connected. Certainly social customers are social. But it is the empowerment they've taken and the influence they exert that changes everything. No, social customers are not looking to be "managed." Nor are they looking to succumb to the 3Fs (friends, fans and followers). They're looking to engage on a peer-to-peer level where mutual value is now the ante to engage.

Adam Metz and I go back many years. In fact, we were active on many fronts together during the rise of social media. Here, Adam is at his best. After reading this book, you'll not only understand how to acquire, monetize, and retain the social customer, you'll learn something far more important. By the time you reach the last page, you'll find that the future of business lies in the ability to adapt processes, methodologies, and frameworks to not just react to a new type of customer, but instead help guide their experiences as a peer and as a leader.

ACKNOWLEDGMENTS

It's impossible to string together a social business book without a huge string of thank-yous.

To the godfather, Paul Greenberg, your writing has been a huge influence on me, and your good business sense has guided me well. I look forward to many more years of guidance. Rich and Brian, thanks again for your contributions to the afterword too. The book would not have the same flavor without any of you. To Jeff Seroy and Christina Harcar: this whole project would not have come together without your input.

Christina and Melissa, you guys were my super-amazing support team through the years at Metz Consulting, and I'm so proud of both of you. Also, to Jason, Jesse, Throck, and Brett at LaunchSquad; I couldn't have ever gotten here without Brett's encouragement to get me to write my first book.

Ethan—you've been a great editor, and have always kept my feet planted firmly on the ground. Knox, Zach, and Daina—thanks for the tireless attention to detail and the constant reality checks. Sara, Elizabeth, and Ann—you are three of the best publishing marketers and PR geniuses that a guy could ever hope to work with.

Steven Kiefel and David Libby—you two have been trusted advisors to me over the years, and I really value your influence on this book.

To the vendors, especially Oracle—I really appreciate your timely help on this book.

Dad, your influence on my growth as a consultant was tremendous, and I want to thank you, Mom, Rachel, and Noah for the big support in the last year—the good parts, and the not so good parts.

J, you were a huge influence on the proposal process; your feedback and friendship means a lot to me. I could not have done this project without your support and kindness.

Alie, I wanted to thank you for your support in the very early days of Metz Consulting; I would not be where I am today without you.

Last but not least, Susie—I love you so much. Thanks for being my best friend, my editor, my client coach, and my Teddy-fan roommate. I hope to write many more books to Thin Lizzy with you building terrariums in the next room.

INTRODUCTION

It's possible that many of the readers of this book will understand how I grew up, and how it has influenced my worldview, and how it can make their lives—and the lives of their colleagues, friends, and customers—a lot better.

Although I was born in 1977 during what became known as the first punk era, six days before Elvis Presley died, I was a child of the *second* punk era. I grew up in the confused late '80s and early '90s, in the middle of a DIY punk culture, in an affluent San Francisco suburb, Palo Alto, at the top of the Silicon Valley, at the beginning of the boom years.

I bought my first punk CD at the tender age of 12, at the CFY record store near the railroad tracks in downtown Palo Alto (it's long since been demolished to make way for the Palo Alto Medical Foundation). But I bought most of my "corporate" Clash and Sex Pistols tapes at Tower Records in the strip mall.

I spent my formative high school and college years of 1994 to 1999 promoting punk shows in California and Wisconsin.

The reason I'm telling you all of this is because the culture I grew up in was one that was *DIY*: do it yourself. We put on our own shows, posted our own flyers, put out our own records, and hauled our own gear. We did these things because there was no one there to do it for us, and because the record industry in the '80s and '90s ignored what many of "the kids" really wanted, spoon-feeding us Madonna, Milli Vanilli, and Prince. The DIY punk scene responded with Nirvana and, later, the tech-geek DIY scene gave us Napster, and, well, you know what happened to the music industry after those guys hit it.

Even before that, however, DIY culture in the '80s, in my opinion, helped give rise to the social customer. Consider, for example, Los Angeles hardcore punk band Black Flag, who are frequently thought of as the first or at least the archetypal American hardcore punk band.[1] Their cultural influence on DIY culture was tremendous. Black Flag not only influenced thousands of individuals to start bands and play music, but also to rebel against American cultural norms, to *think different*, and really *act different*, years before Apple Computer turned the phrase into advertising copy.

I don't think that the social customer, as we know that customer, today, could exist without that DIY culture that arose in the late '70s and early '80s. It wasn't just a "punk" thing; DIY inspired all of the computing culture, too—the geeks who got together and formed BBSs (bulletin board services), home computer developers, and even early computer graphic designers and video editors. Is Facebook's Mark Zuckerberg "punk rock"? Hardly. But the type of thinking it takes to create something like Facebook? Absolutely. While using social media and becoming a social customer is hardly an act of rebellion, at some point it was. My Yelp.com profile, which contains a few hundred restaurant and hotel reviews, is hardly controversial today, but when I launched it five years ago, in 2006—it was a pretty controversial platform, because it undercut Zagat and the local newspaper.

A lot of people in my field call Paul Greenberg "the Godfather"— he's known as the preeminent voice in Social Customer Relationship Management (his book *CRM at the Speed of Light* is probably the clearest, best book on the subject). The combination of DIY culture and Paul Greenberg's words represent, to me, the yin and the yang of the social customer. Greenberg's eye-in-the-sky view reflects on the decades-long series of business changes that have brought us to this point, and the DIY feet-on-the-street view illustrates the cultural changes that have been percolating for over 30 years, making this evolution possible.

I've been on the Internet, in one way or another, for over 20 years, since I was 13, in 1990. Technically, as a 33-year-old, I'm a Gen Xer, but in my heart I *feel* more like a Millennial because I was handed my first computer at the age of five (a Commodore 64), and taught to program by my physicist/management consultant dad, Phil.

I'm going to make one promise here: to the best of my ability, *The Social Customer* will explicitly tell you how your company can drive revenue from the social Web and have mutually valuable and profitable relationships with the social customer. Driving millions of people to interact with your brand (10 to 500 million) and making that kind of money, on a large scale, is extraordinarily resource intensive, but it usually yields amazing results. Nearly three-quarters of your customers (B2B and B2C) are now the social customer, according to Forrester Research's 2008 and 2009 Social Technographics studies. If your customers are under the age of 25, nearly 90 to 95 percent of them are the social customer.

If you're into recruiting dozens of people from different departments and mobilizing them into a million-dollar social-business action machine that generates huge business outcomes, awesome. If not, you might want to put this book right back on the shelf and get a more low-key business book that will help you fulfill more modest expectations. (If you're looking for guides to the tools of social media and how to turn your public relations into "social media PR," just enter the code BOOKSTORE on www.adammetz.com at the bottom of the page or go to tinyurl.com/metzbooks. This book won't help with those objectives, because it's about *social business*, not social media.[2])

For any consumer brand, when it comes to social media strategy or Social Customer Management, there are many paths to take, and many ways to screw it up. Companies have been engaging and selling their wares on the Internet since the pre-Web days, in the early '90s, and this is no longer an immature discipline. The fresh-faced college graduates who launched the first consumer-brand Web sites are now 39 years old. Those days are two-thirds of a generation behind us.

I remember seeing consumer-branded content online the first time I logged on to Prodigy, one April night in 1991. As the Web evolved, some brands jumped on earlier than others. For example, Pizza Hut crafted the world's first online pizza storefront in 1994.

Other brands, like airlines, waited until nearly 1999 or 2000 to bring their offerings to the digital space. One of my clients, Chris Clark of the San Francisco Travel Association, was largely responsible for that push for USAir. Billions of dollars were made in e-commerce in the 1990s, and U.S. e-commerce revenues hit the $20 billion mark around 2006, no small amount.

Since 2007, with the rise of the social Web, and so-called Web 2.0 and Web 3.0 technologies, consumer brands have found themselves in an awkward place: Yogi Berra's proverbial fork in the road: "If you find a fork in the road, take it." Some brands desperately want to engage with their customers and prospects on the new social Web. Some are deeply fearful. Most are somewhere in between. There's no easy extreme to point to.

My client, Christina Harcar, Director of Business Development at Audible, put it best: "A lot of brands are accustomed to thinking proactively and strategically, but they just don't have the tool kit to be proactive and strategic at work anymore." To complicate matters further, most companies confuse strategy with planning, and planning with strategy, to paraphrase Alan Weiss, the author of *Million Dollar Consulting*.[3] MILLION

In 2009, I spoke with Lorelei (some names have been changed throughout the book), a senior-level Hawaiian hotel executive. She was unsure about whether deploying a social Web strategy for one of her properties would be a good idea.

"From everything I've heard," she said, "the travel industry and hotels in particular are still having challenges monetizing social media. I can completely understand how important it is to manage customer feedback on [travel review] sites like TripAdvisor, but I'm having a very difficult time figuring out how I could sell my company on spending money on a social media strategy when I have no data to prove that it will work."

Well, it's a tough question, but it's one that I'm going to answer in this book, with case studies and examples that actually contain value assessments like sales figures, profit metrics, and market-share stats.

There are two types of social customer management strategy I'll address in *The Social Customer*: structural and tactical. The structural strategy is more goal-oriented, and it dictates when certain initiatives will be phased in, how certain metrics will be achieved, and how key performance indicators will be measured. Tactical strategy shows you how to build the humans-and-technology infrastructure that supports the structural strategy.

The notions of lifestyle marketing, branding, and behavioral targeting are still new to many consumer brands and have not been addressed thoroughly in previous books about the social Web. Here's how lifestyle marketing comes into play: when the average consumer thinks of a consumer brand, 90 percent of the time they're thinking of a lifestyle brand (Victoria's Secret, Nike, Abercombie and Fitch). These are brands that symbolize the dreams and aspirations of the groups to whom they belong. The reason they succeed is because they convince their potential customers that the identity they dreamed they would have will become a reality, if they continually purchase this product.

Lifestyle marketing was all the rage around 2003, and there was even a good book written on the subject.[4] But with the rise of the social Web, the basic tenets of lifestyle marketing have fallen by the wayside for many consumer brands. The big idea with lifestyle marketing was that brands had to learn to go beyond examining their consumers in demographic segments and break them up into segments according to what we can now call "light" behavioral segments such as Singles, Teenagers, College Students, or Seniors. The rationale for this type of customer view is that gender roles have drastically changed since women entered the workforce two generations ago, and that typical gender-based purchasing roles ("the man buys the car, the woman buys the flatware") are long dead.

Although the researchers behind lifestyle marketing didn't tell us how to engage the social customer, their research serves as the crucial missing link between the demographic-driven customer "conversations" of the '80s and '90s (if you can call them that, as they were particularly one-way), and the full-blown social customer conversations of today. To put a rock 'n' roll metaphor on it, if demographic marketing was the Blues, lifestyle marketing was late '40s and early '50s Rhythm and Blues. That would make early social media and social customer management sort of like Bill Haley or Chuck Berry—the sign that something new had hit the scene, changing the environment, permanently.

Since 2005 the push for brands to construct meaningful, assessable social Web strategy has come from two big developments: (1) consumer intent-driven enterprise is becoming the most successful way to run a consumer brand, and (2) established, nonassessable communications media like radio, television, and newsprint are falling away, and matter less and less to young consumers every day. Remember, even if only the forms of media consumption (i.e., watching TV, reading the news, listening to music) are shifting online, there is a clear case that the way people under the age of 50 are consuming media has drastically changed as well. You don't need a $1,000 Forrester or a $100 Pew Internet and American Life study to tell you that.

The very nature of the way consumers "consume" content has profoundly changed. People don't just watch TV anymore—they stack playlists of their favorite shows, comment on them, share them with friends on Facebook, and vote on them via text messages on their mobile phones. The same radical changes have happened to the way consumers research their purchases (like Lorelei's Hawaiian resort hotel rooms) and the way they complete those purchases (by purchasing movie tickets on their iPhones, standing on the corner, a block from the theater).

Before we go any further: if you want to cite Malcolm Gladwell's "10,000 Hour Rule" as the criteria for being an expert on a given subject, it's a test that I've passed. I've been writing on and executing social Web strategies since 2005, and on that time, I've worked for over 75 companies. When you add up all of the time I spent working on behalf of my clients and employers, you get more than 10,000 hours. What I'm saying is, I can safely call myself an expert on the subject of managing the social customer.

But being a "social media expert," "social media strategist," "social media consultant," or even a "social CRM consultant," is only a passing title. At the time of this writing, 16,000 other people on Twitter claim to hold the same title. I'm fairly certain that this occupation will change names and duties over the coming years, but I also know that people who engage in crafting solid brand strategy will be around as long as there are brands, and as long as there are customers who purchase the goods and services provided by those brands.[5]

Let's take 30 seconds to dissect the title of this book.

The social customer is the type of customer brands have essentially been dealing with since consumer-generated media began. You can trace this lineage back to the punk rock 'zines of the 1970s (when cheap photocopiers made it possible for consumers to make their own content), right through the rise of the Internet in the late 1990s (where you didn't even need to have a 'zine or a copier). Slowly but surely, since around the mid-'90s, the customer took control of the conversation about brands, and has begun talking to other customers.

When I worked in Palo Alto's famous Peninsula Creamery, in high school, if a customer was dissatisfied with the way I made their milk shake, all they could do was complain to the manager, and statistically speaking, an absolutely irate customer might tell 11 friends about this negative experience. These days all an angry customer would need to do is take 60 seconds to write a bad Yelp.com review on their iPhone, on the spot, and potentially millions of people could read it.

If you don't believe me about the rise of the social customer, go to blog search engine Google Blog Search and type your company's name into the search box. Brands are standing on a precipice, trying to dance with the social customer. Sometimes the "dance" works out wonderfully. Sometimes it sends the brand into out-and-out disaster.

On the social Internet, some consumer brands have fallen flat on their faces in recent years (Wal-Mart), some have succeeded beyond their wildest dreams (Carnival Cruises, Jack in the Box, Marriott), and some have emerged loudly flailing, with no clear results either way (Skittles, Snickers). The infrastructure that served consumer brands to communicate with their constituents for the better part of the last eight decades has pretty much fallen away. Young people are abandoning television and radio for the Internet at an incredible rate, and regardless of radio analysts' manipulation of the numbers, the number of young adults and teens flocking to radio is still less than 93 percent, proving that radio has barely rebounded from its all time low in September 2005, declining 22 percent from its 1989 peak in 155 top markets.[6] And then there's the assessment piece: most brands don't know how to quantitatively measure their success on the social web, or track and monetize social customer data. They just don't know which metrics matter around the social customer.

In a 2008 blog post, Clay Shirky quoted *New York Times* online editor Gordy Thompson as saying, "When a 14-year-old kid can blow up your business in his spare time, not because he hates you but because he loves you, then you got a problem." Thompson said this 15 years ago, after the early online piracy of Dave Barry's newspaper columns was traced to a Midwest teen, who had been copying the work and posting it online for the sole purpose of sharing it with others—simply because he couldn't find the Dave Barry column in his local newspaper. As Shirky suggests in his prescient essay, we're now in that awkward in-between time where the old "stuff" has been thrown in the garbage but the new "stuff" has not yet been completely adopted (or normalized).

That's the other thing we're going to talk about: failure.

I ran into Zynga's Alex Le[7] at a cocktail party. He was raving about a conference called FAILcon, which goes against the grain of those who celebrate brands that have "won" or accomplished their business objectives. FAILcon highlights folks brave enough to explain why their companies' initiatives have failed.[8]

It would be myopic for a book like this to characterize the entire state of the brand-customer relationship as diffuse chaos, and then prescribe a single panacea (or a single set of tactics) to fix it all. *The Social Customer* only strives to illustrate the higher-level strategic decision making needed before any execution can take place and before the customer can be managed on the social Web. The tools and technologies will continue to change, but the strategies will remain. One question remains: is your brand ready to engage customers head-on, and allow them to sell your product or services to each other, perhaps disintermediating parts of your supply chain?

Readers, we did something really cool in this book. In a few dozen places, there are words in the text that are called out LIKE THIS. To download the bonus content—cool stuff like whitepapers, presentations, videos, mp3s or even conference ticket discounts—just go to our Web site at www. adammetz.com and look for the MetzBox. It's at the very bottom of every page inside the Web site. Just enter the words from the text, and your downloads will be served up to you, super-fast.

By the way, if you're thinking this is a completely original idea, I completely stole it from sales genius Jeffrey Gitomer.

DISCLOSURES

The following brands mentioned in the book have been Metz Consulting clients: Hollywood Park Racetrack, Waggin' Train (now a part of Nestlé), Wente Vineyards, The San Francisco Convention & Visitors Bureau (now the SFTA).

Regarding vendors, my company, Metz Consulting was vendor-agnostic, and we recommended the best technology selection for each client. We were a Salesforce customer and we *were* a Salesforce partner until March 31, 2010. Metz Consulting did not accept kickbacks or year-end rebates for any vendor-recommended products. Metz Consulting also did not accept referral fees for referrals to other service providers. We are not currently formally partnered with any software brands.

That said, Metz Consulting did allow our clients to use our Campaign Monitor e-mail system for a small surcharge (a few hundred dollars per year), and we do use a number of affiliate programs, including Amazon Associates, for books that we recommend. We also receive no-cost software from InsideView, valued at about $3,500 per year, in exchange for limited comarketing, and a few blog posts. We also attended conferences at no cost—probably four or five per year, in exchange for blog posts—but we generally pay our own way for travel. Any other disclosure-related questions can be sent to adam@adam metz.com, and we'll reply right away. It's critical that you can read this book and know where any bias might come from. Also, pretty much none of the vendors like me all that much, because I'm always poking holes in their game and giving them grief about how they could make their products better, while leaving them with the bar tab.

1

THE BRAND AS A SOCIAL OBJECT AND THE BUSINESS CASE FOR SOCIAL CRM

W hy would a brand want to be a social object? And what in the heck *is* a social object?

Brands want to be talked about so people will buy their products and services. Consumers want to interact with brands that make the products and services they purchase, day-to-day. Brands also want consumers to relate to them, become highly loyal, and buy that same brand for the rest of their lives. Brands will disclose that lifetime customers can have values (customer lifetime value, or CLV) of tens or hundreds of thousands of dollars, depending on the brand. Even a brand that sells a seemingly low-value product can have a relatively high customer lifetime value.

A social object is something that people look at, discuss, and pass from person to person, putting their own stamp on it. An iPod is a social object—people make (or buy) custom cases for them, and integrate them into their outfits as accessories. A Lady Gaga song is a social object, when 400 people record their own interpretation of it and post it on YouTube. Post-it notes are social objects when employees at your company cover a departing coworker's cube with them and post it on the Internet. So, why would your company want to become one? Notoriety? Fame? Wealth?

THE BRAND LIES DOWN ON BROADWAY: HOW DID WE GET INTO THIS MESS?

A legendary (and bad) marketing joke comes to mind. A client walks into their ad agency's conference room and says, "I want a chicken." What this means is that the client wants the marketing agency to create something that will make their brand "viral," just like Burger King's groundbreaking "Subservient Chicken" campaign. They want customers of the brand (or people who, until recently, had never heard of them) to evangelize the brand, and get their friends to go out and purchase whatever the brand sells. But to say that the whole brand-as-social-object idea started with Burger King's Subservient Chicken would be a gross oversimplification. Consumers have been interacting with brands long before that.

A Brief History of Consumer Brands that Tried Very Hard

Let's get one thing straight: brands are nothing new. Four hundred years ago companies and multinational brands fulfilled consumers' needs for products and services. The notion of branded consumer products (like the shoes on your feet or the granola bar you had for lunch) emerged in the years following the Industrial Revolution. Nineteenth century factory owners realized that the mass-produced goods they were creating (e.g., a pair of leather boots) needed some way to be differentiated from locally produced goods, to allow consumers to place their trust in a product that was not created in the local area.

Consumer brands, as we know them today, didn't really exist until the middle of the nineteenth and into the early twentieth century, and the roots of the earliest consumer brands that are still well known today. Food brands like Campbell Soup Company (1869) and Kellogg Cereal Company (1901) date back to this time. Big-box retail giants like Macy's and Sears began in 1858 and 1886, respectively. The big automotive brands like Ford and GM didn't come along until over a generation later, in 1903 and 1908, respectively.

The first major milestone on the road to "brand as social object" was simply the birth of the concept of "brand personality." We see this concept begin to emerge in late nineteenth century advertising for brands like Aunt Jemima, and soon after, in the early twentieth century, Quaker Oats.

If the years between the Civil War and World War One mark the first phase of consumer brand evolution, then the second phase would be the transitional period between the latter and the early 1960s, where brand personality (the notion that a brand can have a set of emotional characteristics, much like a person) became truly ubiquitous. It became necessary then for a brand to take on a personality or a set of emotional characteristics.[1] PERSONALITY

The second major milestone on the road to "brand as social object" was the Creative Revolution, the watershed era in brand advertising. The Creative Revolution was to brands what the Beatles' *Sergeant Pepper* was to rock 'n' roll: it threw away the old rulebook and made it okay for all brands to have their own personality. Brand advertising emerged into its modern age in the late 1950s and early 1960s, and this came to full flower in the Creative Revolution. Led by agencies like Doyle Dane Bernbach, Young & Rubicam, BBDO, and Ogilvy & Mather, consumer brands began to make a conscious effort to drive the conversation with consumers, rather than take earnest stabs at what would today be seen as annoying "suggestive" conversation: "Try a Lucky instead of a sweet!" An example a of brand-driven conversation can be seen in Volkswagen's famous "Think Small" and "Lemon" ads (DDB, 1959).

For about 35 years, after the late 1960s, brands existed in a murky in-between stage where they could talk to consumers and consumers could talk back, but through a variety of different channels, not directly through one single channel. Consumers could write letters to their favorite brands or show their support (or lack thereof) at the cash register, but brand-consumer interaction was still fairly limited. Around 1990 this all changed, when brands began developing interactive content. The whole notion of brands being interactive grew as CD-ROM drives started becoming a standard feature on computers.[2]

The third milestone on the road to brands becoming social objects occurred in 1993, when branded content began appearing on the Web. (Although the World Wide Web was invented in 1989, consumer-generated, branded content actually appeared on the Internet before the existence of the Web. Conversations about brands repeatedly had been popping up on pre-Web bulletin board systems (BBSs) from the late 1970s until the 1990s.) Some of the early notable brands on the Internet included MTV (1993), now-defunct early e-commerce brand First Virtual (1994), and Pizza Hut. At this point brands became something that could be interacted with, in a direct manner. In 1994 a student at UC Santa Cruz, using a fast Internet connection in the campus library, could direct his browser to a primeval version of MTV.com, interact with 10 or 15 different facets of the brand, and even communicate directly with the brand and its employees.

The fourth and final milestone in this evolution to "brand as social object" was the Groundswell phenomenon,[3] the final, sweeping convergence of social technologies and Internet user behaviors that allowed the voice of the individual consumer (or groups of consumers) to become as "loud" as the brands themselves. While a broad definition of the Groundswell would paint it as a 15-year growth, this milestone chiefly occurred between 2003 and today, when social technology use grew most quickly.

Just like the second milestone (the Creative Revolution), the timing of the Groundswell is also fuzzy, because it didn't occur all at once. In fact, it's still occurring. GROUNDSWELL The Groundswell took a lot of consumer brands by surprise. Some brands experienced tremendous growth and measurable results (Proctor & Gamble, Dell, Starbucks), while others have endured painful, awkward, unexpected surprises, Domino's Pizza and Yum Brands/Taco Bell, to name two.[4]

The Few that Became Social Objects

Whether consumer brands ever aspired to become "social objects" for much of the last 100 years is questionable. Brands have always wanted to be talked about, but whether they wanted to be talked *with* is up for debate. I know plenty of marketing managers, VPs, EVPs, and CEOs who would prefer *not* to interact with their customers. Luxury brands, especially, pride themselves on being completely aloof— their appearance of not caring what their consumers have to say (or think) is part of their appeal. This cool and distant brand personality is actually part of their brand concept, and to surrender some of this to a socially influenced openness would dilute their brand equity.

After reading Ralph Lauren's biography, *Genuine Authentic*, one would be hard-pressed to imagine Lauren trying to tap the wisdom of his longtime consumers for advice on how their next men's fashion line should look—this "wisdom of the crowd" notion goes *completely* against the line of thinking of most consumer brands over the last 100 years, if not longer. And believe me, there are pundits and writers who vociferously cry out against the "wisdom of crowds"—you'd only need to read the first page or two of Andrew Keen's controversial *The*

Cult of the Amateur to understand this sometimes cogent argument.

Consumer brands cut from the "I don't care" cloth have cast their brand concept and personality on the premise that they do not need to take advice from their consumers or become a part of the conversation. And they usually feel this way until times get tough, revenues drop, and market share begins to erode.

The common thread I hear from brands afraid to become social is that while they want to know what their customers are saying, they realize that they can use relatively inexpensive software (and their PR firm or demand generation agency) to figure this out for no more than about $100,000 per year. That's small change to a multinational or enterprise brand.

The entire notion of monitoring what consumers are saying about a brand is somewhat of a new thing as well. Until about 2007 full-scale assessment of what consumers were saying about a given brand was dependent on extrapolating conclusions from representative survey samples or performing a qualitative assessment. Until relatively recently it was almost technically impossible to monitor or detect changes in sentiment in what millions of consumers were saying (or feeling) about a given brand. Prior to the advent of the social Web, the University of Michigan launched American Customer Service Index (ACSI) surveys (1994), but customer satisfaction trends had been "flat as a pancake" since then.[5]

What trips up consumer brands in terms of becoming "social objects" is that brands are sold on the value of knowing consumer sentiment and being able to act on it: "Do consumers like and trust our company, the Gap? Are they still open to the idea of buying things from the Gap after learning that we had to terminate business with 23 factories because they were using child labor?"[6] They're not yet sold on the value of letting consumers interact with them. For example, as of late 2010 Southwest Airlines had a little over a million people interacting with ("following") their brand on the microblog platform Twitter, but the actual "hard value" of that marketing asset is unclear.

To calculate the financial value of a piece of social collateral like this Twitter account, I propose that brands use what is called "Crisis Valuation": How much would the brand be willing to pay, *in a crisis*, to have this asset. You may recall the Menu Foods 2007 Melamine tainting scandal in which certain pet food made by the company were sickening and killing household cats and dogs.[7] In such a crisis, the company would have wanted to directly communicate with a few million customers and prospective customers before or just as news of the issue hit major news sites. While it may be possible for a brand to make fast, sweeping changes to a branded destination Web site (i.e., changing Menufoods.com on a moment's notice to reflect news of the incident), or plan an impromptu press conference, it might be more valuable to the brand, a better crisis response, and simply more calming to consumers to first respond through two-way social channels.

Sometimes, becoming a social object is actually the cheapest, easiest option. How much is this social asset worth to Menu Foods? Ask their PR department what they'd be willing to pay to communicate directly with a quarter-million customers within a few minutes of the first sick pet. I'd be willing to guess that the answer is about a million dollars, maybe a little more. In a crisis event, I'd envision a brand communicating with customers roughly every 15 to 30 minutes for the first 48 hours; the location-based expectations, for the social customer, sometimes differ.

"With real-time social media like Twitter, the user expects real-time feedback, which is not always possible," according to Dave Andrews, founder of Devious Media. "With a stand-alone community based on the company's brand [a branded community], they are more accepting to turnaround times within 24 hours."

As managers of organizations, we didn't reach this early point of "brand as social object" by accident. We arrived at it because people wanted the ability to communicate with the things they touch and feel every day. They wanted the ability to tell Apple that they disliked certain features of the new iPhone, or to tell the local supermarket that they wanted them to carry more organic produce. More and more people are becoming "social customers."

The Social Customer

This entire book is written about the social customer, and the social customer is *your* customer. It's the customer who didn't exist at the turn of the twenty-first century, because the social technologies that exist today—social networks, geolocation technologies that let customers "check in," and so on—weren't yet invented. (Though blogs existed 10 years ago, the user base was very small.)

There are *two* criteria you can use to determine whether a given customer is a social customer. The first one is that the social customer uses social technologies with regular frequency. As of this writing, it's safe to say that if you're doing business in the United States, at least 73 percent of your customers are the social customer[8]—if they are anything like the teenage customers of the clothing chain Wet Seal for example, which we'll examine later in the book, your customer base might be 90-plus percent social customers. GROUNDPROFILE If you're in other countries, like metropolitan parts of China, this number could be as high as 80 percent, and in less "socially technographic" nations like France, that number could be as low as 50 percent. (To check where your consumers are, using demographic information, [9] have your team utilize the awesome Forrester social technographic tool, which came out alongside Josh Bernoff's book, *Empowered*.[10])

The second condition for "social customers" is that they are equipped with the tools to talk about your brand to your brand and to other consumers (their "followers" or "friends," usually) in an *uncensored* environment. For example, if your company is a multinational beer brand that has less than stellar labor practices, and you erase your customers' comments about this from the brand's Facebook page and send takedown notices and cease-and-desist letters to bloggers that write about it, you're not engaging with social customers—you're harassing and alienating them. To engage social customers, in this case, would be to dialogue with them, and state the brand's case. And to track and code all of the negative and positive responses, and turn the relevant ones into actionable items.

We're at a strange point, where some brands have fully completed a social transformation, catering to the social consumer, and some haven't. We're now at the culmination of a 25-year transformation in the business ecosystem.[11]

VALUE, SUPPLY, AND DEMAND CHAINS

A *value chain* is a business management concept invented by Harvard business economist Michael Porter[12] in the '80s, referring to a chain of activities for a company that operates in a specific industry. For example, a value chain for an airline would include *primary activities* like marketing and sales, inbound logistics (getting all the physical components to have a functional airline), operations (making sure planes take off and land safely on time), and outbound logistics (selling excess inventory, repairing planes). *Secondary activities* support the primary activities, like human resources (hiring/firing/supporting airline employees), firm infrastructure (structuring how the airline will work, internally), technology (figuring out what technology the airline will run on), and procurement (buying planes, fuel, and that yummy airline food). If you break it down further, the value chain is basically made up of a supply chain and a demand chain.

Back in the late 1980s the corporate world was driven by product and demand—an arrangement called the corporate ecosystem. Back then there were *separate* demand and supply chains. Supply chain technology was growing, especially with booms in information technology, process analysis, and cost analysis. If you were a supply chain focused on purchasing, manufacturing, and distribution, this growth was great.

The demand chain, however—composed of marketing, sales, and

service—had a much slower evolution. When your supply and demand chains are growing at a different pace and are therefore not linked, the supply people can't get good demand forecasts from those people driving demand (sales, marketing, and product development people). When projections are off, it causes merchandise to be out-of-stock (no available seats on airline flights, for example). Even worse, the excessive cost of supply, when demand spikes, goes up and down. The supply and demand people begin to freak out on one another when experiencing something called the *bullwhip effect*. This happens when demand patterns get volatile, sometimes as a result of big sales promotions, which unintentionally drive up supply chain costs and service issues. The social customer *really* doesn't like this.

Partly driven by evolution in the supply chain, in the late 1990s until about 2006 we entered what is now known as the customer-driven corporate ecosystem. The fancy phrase "enterprise value chain" was born then, meaning that customers are actually active participants in creating value, not passive recipients of it.

The Personal Value Chain

Around 2006 everything changed again, and the customer ecosystem finally arrived. This is when the era of the social customer truly began. The definition of the customer was completely altered. Before, a customer was a person who gave you money for goods and services. Today, a customer is *anyone* your company exchanges value with—for the airline we mentioned, it could be the person who pays money to get on the flight from New York to San Francisco, the employee who repairs the plane, or the people who work at Travelocity who help the airlines sell tickets.

This marks the development of the *personal value chain*, a term coined by Paul Greenberg implying that each person actually has their own value chain, and that they're consciously aware of it. Today's customer wants to cocreate value with their "suppliers" at varying levels of interactivity. In the mid-'90s, customers were thrilled to come home from 7-Eleven with a mini CD-R that was attached to the top of their Slurpee Cup. In the eyes of the brands, that alone was cocreation—customer comes home from 7-Eleven, plays with the interactive content, maybe even goes to the brand's Web site. The personal value chain is the evolution of that 7-Eleven CD-R promotion. It's when Virgin Airlines offers customers a 33.3 percent discount on their plane ticket, in exchange for posting an awkward family photo in their Awkward Family Photo contest. This evolution didn't take very long (1996 to 2010), but it was a *total* shift in the way customers and brands interact.

Let's take another look at the airline industry today, through the eyes of the present-day customer ecosystem. A few brands that are decidedly "social": Southwest, Virgin America, and JetBlue are three of them. About a dozen are not, among them some of the largest brands in the industry, including United/Continental, American, and Delta. The big difference between the social ones and the nonsocial ones is that the first three generate content, engage with their customers on a daily basis, and have an enormous "intake valve," allowing them to be constantly in touch with their customer base.

WHAT IT TAKES FOR A BRAND TO BE A SOCIAL OBJECT

Whereas back in 1973 it might be enough for a brand to have a cute mascot, a catchy jingle, and feature real customers in their ads (think: "Leggo my Eggo!"), today the rules have completely changed. I would like to propose three criteria of a social object (as a useful tool to the social customer):

1. Near real-time response to the social customer (or at least the influential ones), on the social Web
2. Synthesis of social customer community data through Social

Customer Relationship Management systems (we'll explain how to do this in Chapter 4)

3. A strategic engagement model around the social customer (the "where" of the social customer, within the organization) that takes social data and pipelines it into operational work flows

These three criteria *couldn't* have been met in 1995 or even in 2003—the mass of social customer data just didn't exist yet. When brands act as social objects, customers hear them, but brands hear their customers, too. Now that all the technologies have arrived to allow brands to directly engage with their customers, and as there are fewer and fewer customers who have no interest in using this type of technology,[13] one question remains. Should all consumer brands pursue this objective—to become a social object—or do the risks outweigh the benefits?

What's held a lot of brands back from becoming social objects is the idea of the brand hijack, described more thoroughly in the Alex Wippurfurth book, *Brand Hijack,* published in 2006.[14] HIGHJACK Timothy Jones, CEO of social media monitoring and management company Buzzient, was telling me about experiences he had in the early '90s with brands that were reluctant to even get on the Internet. "They say things like, 'We're never going to have a Web page. Most of our people have no need for e-mail, so we're not going to even give them e-mail addresses.'" This view toward the customer-driven corporate ecosystem lasted about six years, from 1993 to 1999. By 1999 the Internet had become so engrained in consumer culture, it would have been reckless for a business or organization not to have a Web presence.

Should Your Brand Become a Social Object?

There are a few key questions to consider when a brand is trying to determine whether it wants to become a social object. It's assumed that brands will know consumer sentiment regardless of whether they wish to become social, due to the recent decrease in the cost of social media monitoring software. These questions are serious questions about your brand's values, and how far the brand wants to move into this new worldview, the customer ecosystem:

1. Does the company want to be able to talk to its customers immediately and directly without a third-party intermediary (i.e., a television station, journalist, etc.)?
2. Does the company want the ability to directly engage with customers on a day-to-day basis?
3. Does the company want to be perceived as highly engaged, proactive, and responsive to customer needs?
4. Is the company willing to monitor these conversations and turn them into actionable items?
5. Does the company want the ability to solicit instant customer feedback on important questions?
6. Does the company want to face the responsibility of living out its "personality" every day?
7. Does the company want to drive demand, from the social customer?
8. Does the brand have, at least, a full-time staff of two to 30 people who can be allocated to the brand's engagement of the social customer? (Most basic social media programs take between 5,000 and 30,000 worker-hours per year, and most Social CRM programs take upward of 15,000 worker-hours per year to implement, so you could be looking at a serious price tag of $350,000 to $1 million per year.)

If the answer to any (or all) of these questions is yes, then keep turning these pages so we can dive into the metrics and rationale.

Beginning Your Relationship with the Social Customer

You will need to figure out where your brand is *right now* in relation to the social customer, and where you want to be 12 to 24 months from now. Timing: that's a given. To move ahead with the social customer, your brand *can* show some early wins, but real progress takes one to three years. Why, you ask, does it take two or three years to get ahead with the social customer? Your competitors built a Facebook page and engaged 665,000 customers inside of six months, right? And now they're getting 6,000 of those fans to redeem a coupon in their retail stores every weekend — isn't that a win?[15]

Your competitors did *something* right. They were able to gather a mass audience, and they *were* able to create outcomes. But this kind of customer relationship is a tenuous, not-so-sticky kind that has "weak ties." I know, I know: you've been told by all of the business-book gurus that it's wiser (and more profitable) to have lots and lots of weak-tie relationships.

Well, what works in personal networking doesn't really apply in Customer Relationship Management on the social Web. By only having access to that customer data through a "filter" (i.e., Facebook, or some social network that's a "walled garden," providing limited, nonscalable access to the social customer), brands are throwing the equivalent of a frat party, one where no one's able to exchange phone numbers. The big "fail" here is that brands think they're *owning* the social customer when they're not even renting.

What brands truly need when they're beginning the dance (oh, and it is a dance) with the social customer is a series of speed-dating events, where information is exchanged at the customer's level of comfort. Some customers share varying levels of personal information with the brand, some share with other social customers, and some give you little information. This all begs one critical question: *What is one marginal piece of social customer data worth to your brand?* (We're going to explore ways to valuate this in Chapter 3.)

THE BUSINESS CASE FOR SOCIAL CRM

Before you move forward, you're going to want to know the business case for Social CRM, and the value of the demand the social customer drives. I've read a number of explanations for this in a number of different journals—mainly key CRM publications where existing big CRM vendors, multimillion and billion-dollar software companies, are trying to make inroads into Social CRM because their customers—big brands like yours—are demanding it.

You can monitor what customers are saying about your brand all day long. Heck, you go to HootSuite and get yourself a free account, or even a decent paid account for probably about $20 a month for a small company. This account allows you to track a majority of content from all of the different social networks and discussion forums, and all of the important places on the social Web. This monitoring will tell you what people are saying, but the $20 HootSuite account won't tell you (1) what to do with it, (2) how to derive insight from it, or (3) what any of that data is really worth. Hence, the business case for Social CRM, which combines the ubiquitous amount of chatter about your brand (and your market and your competitors) from the social Web with the tools you'll need to strengthen customer relationships. Your brand shouldn't have to struggle to figure out which conversations are truly relevant, how to embed the voice-of-the-customer into routine company decision making, and how to proactively serve customers.

The business case for Social CRM has six key points to remember:

1. **You've got more types of customers than ever before.** To consider the social customer set limited to, say, the folks who buy the bottle of wine at the grocery store your company manufactures, is a pretty shortsighted way of looking at the situation. Your customer set includes partners, vendors, employees, ex-employees, prospective and current customers.

And they're all talking about your brand, your market, and your competitors right now.

2. **You need to obtain direct and actionable customer insight.** You can "social media monitor" until the cows come home, but it doesn't make a lick of difference to your brand until you can verify that these social media actions come from real prospects and customers, and that you can take action with it after you've made sense of the data. Social CRM isn't black magic—it's a mixture of business science and art. Some Social CRM solutions even use Natural Language Processing (NLP) to help brands separate the wheat (important things that your customers are saying) from the chaff (chatter, essentially just noise). Other solutions depend on human interaction that trigger systemic work flows your company has codified, because they've been proven to achieve business objectives over and over in the past. If your data doesn't show a stark black-and-white picture of the "at this moment" relationship between you and your customers, then you're not going to be able to take useful action.

3. **You're trying to keep costs down and increase engagement with your customers.** When a brand reaches out to a customer on the social Web, it can't feel fake or forced—customers will feel alienated, like their relationship with your brand is meaningless. They'll eventually seek someone else to provide the service or product you provide if engagement remains low. If you can't afford a high degree of customer churn, but you *don't* want to be forced to build a nonscalable solution for dealing with the social customer (imagine Southwest airlines hiring a new employee to engage every new 10,000 fans and followers they have on Twitter—this would mean they would have had to hire 106 new employees in the last three years!), Social CRM is the highly scalable and a highly engaged way to "divide and conquer" your customer sets.

The idea is that you'll take all of this data, from your sets of customers, prioritize the key messages that are coming in, systematically route them to the most important people in your enterprise, and use the smartest people to make "micro" decisions triggering automated work flows that make your customers happy. And proactively engage the customers when you anticipate trouble spots—the flight that your company knows will be canceled tomorrow, the truck of really hip sweaters that will not arrive at your customers' favorite stores until next week, when they were expecting them this week. When your team is powered by Social CRM, they'll have the information and the scale to engage the right customer at the right time, creating win-win outcomes. And you'll have a 360-degree view of these social customers, to know whether you delighted them or they were just giving you lip service.

4. **You want to deliver the best products and services possible.** Developing products with your customers actually reduces costs and increases market share and sales. If you're looking to plow through design flaws, infer possibly unexpected customer intent when they're buying your products and services. You can't target innovation without the right customer data, and you can't get the right social customer data without a powerful Social CRM solution, and a team (read: cross-functional) that's totally on board.

5. **You've got to protect the brand, at all costs, while you constantly promote it.** Protecting the brand is the reason a lot of brands get into social media monitoring, or even Social CRM—totally reactive, but totally valid. There's a lot to lose if you don't do this. If all of the cool product-innovation and customer service is the foundation of the house that supports your business around the social customer, the protection and promotion of the brand is the flashy neon sign that draws people in off the street. In a word: critical.

6. **You're trying to create an agile business that can stop on a dime.** Ten years ago, with no knowledge of the rise of social media or Social CRM, top business analysts and consultants were telling us that the need to create an agile enterprise would be key in the early twenty-first century. Mike Fauscette, a top IDC technology analyst calls this concept "organic business"; it's any business that can dynamically (or at least quickly) reallocate value to any part of the business, or any part of the customer ecosystem (this is a core concept of the march toward Social CRM that many businesses have undertaken). We're all shooting for that, right? Wow, how in the heck do you plan on doing this without some kind of real-time voice-of-the-customer embedded in your every business function?

Now that we know the business case for Social CRM, let's examine the Four Social Customer Scenarios—this will tell you where your brand is around the social customer, and where you're trying to go. Then we'll get into the "how" of engaging the social customer, before we get to the "23 Use Cases of Social CRM" and really blow your mind.

2

THE "HOW" AND "WHERE" OF ENGAGEMENT AND THE FOUR SOCIAL CUSTOMER SCENARIOS

B efore we can examine the Four Social Customer Scenarios— where your brand is, currently, in relation to your social customers—we must look at the Social Customer Engagement Models, the "where" of the social customer, within your organization. These five models were developed most thoroughly by Jeremiah Owyang, of the Altimeter Group. He wrote a ground-breaking white paper where he profiled five different models of Social Customer Management. These are the ways that brands attempt to "grab" the social customer.

Maybe your organization is using some of them right now—

maybe you're using none of them. No matter; just look them over so you gain a cursory understanding of organizational approaches to the social customer, and then we'll use the Social Customer Scenarios to figure out where your organization is right now.

SOCIAL CUSTOMER ENGAGEMENT MODELS

Each of the Social Customer Engagement Models is profiled below, with their respective graphical representation, pros and cons. By reading them, you'll figure out where your company currently stands around the "where" of the social customer, and maybe get an idea where you want to go.

Model One: Organic

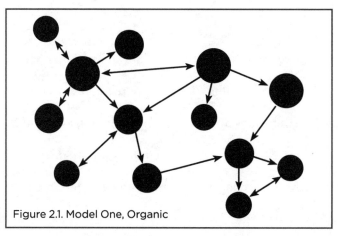

Figure 2.1. Model One, Organic

What it is: A model where the social customer is engaged, organically, by departments or business units, as they launch strategies (sometimes ad-hoc) to manage the social customer.

Pros: Springs up naturally, allows departments/business units to follow their natural cultural bent. Very authentic. Occasionally, success stories and/or best practices are shared.

Cons: Very difficult for any kind of central management or governance, scares the heck out of most brands. Can create severe scalability challenges and "blockages" if one team (e.g., sales) is much larger than another (e.g., customer service). Makes most I.T. managers/ CIOs nervous due to inconsistent business practices against shared infrastructure (CRM or ERP systems).

Percentage of companies using it: 10.8 percent.[1]

Model Two: Centralized

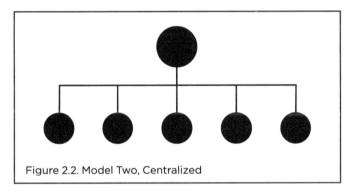

Figure 2.2. Model Two, Centralized

What it is: One central group represents all business units in initiating the conversation with the social customer (and relaying everything between the social customer and the executive team, as well as the other business units). This would be what happens when a marketing group, or a corporate communications team, takes ownership of a social customer strategy (or when it's outsourced to a PR firm, ad agency, or demand generation agency).

Pros: Consistency of message (or brand value promise). Marcom and communications teams typically have strong buy-in because it fits with dominant 1980–90s marketing paradigms. Easy to tell "who said what." Successes are easily visible because this type of strategy is usually implemented by high-visibility departments or partner agencies.

Cons: May cause skirmishes across business units, when other teams wish to engage directly with social customer. When outsourced, there can be drastic delays in turnaround time, and relationship-damaging scope creep (e.g., the PR firm and ad agency can become de facto customer service agents, and that was not what they signed up for). In general, people with very little customer service experience frequently end up handling engagement.

Percentage of companies using it: 28.8 percent.

Model Three: Coordinated

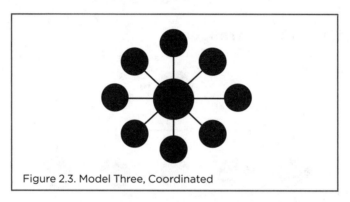

Figure 2.3. Model Three, Coordinated

What it is: A central (usually cross-functional) team makes sure that all connected business units get equal experience (and education) on how to work with the social customer. The cross-functional team sits in the middle, working with connecting business units (e.g., sales, operations, HR), and provides education and support to work with the social customer. (We'll see an example of this model when we get to Whirlpool, later in the book. Their corporate communications team set social media guidelines and shared best practices with all of their brand units.)

Pros: Generally, a consistency of vision and technology practices. All teams are roughly at the same skill level (and ideally, the same response time) as one another, when engaging the social customer. Best practices are shared. Generally, highly effective.

Cons: Takes a long time to implement, requires a shared vision on customer experience management and technology and consistent key executive buy-in.

Percentage of companies using it: 41 percent (the dominant model, at this point in time).

Model Four: Multiple Hub-and-Spoke

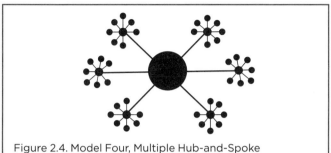

Figure 2.4. Model Four, Multiple Hub-and-Spoke

What it is: Owyang refers to this as the "dandelion" model. Each business unit has semiautonomy, but there's an overarching tie back to the central group. More common in large companies with multiple smaller brands (i.e., multiflag[2]/multibrand) or products acting essentially autonomously from one another under a common brand (i.e., CPG, food/bev). For example, a large hotel brand would be the central group, and the smaller properties owned by the chain would operate independently of one another. In my opinion, the best one for medium and large enterprise, and the most scalable.

Pros: Realistic, for consumer brands. Among the easiest of the models to manage. Allows for the use of shared resources and the sharing of best practices. A good fit for huge consumer multinationals (e.g., Proctor & Gamble, Unilever).

Cons: Requires a tolerance for cultural differences across product lines or brand extensions and a versatile, agile touch in managing the social customer. Not ideal for inexperienced organizations.

Percentage of companies using it: 10 percent.

Model Five: Holistic Honeycomb

What it is: This model acknowledges that *every single employee* in the organization is socially enabled. This means that any employee could play the role of customer service, support, or sales, *if* they choose to be social, or engage with the social customer. Owyang noted, in an April 2010 blog post, that this model rarely occurs naturally and should not be forced. Essentially, if this type of approach to the social customer is not a part of the company's DNA, then don't force it.

Pros: Perhaps a better fit for newer companies, or companies that "grew up" with the social customer. Examples include Zappos and Dell. Has a very "real" feel, almost folksy.

Cons: Requires consistent education, across all business units, and a deep cultural desire to manage and thrill the customer, at all costs. Trades "polish" for presence.

Percentage of companies using it: 1.4 percent (according to that study, that's two brands out of 140).

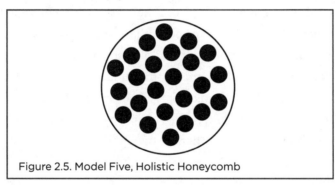

Figure 2.5. Model Five, Holistic Honeycomb

THE FOUR SOCIAL CUSTOMER SCENARIOS

This brings us to a critical black-and-white snapshot of the places your brand could be (and where your brand is, right now) on the social Web. Some people like to think of the Four Social Customer scenarios as "social customer maturity models." I've never been one to use fancy management consulting phrases, so I just like to think of them as "where are your people at?" around the social customer.

Typically, the brand won't effortlessly glide from Scenario One to Scenario Four. More likely, the brand will sputter, gradually moving across the "spectrum" of these four scenarios. Again, this kind of transition should take 18 to 36 months.

"We're looking at this as an *enterprise-class* data problem," Buzz-ient's Timothy Jones said. "Nothing [huge] is going to happen in two or three years. People are still going to be working on their first major social project five or 10 years from now."

Then there's the question of executive ownership. Even in small and medium-sized companies, the social customer should be owned by the senior executive team.

"I think in [say], a 200-person company, this is a lead initiative for the CMO. In fact the CEO themselves needs to be very heavily engaged in it," Mark Woollen, VP of CRM Product Strategy for Oracle, said.

"I would say that basically the champion of it for all external pur-poses is the CEO," Woollen explained, "but you need to make sure you have a day-to-day owner of it, who is as passionate about it, which is the CMO."

"When you look at a company like Starbucks," Woollen continued, "that has a huge loyalty program, run by a very large team, working for the CMO, what you need to do is actually embed [Social CRM] into the program itself. So, the program takes preeminence over the people. You still have the need for a very, very keen leader at an executive level, like the CMO. It's gotta be a C-level executive."

First, you have to decide what your company's burning need is, before you can figure out what kind of resources to deploy against that need (or what sacrifices you're willing to make, in order to sat-isfy that need).

> **Scenario One: No Engagement.** This means that your brand has no data on the social customer, no model to try and en-gage the social customer, and no idea what the value of the social customer will be to the brand. Whether diffuse depart-ments at your company have engaged the social customer (e.g., marketing started a Facebook page) is irrelevant here.
>
> **Scenario Two: Partial Engagement.** This is the muddiest place to be, but it's further along than Scenario One. This

means that multiple departments or business units have conflicting agendas around the social customer (sometimes using multiple or disparate CRM technologies). Also, there is no clear engagement model for how the social customer is managed throughout the company. Also, this is what nearly always happens in a merger or acquisition. Also, it is very common in multinationals or multiflag hospitality brands, like a chain of hotels, or a software company that's recently acquired 10 other smaller software companies but has not integrated all of them into a coherent single company.

Scenario Three: Modeled Engagement. This means that the company has a strategic model for engaging the social customer (typically with multiple business units engaged), end-to-end customer experience management (CEM[3]) processes,

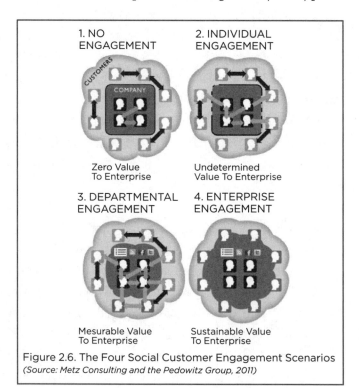

Figure 2.6. The Four Social Customer Engagement Scenarios
(Source: Metz Consulting and the Pedowitz Group, 2011)

and some set of data on the social customer (e.g., a CRM system that has partial data on end-user customers of the brand). CEM A company with 100,000 Facebook fans and a loyalty system database (e.g., airline miles, hotel points) could be an example here.

Scenario Four: Social Customer Engagement. This means the brand meets the three criteria of a social object: (1) near real-time response to the social customer, on the social Web; (2) synthesis of social customer community data through Social CRM; and (3) a strategic engagement model around the social customer (the "where" of the social customer, within the organization). Examples of this would be organizations that fully "own" the social customer, through their use of integrated Social CRM, such as Comcast, Dell, Zappos, and Hollywood Park Racetrack.[4] HOLLYWOODPARK

Where Is Your Brand?

Here's how to figure out *which* of the scenarios your brand is currently in. Copy the four scenarios and write above them, "Which one are we?" Bring a bunch of hot chocolate chip cookies to the meeting. Keep the cookies in front of you, and pass out a copy of this material. Tell each person that they need to select their assessment of where the organization is and where the organization should go. For each assertion they support, they may have *one* cookie. You'll have 20 perspectives in 20 minutes.

Put them all on the whiteboard and then see which category they land in. The most common scenario that I see, with consumer brands, is that the Ones want to become Threes (due to some logical or technological impediment that dictates that they cannot become Fours, which I disagree with), or that the Twos want to become Fours. My advice here is to take this shift *one scenario at a time.* (If key executive stakeholders like the CEO and COO of your organization don't have direct input at this stage, then shifting through the scenarios is not likely to happen.)

SUCCESSFUL SOCIAL OBJECTS

Before we wrap up we'll want to spend a bit of time examining what makes a brand a good "social object," and what, honestly, makes a brand ill-suited to be a social object. A couple of years ago I spent a bit of time working with a Bay Area luxury hotel brand—they came to our company because they wanted to monetize the social customer effectively and get more customers from the social Web. In the end they executed a little less than half of the strategy my company wrote with them—they felt that a lot of the recommendations were aimed at an audience that was a little down-market of their target audience (i.e., people who couldn't afford to stay at the hotel).

Since then the hotel shied away from Social Customer Management, and they have a minimal presence on the social Web. There's a few reasons for this. First, the brand honestly doesn't want their customers' input on how they should do business. One part of the "brand value promise" of being a luxury hotel, from their perspective, is that they create the experience for the customer, not the other way around. To them, managing the social customer simply means promoting the brand in social channels, without embedding the voice-of-the-customer. Does this make this hotel brand a social object? No, but I guess that was never what they sought to achieve in the first place. This all begs a critical question: *what are the conditions that make a brand a successful social object?*

First, the brand needs to accept the six foundational premises of Social CRM. Here they are, as elucidated ever so clearly by Paul Greenberg in his landmark book, *CRM at the Speed of Light:*

1. If the customer likes you, he will stay with you.
2. If a customer doesn't like you, in time she will leave you.

(This statement totally accounts for the economic concept of switching barrier or exit fees; in other words, the reason you don't terminate your cell phone plan everytime you see your outrageous phone bill is because it would be a royal pain to start a new phone plan every month).

3. People are looking to control their own lives.

4. People are looking to fulfill their own agendas; they're self-interested. This goes a bit beyond number 3 because it states that within people's lives, at different times, they have different agendas.

5. If you help people control their own lives and fulfill their own agendas, and you're nonobtrusive and valuable, and provide memorable experiences, they will like you.

6. If you fail to help them, they won't like you, and won't continue with you because someone else will help them. (There's those switching barriers again.)

It's pretty common-sense stuff, and I can almost picture Sam Walton dispensing this kind of advice from a parking lot in the sweltering summer of '64 in Bentonville.[5] These switching costs (or switching barriers) mentioned in the foundational premises of Social CRM above are a big deal. I sat down with one of the smartest people in Social CRM—Oracle's VP CRM Product Strategy, Mark Woollen—and he had a singular perspective on this.

"If becoming a fan [of a brand] results in someone being peppered with connection requests [or messages] from a brand that they don't have a connection with, the switching cost is not too high," Woollen said. "The switching cost would be much higher if the social channels were better integrated with the rest of the channels the company is using to engage with the customers."

This means that your brand will lose fewer social customers, and be a better social object, if your social channels (social networks, mobile, etc.) are better integrated. What does that integration look like?

"What you're going to see is that right now social media is very separate, basically to make it an integrated part of the customer service, sales, support, and marketing processes, along with the other channels that the company is going to use in a cross-channel or multichannel fashion," Woollen said. Then he brought up a crucial point about "right-channeling," something the best social-object brands do really well.

"['Right-channeling' is] basically allowing a company to optimize, not just for the right person or community or time with which to engage or harvest them from social media, but to determine if—in this place in time, given this request, even though [the brand] saw it in social media and they may respond immediately there—they *may* take it to another channel. How do we 'right-channel' this, if you will?" he asked, pointing to one of the highest-order skills of Social Customer Management.

"Right-channeling" is a tough thing to do, and it's not for lack of corporate intelligence. It's usually for a lack of business "emotional intelligence," also known as EQ,[6] that companies are unable to become social objects, and work with the social customer.

"In general, in life," Woollen said, "there's IQ and EQ (emotional quotient or emotional intelligence). Companies have got IQ, and [Social Customer Management] is an area, like e-mail, it's one-to-one—in this area, who need a whole lot of EQ [emotional intelligence]. Enterprise EQ is *hard* to get."

UNSUCCESSFUL SOCIAL OBJECTS

Conversely, what are the conditions in which a brand would be unable to become a social object, or would become a poor social object? The answer is a three-parter:

1. **Bad or poorly differentiated product or service.** If you're simply selling junk, hoping that people will never find out, or that

you will have their money before they do (fake fitness supplements, cheap, shoddy products, etc.), your brand is absolutely unsuitable to be a social object because of the brand's lack of remarkability, and the fact that any conversation around the product or service would be inherently negative. That said, even if you're perceived as a "negative" brand—say you run the largest bail-bond service in Tulsa, Oklahoma—there are still remarkable positives that would cause customers to want to socialize your brand. In this case you might help more people get out of jail than anyone in Tulsa, and that's something to talk about. (We'll get more into product differentiation when we talk Blue Ocean strategy, in Chapter 13.)

2. **Lack of a brand orientation around win-win outcomes.** When I was fresh out of college, I was a corporate account manager at a big multibrand computer reseller, CDW and they had this slogan emblazoned on the walls: "It's only good if it's win-win." At the time, I thought it was a little hokey, but as I grew older I realized that unless a brand is centered on win-win outcomes for employees, suppliers, vendors, ex-employees, and customers, it will make a pretty crummy social object. What does it matter how many fans your brand has on Facebook if 90 percent of your former employees are slamming the company on Glassdoor.com, the social Web site where employees review their employers?

3. **Lack of desire to embed voice-of-the-customer in the brand, due to brand value promise.** This is a really interesting reason. If your brand has a constant desire to tell the customer how it's done (essentially, operating from the point of view of the *corporate ecosystem* rather than the *customer ecosystem*), then your brand may not be ready to be social. You find this with brands that fear that embedding the voice-of-the-customer will devalue their brand value promise as tastemakers.

Let's take a look at what made Apple Computer one of the first so-cial brands in the tech industry. If you think about its first 20 years (1976–'96), they were a quirky, iconic brand—the kooky Californians who simplified computing and brought you the Mac computer.

Now, though, when you think of the technology space, you think of one brand that absolutely sets customers' hearts aflutter: Apple. How-ever, when you think of brands that listen to the customer at times, and completely ignore the customer's wishes at others, Apple also definitely comes to mind. Here's how to prove it: just ask yourself whether Apple accepted Paul Greenberg's six foundational premises of whether the brand succeeded as a social object:

1. **If the customer likes you, he will stay with you.** Post-1984 (when the Macintosh came out), it's safe to say that's when Apple began to engender deep brand loyalty. The 2010 sta-tistics said that 77 percent of the iPhone 4 purchases were upgrades.[7] These are nearly *unheard-of* levels of brand loyalty.

2. **If a customer doesn't like you, in time she will leave you.** Well, this is true, but it's way more applicable to the ads that Apple has been running—first the Apple Switch and then the wildly successful Get a Mac ad campaigns—for nearly a decade, to try to convince frustrated PC users to switch to their comput-ing platform.

3. **People are looking to control their own lives.** This is where Apple has been hitting a friction point (and backlash) from their loyalists. While Apple has allowed people to drastically customize their music and television viewing experience (Apple TV, and the paradigm-shifting iPod), it also has had customers "jailbreaking" their phones for nearly four years, and is seeing both sides of this one.

4. **People are looking to fulfill their own agendas; they're self-interested.** Apple has based nearly all of its marketing around

this, since their ground-breaking 1997 ad campaign, Think Different.

5. **If you help people control their own lives *and* fulfill their own agendas, *and* you're nonobtrusive and valuable, *and* provide memorable experiences, they will like you.** For the most part, Apple's customers would agree with this statement, and even though you'll occasionally run into a "former Mac user," you're more likely to run into individuals who have switched from PCs to Macs.[8] How many other brands do you know of that have to actually *restrict* how many of their products come out (iPad, iPhone 4) to make sure everyone gets one?

6. **If you fail to help them, they won't like you, and won't continue with you because someone else will help them.** Well, this explains where Apple gained a lot of their new customers—because the PC brands (or the folks that made other music players, like Microsoft, Creative, and SanDisk) lost millions of customers to Apple over the 10 years.

Did Apple use Social CRM to get to where they are? No, they didn't. And don't even look at "right-channeling"—Apple is famous for being nonresponsive. The brand actually approached me in late 2008 to explore using Social CRM inside their iTunes product and decided not to do it.

In fact, the brand just began playing in the social space in 2010 with their Ping feature, which attempts to get users of their iTunes music software to share what they're listening to with friends. So, why should your brand use Social Customer Management to be successful with the social customer, if Apple didn't have to? One of the key reasons that Apple didn't have to is because they were experts at something called Value Innovation. We'll get way more deeply into this in the strategy chapter of the book. The other key reason is quite simple: you're not Steve Jobs.[9]

3

SOCIAL CUSTOMER RELATIONSHIP MANAGEMENT

Social Customer Relationship Management (SCRM) is something that the "godfather of CRM," Paul Greenberg, first defined in his groundbreaking book, *CRM at the Speed of Light*,[1] a few years ago. CRMSPEED The way he wrote the definition was true to the social Web: he gathered a bunch of CRM consultants to write it, collaboratively, on a wiki (a Web site that allows for easy collaboration through interlinked Web pages). The resulting definition is completely accurate, but also consultantese (a language spoken only by management consultants):

> Social CRM is a philosophy and a business strategy, supported by a technology platform, business rules, work flow,

processes, and social characteristics, designed to engage the customer in a collaborative conversation in order to provide mutually beneficial value in a trusted and transparent business environment. It's the company's response to the customer's ownership of the conversation.

Let's call that the 60-second version of the definition of Social CRM. When you're writing a definition that's going to be seen as an elevator pitch by much of your team, however, you'll want to make it short enough so people understand it in a sentence or two.

Here's the 30-second version of the Social CRM definition:

The customer owns the conversation now, so companies need to change the way they do business. Social CRM is a philosophy and a business strategy that uses technology, work flow, business rules, and social information to talk with (not at) the customer in a transparent way, to make value for both parties.

The 10-second definition is even simpler:

Social CRM is strategy to make conversations with customers who bring you money and make your customers happy.

There you go. Three flavors, all pointing to the same big idea. While you use technology and work flow and all of this crazy social Web data to facilitate Social CRM, it all comes down to this: get the feedback you need to amaze your customers, then actually amaze them with your brand and the total customer experience your brand provides, end-to-end.

THE 10 COMMANDMENTS OF SOCIAL CRM

I was reading a blog post the other day by Radian6's Lauren Vargas (Director of Community) that gave a few solid best practices,[2] and I realized that no one had yet written the 10 commandments[3] of Social CRM. So, I'd like to run through them so you get a better idea of Social CRM best practices.

1. Executive-level shared vision of what defines "customer relationships" shall be more than "understood" universally through your organization. You should be able to ask any employee what a customer relationship is, and what it means, and they should be able to give you a straight answer.

2. From your company's perspective, a relationship with your customers is not what you need most. You must understand the job your customers are trying to get done and help them make that happen.

3. You shall not address the social customer in a nontransparent manner, because if you are dishonest with them, they will figure it out and it will come back to haunt you.

4. Remember to define clear, measurable business objectives and base all social customer strategy on achieving those objectives.

5. Honor your customers and your community by asking them what they expect from you, and delivering it.

6. You shall not think that software or technology, by itself, is a solution strategy. Educate your work force by building their abilities and skills, and only deploy software once you have the culture and cross-functional buy-in to support it.

7. You shall not necessarily keep existing business processes if they don't fit with the new vision.

8. You shall not be foolish enough to not have a change management strategy.

9. You shall not expect your employees or customers to converse with one another unless clear expectations have been set with both parties by your company's management.

10. You shall not covet your competition's social customer strategy or think that what they're doing is right; they may have just confused strategy with planning.[4]

If you can get your company to stick to these 10 guiding principles around the social customer, you'll be in pretty good shape. But doing that is going to take senior executive–level buy-in. If you want departmental-level ownership of the social customer, keep reading (and following the pointers), but don't expect to get anything besides the organic model of social customer engagement (or past Scenario Two), if you're *not* going for top-level buy-in.

Some readers may say, "Hey, I think that's the best I'm ever going to get on this project," and pursue a fair-to-middling objective. This is where I invoke the aphorisms of superintense GoDaddy CEO Bob Parsons (sort of the Mr. Clean of the technology world). On his list of "16 Rules for Success in Business and Life in General"[5] number three is: "When you're ready to quit, you're closer than you think." Don't let a fear of rejection quash your dream to pursue the rewarding relationship that your company, and your customers, desperately need.

BEFORE THE SOCIAL CUSTOMER AND SOCIAL CRM: THE MICROSITES OF 1999

Before brands had the tools, technology, and "cultural values" to engage with the social customer, things worked differently. But back then customers were buying things differently, too: there was no Zappos.com,[6] no mobile commerce, and no Facebook. ZAPPOS

In 2000 there were only a few different ways to engage the customer on the Web. Let's go with an example of a consumer brand we all know: Levi's jeans. Remember the year 2000? CD Stores? *Who Wants To Marry a Millionaire?* U2's "Beautiful Day"? Napster, anyone?

Let's take a look at the Levi's Web site, circa 2000.[7] Their entire site consisted of 15 pages at the time (today it's at least four times that size). Back then there weren't too many ways to engage with the customer on the Web. Most brands simply posted an e-mail address, where customers could reach out to the brand's marketing team if they were having a problem. Doesn't sound much different from putting a customer service P.O. box on the back of the tag attached to the jeans, which in fact was done in the 1980s.

Around 1999 or 2000 a lot of consumer brands got the idea (or their ad agencies planted it in their heads) to launch a microsite whenever a brand launched a new product, product line, or contest. These sites were wonderful for brands in that they focused all the content around a specific initiative (e.g., the new Levi's hooded sweatshirts) and diverted all pay-per-click (PPC) advertising to one specific place. They weren't particularly good for the consumer, however, as they did nothing to enhance the consumer's ability to understand the brand as a whole, and also offered little to no way for the consumer to convey their thoughts on this "focused" content.

The one step in the right direction that these microsites gave the social customer was content. They were big enough—or, shall we say, deep enough—to allow the social customer to dig down into whatever grabbed his or her interest (hooded sweatshirts, hybrid cars, face wash).

Although the customers were, at this point, going exactly where the brands wanted them to go, brands were far from "owning" the social customer with their microsites, as they lacked the technology and cultural buy-in to do three things:

1. **Provide tools.** The brands didn't equip the customer with the tools to communicate with the brand, and also share their feedback with other consumers in an uncensored environment.

2. **Engage conversation.** The brands didn't look at what customers were saying about them, or about other brands.
3. **Create economic value.** The brands didn't put some economic marker on what having the customer engaged would be worth, to them or to the customer.

The technologies to fully engage the customer *just didn't exist* in 1999. Using a microsite 12 years later to launch your juice company's new brand of, say, Acai Pomegrante juice, would be downright disastrous. Let's take a look at a recent product launch that tried to do so *without* engaging the social customer, and how much it cost the companies.

Case Study: Tropicana Orange Juice

Tropicana Orange Juice, part of the PepsiCo brand family, learned the hard way, in January 2009, that not engaging the social customer could be *very costly.*[8] The brand launched a full-scale package redesign, replacing their decades-old "straw in an orange" packaging with a minimalist, sans-serif design. Customer complaints ensued to the point where Tropicana eventually reverted to the original packaging the next month, in February 2009.

The *New York Times* called the incident Pepsi's "New Coke," referring to Coke's ill-fated 1985 product launch.[9]

Neil Campbell, the president at Tropicana North America, part of Pepsi's Americas Beverages division, stated that the brand reverted to the old packaging not because of the number of consumer complaints about the change. Rather, Campbell said, Tropicana made the change because the criticism came from "[Tropicana's] most loyal customers." I think he was talking about the social customer, don't you?

Conventional wisdom on the social Web dictates that Tropicana could have figured out what their customers wanted for under $1,000 (16 hours of a marketing manager's time), by simply posting a few of the design comps on Facebook, Twitter, or wherever they calculated their most vocal customers would live online. Even if the design comps were too complicated for Facebook's Polls product, they could have used a basic contest solution like Wildfire or Strutta for under $1,000.[10] SOCIALCONTEST And the bloggers at *Fast Company, Advertising Age,* and many other publications were quick to tell them that.[11]

"You used to wait to go to the water cooler or a cocktail party to talk over something," said Richard Laermer, chief executive at RLM Public Relations in New York, and author of the go-to shake-up-your-company marketing book *Punk Marketing.*[12] PUNKM "Now, every minute is a cocktail party. You write an e-mail and in an hour you've got a fan base agreeing with you."

Or, not agreeing, in the case of Tropicana's repackaging.

THE SOCIAL CRM PROCESS

The diagram of the Social CRM process below, developed by my friend Jacob Morgan from Chess Media Group,[13] shows what a company like Tropicana should have done in its repackaging efforts. MORGAN (The diagram is one of many in this book, all of which will also be kept on the book's social workspace, The Social Customer.[14]) SOCIALCUSTOMER

Since the brand was asking a question, they should have begun by amassing a community on the social Web. That actually takes a little time, but a huge brand like Tropicana (whose products have been part of PepsiCo since 1998) could amass a big ol' community within 30 days, if they put five or six people behind the effort.

The next thing they'd need to do is engage, cross-channel (social Web, mobile, message boards, everything) and cross-language. The key to allocating effort here is spending the team's time where the customers are. For example, if Tropicana determined that 50 percent of their North American customers were in Canada, they should spend 50 percent of the "engagement hours" on the project speaking with those customers.

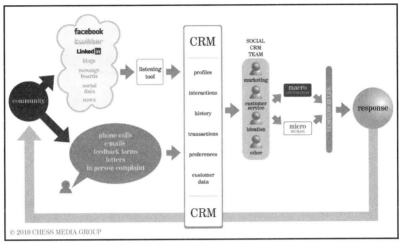

Figure 3.1. Social CRM Process

Following Chess Media Group's Social CRM Process, (see Figure 3.1) the *next* thing they'd want to do is aggregate that data with their nondigital data (phone calls, e-mails, feedback forms, etc.). Why bother with this? Well, when my Bubby Burnis (my grandmother) goes grocery shopping at the Wegman's in Fayetteville, New York, she's not going to be comfortable text-messaging her packaging choice back to Tropicana. But she might be okay with filling out a voting form in exchange for a two-dollars-off coupon. Tropicana could then have each of those point-of-purchase displays picked up by a home-sourced contractor in each local market. One hundred grocery stores times 500 ballots per store times six hours counting time equals $6,000 to get a statistically significant sample of what each nonsocial customer, nationwide, thinks of the new Tropicana packaging.[15] MEASURE

So, now, the Tropicana team has all of their community data and their offline data. How do they filter it into their CRM? They need to use a listening tool. As mentioned earlier, there are plenty you can use, and many of them are even integrated with social media management systems (SMMS). But let's say you wanted to use a basic, effective low-cost tool like Lithium (or even HootSuite, which is dirt-cheap, but not as capable as Lithium or Radian6). Their product could do this for $249. With a small amount of custom coding (it would take a decent programmer 16 to 40 hours), they could pump this data into their CRM (OracleCRM, Salesforce, etc.), and then make a human decision, based on whatever the data says: "Customers in New England preferred Times New Roman and a pink background ... New Yorkers stated in no uncertain terms that they want us to leave the packaging alone ... Los Angeles residents specifically didn't care."

Since this is a major decision, they could then follow up with a series of micro responses (a press release) and macro responses (thank-you coupons to all customers who voted). Then, upon release of the new packaging, they could reassess the success. Where Tropicana erred was skipping everything except the last part of the diagram.

Hospitality Brands and the Social Customer

Now that we've seen where a food and beverage brand tripped up, let's take a quick look at where hospitality brands typically drop the ball with the social customer. Here's a little guest advice from my friend Casey Phillips, a digital media consultant who handles social strategy for the well-known Los Angeles rock clubs The Mint and The Viper Room. In his own words Phillips says the following concepts are three big ones that hospitality brands do not understand about the social customer:

1. **Engagement.** "You can't market at people—it's more about the community around you than about your brand. It's about engagement and transparency. A lot of time and resources go into becoming a tastemaker. It's hard to teach brick and mortar clients how to get that voice and philosophy across through social media but they're getting there."
2. **Metrics.** "They really don't seem to get it. They want to see hard metrics. If it's music, they want to see ticket sales. If it's a bar,

they want to see bar sales. They need to understand it's a long-term play; it's not there to come out of the gates and scream—it's about building an 'organic funnel.'"

3. **Spend money.** "[Social customer management] is the most cost-effective advertising (with the exception of word-of-mouth), but it's the most labor intensive. The brands that are consistent about their outreach are pretty humble about it, but even they find it really difficult to spend on digital ads to support their 'free' outreach. Clients will spend $1,000 on a quarter-page ad in the LA Weekly, but shiver at blog and Facebook ads. I have brands that are convinced that print is still 'the way.' They ask, 'Is it hurting us?' Maybe not, but the ROI is disproportionate to their budget. Getting people to take the leap, even in the entertainment vertical, is still a struggle, to convince people to reallocate their advertising funds away from traditional. It's still difficult to convince them to spend money on something they can't taste, touch, or feel."

Phillips further explains the concept of franchising your brand utilizing Social CRM:

A few of the brands I work with are in the infancy of franchising. It's not just about your outer message, it's about internal communication. No [social customer] has time to come and look at your blog. Find a vehicle that works, and use it for customer service. I actually have to outsource that, and bring people in. [My friend] Kyra Reed likes to use the example of the Roxy [another Los Angeles nightclub]. Someone walked into a show and saw that someone Tweeted that the bouncer was rude to him—the owner intervened immediately from backstage, and that customer became an evangelist for life.

Phillips finds that the biggest organizational obstacle for hospitality brands is to cross-functionally manage the social customer.

> You don't have a lot of diversity in those departments; so I
> also find that creatives aren't present everywhere. A lot of
> times people don't see the value in it—they fear what they
> don't understand, but it's not about the age gap either. They
> feel that a post on, say, Twitter or Facebook, might get them
> fired. It's not given a priority, and people just drop the ball.

The ability to not only engage your social customer, but also to foster an understanding of the effectiveness of Social CRM in your employees, is obviously not specific to hospitality; hospitality is just an industry where employees are constantly interacting with the customer, face-to-face, in real-time. Such concepts can be applied across all industries and will prove useful in the growth of your brand's relationship with the social customer.

There's also a whole batch of things that brands just don't get about the social customer, like control and risk. Let's bring back Punk Marketing author Richard Laermer to help explain.

> Brands are afraid of giving up control. They want to be as-
> sured that everything is neat and tidy. Keep in mind, most
> brand or marketing managers are frightened that if they
> take a risk they'll be fired. But social media is the only way to
> reach customers with any depth, so it's not risky any longer—
> not doing such activities is.

Laermer cites a great case about first-mover advantage, when it comes to the social customer, with Axe Body Spray (a Unilever subsidiary):

> I often shake my head at what I call the GMOOT attitude or,
> "Get me one of those," from a [brand] that tells its marketing

manager (or agency) to do something completely off-message just because someone else [i.e., a competitor] in their space is. Why, after all, did Proctor & Gamble do body spray YouTube ads [for their short-lived TAG brand] to compete with Axe—an entirely different demographic! P&G did not gain traction—and the competition was able to largely make fun of their videos.

So here's where the me-too attitude toward Social Customer Management completely backfires. Without a completely coherent strategy behind it, a brand's attempt at Social Customer Management can not only fail, but *cost* them market share, if the customers perceive the brand as idiotic.

"In the end, a lot of people will lose their jobs because a competitor will jump in before they will," Laermer said. Now, here's where he gets really ugly: "The social customer is king. He will talk about you and you will make him do *nothing*. That's something most companies big and small cannot, for the life of them, fathom."

Some brands just can't handle this. But then again, in 1999, some brands just couldn't handle this other new thing—the Internet. "When a firm complains about a negative comment or a nasty video," Laermer said, "it shocks me because—what?—someone took the time to say something about you. Imagine: I can hardly fathom that anyone cares about *anything* outside of their own spheres. So stop controlling. Jump in, damn it!"

How Visible Are Your Conversations?

Here's another example on the visibility of the conversation when your brand manages the social customer. (See Table 3.1.) Let's say you're selling mobile phone service[16] and an unhappy AT&T customer, who we'll call Jane, is frustrated because her Apple iPhone contract ended in June 2010 and she thought AT&T would simply stop billing her. She went to the store, purchased a new Droid phone, and began using a new carrier, Verizon Wireless. She then receives a $150 bill from AT&T and calls customer service to complain. They accidentally disconnect her.

Jane then gets angry and does a Twitter search for AT&T. She comes across numerous other posts complaining about AT&T, some from other consumers and some from influencers (a search today yielded a number from Kevin Rose, founder of the popular social news Web site Digg). Jane decides to get into the action herself, posting on Twitter, "I can't believe AT&T disconnected me when I called to end my contract and get my $150 back; I thought it ended a month ago #attfail." That last part, "#attfail," is the hash tag used by thousands of other frustrated AT&T customers. Jane's complaint is the data input from the COMMUNITY (anywhere on the social Web, really—any public-facing social network or social Web site) that comes from the left part of the slide, and it can come from the social Web (the big cloud including LinkedIn, Facebook, etc.) or the real world (e.g., a phone call, a postcard, or even an in-person complaint). Hopefully, someone at AT&T will pick it up using their listening tool, or perhaps they'll even take a note about it while speaking with Jane on the phone if she calls back.[17] LISTENINGTOOL

Since AT&T is a big multinational, it's a safe bet that they use an enterprise-class listening tool like Radian6[18] (this is what Pepsi, Dell, and MolsonCoors use). Once this piece of information (Jane's complaint) comes into the AT&T office, there has to be a human decision made. Laura, the customer service rep who sees the social media monitoring system (in this case, the Radian6) Dashboard, needs to record this incident in the CRM, and then decide what to do about this complaint. RADIAN6

There are two choices Laura can make. She can choose a macro response—like a work flow, or a series of repeated actions—or a micro response, like addressing the customer directly, either on the social Web or by phone or e-mail. She then makes the response and

Outcome	Value to Customer	Value to Brand	Value to Followers
Jane's able to get her $150 back, ends contract, posts a positive message about the customer interaction	$150	–$1,800 to –$2,400: Their customer service team gets positive response in front of Jane's 450 followers on the social Web, loses $1,800/year customer but may eventually get customer back	Difficult to map: Jane's followers learn that the brand, while unresponsive at first, eventually responds to customer complaints. May lead to favorable buying habits in the future.
Jane has to pay the $150, ends contract, posts a negative message about the customer interaction	–$150	Up to $72,000: their customer service team gets negative response in front of Jane's 450 followers on the social Web, loses $1,800/year customer, which they will never get back, unless Jane has no choice but to work with AT&T again	Difficult to map: most likely will lead to either a confirmation of their previous belief that AT&T is hard to deal with, or a new perception that AT&T does not like its own customers.
Issue not resolved, Jane has to file a second social Web complaint	None	Unknown: what is the cost of a negative "hit" on the brand in front of Jane's 450 followers on the social Web?	Difficult to map until Jane reinitiates the conversation

Table 3.1. The Value of Your Conversation with the Social Customer

records the answer in AT&T's Social CRM solution. If it's a macro response, the SCRM system may even launch a series of other parallel processes, alerting the billing and sales teams. If at the end of this Jane isn't satisfied with the resolution, we go back to the beginning, to the DATA INPUT.[19] R6WHITEPAPER

In this case, the value of a satisfied social customer is a bit difficult to map, so let's examine it across a few different outcomes. Remember, when you're mapping value in these interactions, you have to look at the value to each stakeholder in the interaction. In taking a holistic approach to the social customer, we need to look at not only the brand and the customer, but also the ecosystem (the "friends" and "followers" that surround this incident) in the interaction.

SYSTEMS THEORY AND THE SOCIAL CUSTOMER

Here's the difference between looking at Jane's situation with AT&T from a typical Western management perspective, versus a more holistic systems theory viewpoint. Let's look at the most simple systems theory example we can think of: you, bleary-eyed, pouring coffee from the office coffeepot into your cup at 9:00 A.M. on a Monday morning. Here's how it works, from a Western perspective: you pour the coffee into the cup until the level reaches the level you perceive it should be, in your mind. Case closed. From this same point of view, Jane's story could be told like this: Jane complains, AT&T resolves or doesn't resolve, Jane maybe complains again. Case closed.

On a very basic level those two summaries seem to capture exactly what happened, both with your cup of coffee and with Jane's unexpected $150 phone bill. But they don't tell the whole story. Which is why it's critical to take a holistic view of the social customer. So, from a systems theory perspective, here's how the coffee story would work:

Walking through the coffee diagram (Figure 3.2) is very simple. There's the initial "job that the customer is trying to get done": getting a cup of coffee because they're half asleep. The first thing you do is assess whether the level of coffee in the cup is high enough for you. If not, then you adjust the angle at which you're pouring the coffee. The coffee then rises higher in the cup, at which point you need to choose whether to keep pouring the coffee or stop pouring and drink it ("I am a happy customer because my need has been fulfilled"). Let's now look at the holistic or systemic view of Jane's social customer interaction with AT&T.

Figure 3.3 is a bit more complex, and it accounts not only for what Jane sees, but for interactions seen by the public (AT&T's other prospects and customers). Notice that they touch this interaction at two touchpoints, both of which are in the middle of Laura's conversation with the brand. If you look at the 10 Commandments of Social CRM introduced earlier in this chapter, nearly all of them govern the way

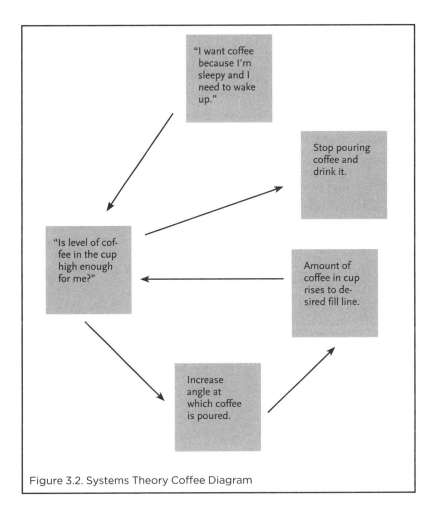

Figure 3.2. Systems Theory Coffee Diagram

this system works. The first commandment—*Executive-level shared vision of what defines "customer relationships" shall be more than "understood" universally through your organization. You should be able to ask any employee what a customer relationship is, and what it means*—is especially relevant here, because it implies that there are multiple customer relationships being affected: Jane's, and all the other customers who witness it.

One of the key failings of most "social media" books is that they fail to address the consumer intent-driven enterprise—only Paul Greenberg's *CRM at the Speed of Light* focuses on this topic. The phrase

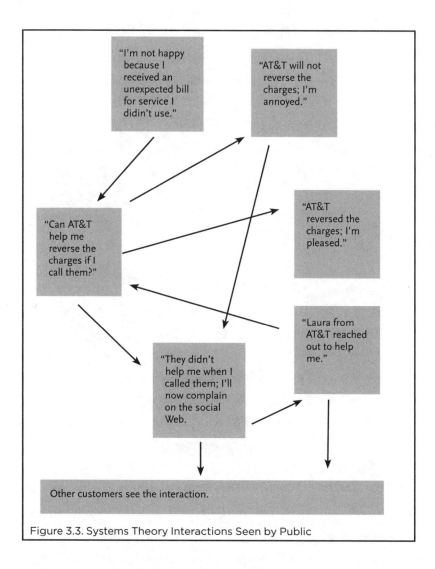

Figure 3.3. Systems Theory Interactions Seen by Public

"intent-driven enterprise" sounds complicated, but the concept is actually simple. It's a big old company that makes a product or a service (vacuums, sports cars, whatever) whose business units are directed and driven by the voice and intention of the customer.

This is precisely what the second commandment of Social CRM focuses on: *From your company's perspective, a relationship with your customers is not what you need most. You must understand the job your customers are trying to get done.*[20]

Jane had a different objective than many of your customers would have. She was actually trying to *break up* with AT&T, "on good terms." Sometimes your customers will want to give you feedback or ideas ("You should invent a new running shoe that's really lightweight, and is available in smaller women's sizes ... You should offer free shipping on all returns, period") and sometimes they're going to want to do things that you don't want ("You should not allow children to be seated in the restaurant after 7:00 P.M. on Fridays or Saturdays so adults can have a quiet dinner"). Sometimes the social customer will want to actually break up with you, in public. You're not always going to agree with the consumer's intent or even feel that it's good for your business. But you're expected to react, because, if you didn't read the long definition of Social CRM: the customer owns the conversation. Your brand doesn't own it anymore. Read that again. *Your brand doesn't own the conversation anymore—they stopped owning it sometime between 2005 and 2007.*

So, let's figure out how to "own" the relationship with that social customer again. And when I say "own," I don't mean "have exclusive title over." I mean that you'll have a productive relationship where you exchange reciprocal value with this customer. Because these days that's what "ownership" of the social customer looks like. Get used to it.

4

SOCIAL CUSTOMER INSIGHTS AND AN INTRODUCTION TO THE 23 USE CASES OF SOCIAL CRM

I've had many an executive ask me, "What exactly can we *do* with social CRM, *besides* field customer complaints and solve problems?" I usually tell them they've already discovered the two key use cases, but there are about 21 more to go, and we better keep moving if they ever want to sell the customer anything. They usually ask me to elucidate all 23 of them right there, in their office. To do this would take about five hours, and most executives don't actually have that much time.

In early 2010, Jeremiah Owyang and Ray Wang, two

sharp ex-Forrester analysts (if analysts in this space were rock stars, these guys would be Mick Jagger and Keith Richards), who were working at Altimeter Group at the time, wrote an amazing white paper called, "The 18 Use Cases of Social CRM, the New Rules of Relationship Management."[1] 18USECASES

As comprehensive and wonderful as the white paper is, I think the authors actually missed five use cases that I would add. I also argued with, modified, and updated a number of their suggestions. What you're getting in this chapter through Chapter 10 is just about everything you can do with Social CRM.

The key slide from that white paper is shown in Figure 4.1 (with my edits—the extra five cases), and it identifies what I think are all of the use cases of Social CRM—there's a lot of them. To say that Owyang and Wang's white paper is the first highly regarded and important white paper on Social CRM wouldn't be fair to three or four other analysts or consultants who have also done great work in this area since 2008. This research is simply the best breakdown of the market demand and technical maturity of the *use cases* of Social CRM. If white papers were rock albums, however, Owyang and Wang's would be the Rolling Stones' *Out of Our Heads*[2]—everything before it laid out the tools, but this one shows you exactly what you can actually do with them.[3] OUTOFOURHEADS

In fact, my only *minor* criticism of the entire white paper is that the use cases lack anecdotal examples. (Probably to make it seem more impartial—not a bad thing!) What you see in Figure 4.1 is a listing of the 23 use cases of Social CRM. We're going to begin by analyzing Social Customer Insights—it's the first of the 23 use cases, and it's a big one, so big it has five different parts: Monitoring, Mapping, Middleware, Management, and Measurement. This is the numero-uno high-level use case of Social CRM. The other ones (numbers 2 through 23) are definitely valid and completely useful, but they're more street-level, as they're the ones that would actually be executed by the members of your company's departmental teams. (Technically, yes, you can use 2 though 23 without doing number 1, but I wouldn't recommend it.)

As you can see in Figure 4.1, Social Customer Insights is the core foundation of all Social CRM use cases. It's the top-level use case, and it breaks down into five categories (the Five Ms mentioned above), that form the baseline use cases. These are the use cases that can cut across multiple departments or even business units. Use Cases 2 through 23 are much more discrete, and will usually be executed by smaller teams within each business unit. Often, *more than one* use case is happening at once. What we saw in Jane's AT&T example in Chapter 3 was one use case from the Sales category, (8, Rapid Social Sales Response) and one use case from the Service and Support category (14, Rapid Social Response.)

Figure 4.1. The 23 Use Cases of Social Customer Relationship Management

BREAKING DOWN SOCIAL CUSTOMER INSIGHTS: THE FIVE Ms OF SOCIAL CRM

Before we get into granular specifics use cases, and what each of them looks like on a day-to-day basis, let's break down the foundation, the Five Ms of Social CRM, so you understand Social Customer Insights and the baseline use cases.

Monitoring

Brands use social media monitoring[4] software every day, all day, to see what social customers are saying about them. MONITORING On weekends or holidays this can be outsourced to an overseas team that can notify the brand in case of an emergency or high-sensitivity incident. This software collects all of the disparate data inputs from the social Web—social networks, message boards, blogs, microblogs, personal Web sites, video sites—then compiles it into an easily readable format (e.g., a few minutes per day) that can be automagically[5] input into a CRM tool.

For example, the marketing team at pet treat brand Waggin' Train gets e-mail updates from Lithium every morning at 8:00 A.M., and logs into their dashboard. Gatorade has a Chicago-based "Mission Control" hub from which they engage the social customer: it looks like a cross between Facebook, NASA, and ESPN Sportscenter. Radian6, Lithium, and RightNow are three vendors whose monitoring software works quite well.

The main issue with monitoring is that keywords need to be incredibly well tested for these solutions to be effective. Also, the monitoring clock needs to be covered 24/7 if you're a big brand. If you're unsure whether this is economically feasible, ballpark what a damaging incident on a Saturday morning would cost the brand if no response was made until Monday.

Mapping

These are the software solutions that identify relationships *between* customers, and they typically live on top of CRM platforms, although they can also exist in stand-alone environments (like Facebook profiles). Social CRM data (in the CRM tool) is enriched by adding this layer of social metadata (yup, data about data) that tells brands more information about who their customers really are (e.g., LinkedIn Profile, Google Profile, Facebook profile), what they really want, and how they're related to one another. If the brand wants to know who the "influencers" are, this is where it's calculated.

The team at my consulting firm uses InsideView to enrich lead and opportunity data as soon as they are contacted by a prospective buyer, making sales close time shorter, and making sales pitches more relevant to prospects. An early example of a mapping solution was Clara Shih's *Faceforce*,[6] which combined Facebook data with Salesforce's[7] CRM data. Salesview (InsideView), Facebook, and Xobni Pro are known for their solid mapping capabilities. FACEFORCE

The catch with mapping is that if users don't enter a lot of their data for you (i.e., Facebook profile information), your team is going to have a *lot of work to do* to manually collect this data. Make it easy for your customers or potential customers to enter data by enticing them with a special offer, faster service, or something amazingly cool (think of this data as highly valuable, so give a high-value perk in return).

Middleware

Brands use *middleware* to automate work flows and apply business rules to events from the social Web. Also, if your brand wants to make things happen (book events, process returns) across multiple systems, middleware is going to be a must-have. ETL technologies (extract-transform-load) would also fit here. Middleware is simply a piece of software that exists between two other pieces of software, allowing them to communicate. Nothing fancy. It basically serves as the lettuce and tomato (middle layer) between the bread (the social data and metadata) and the meat (the CRM). Also, middleware can connect disparate databases (e-commerce, etc.) to your CRM.

A good example of this function are clothing brands that take return requests via Twitter (run through Salesforce Enterprise Edition), and then use a Talend integration to issue a credit through their e-commerce solution, Magento, and grant the return merchandise request through their enterprise resource planning system, Glovia. Three vendors that perform this duty well are Pervasive, Talend, and SAS Dataflux.

The caveat with middleware is that it is usually somewhat expensive, though incredibly valuable in terms of how much time it will save you. The question to ask is: "Can we afford to have a senior manager that makes $120,000 doing 72 cut-and-pastes, every day?" (Annual cost of that is roughly their entire salary.)

Management

Unless there's a connection to a concrete business objective, you can't really do anything with social customer data. This is where the "rubber meets the road," in the words of Owyang, when business rules, work flows, and process meet the social data. Without these management systems, brands won't know (1) which social customers to help first, (2) which macro solutions can help a majority of them, or (3) which micro decisions need to be made immediately (or who should make those decisions).

Dell Computers, for example, uses Salesforce Customer Portal to map customer support data from Facebook and Twitter all the way through to a closed-case (happy customer). Three vendors who perform management well are Salesforce, SugarCRM, OracleCRM.

An issue that arises with management systems, like monitoring solutions, is that they need to be manned 24/7 in order to prevent social customer crises. Just because your work week ends at 5:00 P.M.

EST on a Friday doesn't mean that your customers won't be triggering business rules that require "micro" (human) decisions at 9:00 A.M. Saturday morning.

Measurement

Measurement is a critical piece for all social customer engagement: without it brands can't tell whether things are improving or worsening. Some brands call this "business analytics software." These are basically fancy dashboards that translate everything the social customer says into actionable decision making. Sample metrics that you could calculate here include Net Promoter,[8] trend forecasting, brand evangelism, customer sentiment analysis, customer satisfaction and virality (how far or how fast customers push the message). NETPROMOTER Pull-through social marketing is impossible without good measurement.

Three vendors that perform measurement well are SAP Business Objects, SAS Institute, and IBM Cognos Express.

If you're thinking of trying to measure metrics across multiple brand extensions (i.e., five different brands under the same mother brand), a measurement suite is crucial. If you're not holistically measuring, you may have one of the companies under your umbrella just going gangbusters, and another having severe problems; without measurement software, this won't be clear, in real-time.

An Example Utilizing All Five Ms

Want to see an example of how the Five Ms are used, all at once? Oracle Retail's Duncan Angove told me about how apparel brands are being transformed by the Five Ms:

> Every Monday morning, at the corporate locations of fashion retail, they do a line review; it's called the Assortment Line Review. They hang the top 10 and bottom 10 performers on the wall. Under each style, they hang the colors. Someone has to run around with Post-it notes and write sales figures

on each item, and then they try to suss out what's driving each of them.

What Social CRM (and the Five Ms do) is automate that process and add social data to the Business Intelligence (BI) data.

"What's missing in that room," Angove said, "is the voice-of-the-customer: what's selling with what."

Here's a real-world example, with some serious impact.

A children's retailer had two khaki skirts—one was a top seller, one was a bottom seller. (This kind of stuff drives the data geeks nuts—you'll understand why in a second.)

"Here's what they found out," Angove said. "The hem on one was an *inch* longer—too short for school. How would you ever know? One of the things I always talk about [with clothing] is *fit*—you never know *fit* at corporate. Now, the customer is sitting in the room with you." This is heavy stuff.

GOING WAY PAST SOCIAL CUSTOMER INSIGHTS: THE OTHER 22 USE CASES

So now you've got the *foundation* of what you can do with Social CRM. In the next six chapters we'll look over the "smaller," more granular use cases, so you'll understand the finer points of what your team can do with Social CRM. You'll probably want to write all over the upcoming chapters with a highlighter or a pencil, so you can choose what your team will do with the social customer by picking your use cases based on your brand's most urgent needs. This is where we will get into the really fun stuff.

By combining Social Customer Insights, what we just learned, with your pick of the remaining 22 use cases of Social CRM, you're going to put together something that will really surprise and delight your customers.

Before you dive into these use cases, I should point out that there's an easy way to set all of these technologies up in your mind, in terms of how *widely adopted* they are. Ray and Jeremiah's study divides each of these use cases into four categories, based on their *technical maturity* ("Does this stuff even work yet?") and their market adoption ("Is anyone actually trying to buy this stuff yet?"). As shown in Table 4.1, those four categories are Early Adoptions, Early Movers, Near Tipping Points, and Evangelizables. Here's a quick breakdown of how to look at this stuff.

EARLY MOVERS (Relatively high market demand, low-to-medium technology maturity)	EVANGELIZABLES (Relatively high market demand, medium-to-high technology maturity)
EARLY ADOPTIONS (Relatively low-to-medium market demand, low-to-medium technology maturity)	NEAR TIPPING POINTS (Relatively low-to-medium market demand, medium-to-high technology maturity)

Table 4.1. Use Case Categories

The two types on the right side of the table, Evangelizables and Near Tipping Points, are technologically in pretty good shape—that means they both work pretty well. The two on the left side of this chart, Early Movers and Early Adoptions, are way less technologically mature. It means these use cases are probably newer, less time-tested, and the technology is *definitely* still evolving. Proceed with caution.

For our purposes, the Early Movers and the Evangelizables are what's going to be "early mainstream," and even the technologies in the Early Adoptions and Near Tipping Points categories should be widely used in the marketplace by 2012.

Keep your eyes peeled for the word *Evangelizable*, because that means the use case you just read about is in "early widespread" use among big-name consumer brands. These use cases are a picture of what's either happening *right now*, and will happen in the next four to six quarters. We're talking short-term here. If someone asks if any of your competitors are using these technologies, scroll down and look for the ones marked Evangelizables and Early Movers to find the "Yes" answer to that question.

Without further ado let's move to Chapter 5 and look at the first group of the "smaller" use cases of Social CRM: social marketing. It's probably the most popular, so it gets to go first.

5

SOCIAL MARKETING

When most people talk about "social media," what they're *really* talking about is *social marketing*—the "tip of the iceberg." This is quite possibly the most fundamental misunderstanding of Social Customer Management and social business. Often, senior executives will hire a strategic consulting team, specializing in social business, then hand them off to the company's advertising or marketing teams. This setup sends what *could have been* a cross-functional voice-of-the-customer engagement into an outsourced *marketing dead zone*. Bye-bye executive sponsorship.[1]

Social marketing only embraces one singular use case of social content: the part that generates customer interest in products or services. There is, however, a general misconception on the part of most consumer brands that social marketing is the be-all-end-all use case for social media or relationships with the social customer. I think the reason is what I call the "first exposure" problem: that most senior executives (people over the age of 40 or 45) were first exposed to social media via a big-brand marketing asset on the social Web (e.g., the Chili's Facebook page or the Starbucks Twitter stream). Whatever the reasoning, social marketing is a single use case category (Jeremiah and Ray's study gave it three subcategories, but we'll be adding a fourth here).

SOCIAL MARKETING INSIGHTS (NUMBER 2)

What Is It and Why Do We Need to Use It?

Companies are confused about the gravity and influence of what the social customer is saying about them, because it's simply not enough for a brand to run a Twitter or Google search of their brand name (try it—what action can you really take with the results?).

When a company says, "We're really puzzled and worried because it seems like there's more information about our brand on the social Web than we have customer data in our internal studies and reports, and we can't tell which pieces of the data are the most important," (e.g., "Facebook knows more about us than we do") that means they have a problem with their social marketing insights. There's one overwhelming common phrase in all social media and social customer strategy: listen before talking. Without deploying some kind of social marketing insights solution, a brand will have no idea what their customers are saying. The key value here is that not only will brands know who the influencers are in the conversation, but they'll know which conversational streams about the brand are most important ("Why don't you make a gluten-free pizza crust? Why isn't there more available in plus sizes?").

Which Consumer Brands Are Using It?

The list here is pretty mind-boggling. Unfortunately, social marketing insights are the 20-minute drum solo of the Social CRM use cases; everyone's doing it but very few brands do it artfully or very well. Critical challenges typically faced because of this are (1) competitive differentiation and (2) razor-sharp metrics. At this point I would be hard-pressed to say that I've walked into many medium-sized ($250 million+) B2C companies in 2010 that were not using *some* form of social marketing insights technology. Nearly every one of my clients has used it, from big brands like Hershey's Chocolate all the way down to medium-sized companies like leisure-cruise brand Hornblower Cruises. When we were approached by Hershey's a couple of years ago, they wanted to learn where their premium gourmet chocolate brands (Dagoba and Scharffen Berger) stood in the mind of the social customer relative to the competition.

If you're looking for a quick example of social marketing insights, one place to start is social demand generation, the sub-field of social marketing insights that harnesses social customers to create demand for a product or service. TD Garden (formerly known as the Fleetcenter) is New England's big sports arena, hosting tons of big concerts, the Boston Bruins hockey team, and the Boston Celtics. TD Garden's marketing and communications division, headed up by Laura Zexter, Director of eBusiness, began integration by developing social content (live blogging games, Facebook, Twitter) and embedding social content into TD Garden's conventional content (beat writing, text programs) in 2009. To begin building a full profile of the social customer, they merged three key areas into their Social CRM system: (1) all of their social content, (2) their Web site and its content management system, and (3) their product itself. Check out Figure 5.1; it's pretty clear how they integrated everything.

TD Garden's strategic aims were fairly simple, and they used clear metrics. They sought to:

1. Measure ticket revenue, per channel, from the social customer

2. Measure the amount of new opt-in social customer CRM records created

3. Figure out the lifetime value per: active e-mail subscriber, Facebook page "likes," and followers

Essentially they were trying to take the meaningless[2] media-centric metrics (Facebook likes, Twitter follows, etc.) and link them up to *real-life* outcomes like how many tickets the person bought to a basketball or hockey game. TD Garden knew they weren't about to get a complete picture of the social customer from a single action (e.g., customer entering a contest, or a "like"). They understood that by using discrete campaigns in each social channel, they were gaining incremental amounts of data about the social customer each time. They figured out where all the Boston-area sports and music fans were hanging out on the social Web using—you guessed it—plain old surveys and profiling (see, Social CRM doesn't have to throw *everything* you know about customer management out the window).

And this case study proves, even "at a glance," that the Social Mar-

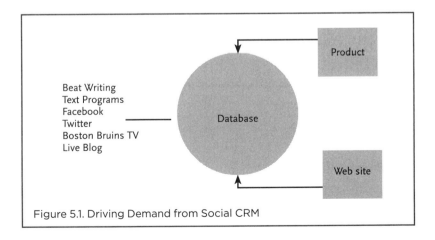

Figure 5.1. Driving Demand from Social CRM

keting Insights use case *aren't just a marketing thing*. TD Garden needed to make operational allocations (HR, staffing, resource allocation) based on what the social customer was saying.

What Is Market Demand and Technology Maturity?

The Altimeter study marked Social Marketing Insights technologies as market-ready (i.e., the stuff actually works) and identified the demand at six to 12 months, so this is a "now" thing, and the technology is nearly 100 percent functional. Out of all of the 23 use cases, this one is nearly the most "baked," and perhaps the most widely deployed. The reason is simple: Social Marketing Insights solutions are poorly leveraged against organizational infrastructure, and are usually purchased by low-level marketing managers and directors who had typically been using a freeware solution previously.[3]

Which Three Vendors Are Doing It Well, for Consumer Brands?

In the small business space (at the time of this writing), Lithium's product offers an entry-level solution in the under-$3,000 per year category. Radian6's product or RightNow Cloud Monitor (part of their Social Experience Suite) would be well-suited for medium and large businesses. Also, I'd be lax if I didn't mention Buzzient, simply because their social media monitoring and management software works well with OracleCRM, Salesforce, and SugarCRM, three CRM systems that are fairly popular with small/medium business as well as enterprise.

In the TD Garden example above, Eloqua was the marketing automation vendor used for capturing all of the social customer data. I'm even going to add a fifth vendor, Hubspot—it's worth examining them from a Social Marketing Insights perspective, since their product is a good fit for small businesses trying to lock up some of the other use cases (Proactive Social Lead Generation, etc.) in an all-in-one suite. While Hubspot is certainly not best-in-class for any one of the use cases, it's definitely a great brand that makes these technologies affordable to brands that otherwise might find them beyond their reach.

What's the Catch?

Some of the less expensive flavors of these software solutions are not quite real-time (hourly or daily updates, rather than minute-by-minute), and reconciling this social marketing data across disparate Customer Relationship Management systems—like our prospective client that has nearly 100 wineries and breweries, all with different CRMs, under their management—can be long and tedious integration. We're talking months or *years*.

RAPID SOCIAL MARKETING RESPONSE (NUMBER 3)

What Is It?

I know, this sounds *just* like social marketing insights, but it's actually the next logical step—defending the brand in a short response time (around five minutes).

This is the use case that *really* validates Social Marketing Insights. For example, let's say you sell all-natural chicken jerky treats for dogs (like one of our clients), and another, separate brand undergoes a gigantic product recall, like the gigantic 2007 Menu Foods pet food recall discussed in Chapter 2. Your brand would use Rapid Social Marketing Response to quickly (say, in under an hour) show customers that your brand is not affected by the recall and that your products are safe.

The Altimeter study cites a document called the Punked List;[4] it's a cringeworthy document that lists brands that have been "exposed" or pranked by the social customer. Again, these incidents only made mainstream media like CNN because the social customer was effectively and quickly engaged.

Which Consumer Brands Are Using It?

The list here is also pretty long because some of the vendors that offer this type of solution are mainstream CRM and social community management vendors (Jive), or even e-mail marketing platforms (ExactTarget recently moved into this space by acquiring CoTweet). A small sample would include Papa John's (HootSuite), Starbucks (CoTweet), and MolsonCoors (Radian6).

What Is Market Demand and Tech Maturity?

This is where I break with the Altimeter report. They say Early Mover, but I say Evangelizable, meaning that the challenge is that while the market demand for this type of solution is actually pretty high, Jeremiah and Ray think the product itself is not yet fully technically "baked." I think it is. The key challenge here is vendor selection—finding one that plays nice with your CRM software. In March 2011, Salesforce and Radian6 announced a Radian6 app that should hopefully do just this.

Which Three Vendors Are Doing It Well, for Consumer Brands?

HootSuite has a nice basic product for under $1,000 per year, and most of the larger Social Marketing Insights brands like Radian6 now have a Rapid Social Marketing Response product built into their Insights solutions; ditto Buzzient, if you're running it on a large CRM. Also, social community platforms like Jive and Salesforce now also have a Rapid Social Marketing Response component built in.

What's the Catch?

You may not need to buy it, because you *might* already own it. Check with your existing vendors before shelling out. The first call to make would be to your existing CRM platform, especially if you're a small or medium-sized brand.

A downside is that it's going to be pretty difficult to coordinate how multiple teams or departments respond to the social customer if the rapid response portion of your Social CRM doesn't share the same platform. Imagine what would happen if your marketing team was using Salesforce, the sales team was using CoTweet and Oracle, and customer service was using a homegrown CRM and HootSuite: a costly Social CRM train wreck would occur.

SOCIAL CAMPAIGN TRACKING (NUMBER 4)

What Is It?

"The one that's going to pop here even more in the next two years or so is Social Campaign Tracking," says Oracle's Mark Woollen.

This is the first use case that directly addresses social advertising, which we'll dig down further into in Chapter 11 when we meet up with experienced social advertising folks. Social Campaign Tracking is the as-we-go or "in flight" tweaking and changing that's needed to massage product or service positioning and messaging in order to meet the dynamic needs of the social customer. For example, let's say that super snack brand Sahale Snacks was about to launch three new flavors at retail. Their Barbeque Almonds turn out to be more popular as a salad topping than as a stand-alone snack. Using Social Campaign Tracking, Sahale Snacks could alter their advertising, on the fly, quickly drafting new ads and deploying them in cooking Web sites and magazines.

Woollen, one of my favorite people in Customer Relationship Management, calls Social Campaign Tracking the "sleeper" hit of 2011–12, meaning that although it may not be the cutest of the use cases, it's the one that may actually provide the clearest and most immediate ROI.

Which Consumer Brands Are Using It?

The name you'll instantly recognize is probably the Republican National Committee (the RNC). If you happened to see the "Fire Pelosi" bus rolling through your town, then you may already be familiar with how the RNC is using Social Campaign Tracking. Their strategic objective in this campaign was pretty simple: to get Speaker of the House Nancy Pelosi out of office. The way they used their Social CRM here was a bit unorthodox, as they didn't rely upon a conventional SCRM system like Salesforce or Oracle to hold the customer data—they used marketing automation software Eloqua, combined with the social media monitoring product Sweet, created by The Pedowitz Group.

When they built their social customer infrastructure, they added what they called a "Custom RNC Layer," which included a few additional components they felt were critical for Social Campaign Tracking, like GOP.AM, a URL-shortening service that lives in the end-user's browser, to allow them to take long Web site addresses and shorten them to something quick-and-easy to share via e-mail, Twitter, or what-have-you. They also added a Points Tracking feature: a mechanism used to track which social customers did the most for "the cause" (I'm guessing they then put this data into Eloqua).

They tracked and measured all of the C2C (customer-to-customer) responses they got from the campaign, then analyzed the data to determine the type of content they needed to push out to their end-users, to figure out what caught on and what didn't. They also heavily promoted their rewards-points system to provide incentive for users to be more social.

Another case study showing the utilization of Social Campaign Tracking comes from Eloqua and their work with Kevin Cote, Digital Marketing leader for the NBA's Golden State Warriors (my home team). It's interesting, because Eloqua is typically thought of as a marketing-force automation software piece, but the social sales function here is clear.

The top-line result of their Social Sales Insights work was "a boost in ticket revenue, greatly increased Web traffic, and record attendance at their NBA Draft Party," according to a case study Cote did with Eloqua. More concretely, the Warriors sold 110 new season tickets and generated $287,000 in additional revenue in two months—not bad for a Social Sales Insights implementation that had a staff of one or two people. (Web site traffic also rose 66 percent, year over year, and the head count for the draft party was 4,000 fans—their biggest ever.)

"Eloqua, our marketing automation solution, was the perfect tool for this contest, as we were able to fully integrate a variety of social media channels while also collecting data on those who participated," Cote said. "We used Eloqua hyper sites and forms and developed a detailed program that was perfect for this sort of contest. Upon registering, users would be able to access the challenge for that specific day and previous days. Once they entered the correct answer to each challenge, a new piece of the puzzle was uncovered, triggered by Eloqua's data collection capabilities."

What Is Market Demand and Tech Maturity?

This is one of those technologies that works at lot better in theory than in reality. Although the social data set is all there and the advertising management systems are well-built, tying social customer data to existing Internet advertising solutions—be they text-ad solutions like Google or Microsoft Search Engine Marketing, behavioral solutions like Rapleaf or Acxiom, or conventional Interactive Advertising Bureau (IAB)-type advertising management solutions—is *really tough* right now. I therefore have to agree with Ray and Jeremiah in marking this use case in the "somewhat mature" Early Adoptions quadrant. There simply aren't enough big case studies to prove widespread adoption yet; not for lack of viable solutions or consulting firms who know how to implement them.

Which Three Vendors Are Doing It Well, for Consumer Brands?

Both Marketo and Eloqua have a pretty clear offering here, especially in relation to medium-sized businesses; Radian6, which we introduced earlier in the chapter, would also be a fit. Other vendors in the space include Attensity (which acquired Biz360) and Overtone.

What's the Catch?

Since this technology is immature, it will be a space to watch, especially from the advertising technology side. Hopefully, some of the ad brands like Google will come up with solutions that better mesh with existing Social CRM solutions, allowing advertisers to more seamlessly alter campaigns on the fly.

SOCIAL EVENT MANAGEMENT (NUMBER 5)

What Is It?

No, this isn't Facebook's popular Events feature or Eventbrite (a ticket sales Web site that integrates with Social CRMs like Salesforce), even though it sounds like it. Confusing, huh? Social Event Management is a collection of technologies that promote and pump up the quality of real-life (e.g., conferences, premieres) and virtual events. Remember the first big virtual fashion show on the Internet? The Victoria's Secret 1999 fashion show, put on by Broadcast.com[5] was a *defining* moment in Internet history because it leveraged off-line media (TV, print, etc.) to promote a huge live event on the Internet, and ended up bringing in an unprecedented 2 million viewers. NEVEREATALONE We're not quite talking Super Bowl size numbers, but this was a big deal, especially at the time.

Then there's the *in-event* use case. Speakers want to know that what they're saying is engaging, whether it's a lingerie-model fashion show or a political speech. (Imagine gubernatorial candidates using a Radian6 console from the podium to change talking points on the fly; it's not that far-fetched.) Want name tags for an event that process all of your customers' social data and tell who they might want to meet at your event? Use something like Pathable.

Which Consumer Brands Are Using It?

If you think about it, a plane flight is basically an event. It only happens once, and Virgin Airlines figured out a way to give their customers a way to reward them for evangelizing their brand—in November 2010 they began giving customers Frequent Flyer points for their location-based check-ins on Facebook or Foursquare.

For virtual events, the big name that comes to mind is Proctor & Gamble, which has been working with InXPO. Also, pharmaceutical brands like Merck, AstraZeneca, and Lilly have been working with ON24, but doing it in a B2B capacity.[6] Social event middleware brands like Gigya seem to be a big hit with consumer-content brands like Alloy Media and MTV.

Although it's easy to figure it out when a geeked-out brand like a tech conference uses Social Event Management (Gnomedex, Future of Web Apps, Le Web), hunting down consumer brands that have explored Social Event Management is much more difficult because this concept is pretty new to the general public. As you can tell, so far some of these use cases are pretty mainstream, while others are still on the fringe or evolving.

What Is Market Demand and Tech Maturity?

Although these technologies have existed since at least 2007, Social Event Management is still a fairly low-adoption technology, and most consumer brands are relying on nonintegrated social technologies (putting the event on Facebook and Twitter, hoping and praying), and receiving unclear ROI. I'm going to push Jeremiah and Ray's borderline Early Adoptions/Near Tipping Points firmly into the Near Tipping Points quadrant, just because the technology actually works.

Which Three Vendors Are Doing It Well, for Consumer Brands?

It depends what you're looking for here, whether you want expertise in real-world events, virtual events, or both. In the virtual events space, InXpo, Unisfair, and ON24 are worth a look.

Gigya now fills an interesting niche in this space: changing the direction from their initial offering, they now act as a sort of middleware between branded content (your Web site) and the social Web (social customer data). This function effectively makes Gigya low-key, flexible social customer middleware. Outside of the mainstream, cool little niche vendors like Pathable are attempting to take conference quality up a notch by creating episodic social networks and communities just for conferences.

What's the Catch?

Generally speaking, there's going to be some custom programming involved to tie these Social Event Management systems back to your single-source-of-truth for the social customer, your Social CRM system. Luckily, nearly all of these vendors have flexible application programming interfaces (APIs).

An API is a pathway that allows one type of software to connect to another piece of software. Great APIs allow all the pieces of software in your business to talk to one another, and prevent your teams from wasting countless worker-hours manually reconciling stuff. I've tried not to use terms like API too much in this book, but to be blunt with you: you're not going to manage social customer data for millions of customers without knowing something about APIs and how different types of software connect to one another.

SOCIAL PULL-THROUGH MARKETING (NUMBER 6)

What Is It?

This is a new use case that I've added, from hearing about it on customer and prospect interviews repeatedly in 2010 and 2011. Pull-Through Marketing is a process where a brand tries to gain market share by increasing sales for a specific product in a particular time period. On the social Web, Pull-Through Marketing is when a brand purposely gathers armies of customer evangelists to solicit a key corporate customer.

For example, a prospective client of mine makes a "green" fossil fuel alternative brand that allows big multinationals like Proctor & Gamble and Unilever to stop using fossil fuels in their cosmetics and food-and-beverage products. They want to cultivate armies of customer evangelists (e.g., political advocates, students, environmentalists, people who have used their product before) to applaud the P&Gs and Unilevers of the world for cutting deals with their company. They're hoping this will help speed up their time-to-market and get closed product deals "live" (essentially, on the shelves) a lot faster.

Which Consumer Brands Are Using It?

To the best of my knowledge, few consumer brands are currently using this use case, although I've spoken with a few that want to. The more familiar use case here would be in politics, and especially in political activism. I expect this use case to break first in the green products space. I've worked with a number of "grass-tops" organizations in the last couple of years, and Social Pull-Through Marketing (to influence legislative outcomes) was a key use case in three different projects.

What Is Market Demand and Tech Maturity?

It's pretty indeterminate at this point, as I don't know of any vendors that have a solution for this use case. I'd have to put it in the bottom-left corner of the Early Adopters quadrant, because the technology is little more than "vaporware" (i.e., an idea, not a prototype).

Which Three Vendors Are Doing It Well, for Consumer Brands?

If a client came to me today and said they *had* to do Social Pull-Through Marketing, I'd recommend that they integrate two different technologies to make this concept a reality: (1) a CRM platform, to aggregate all data and results and track the actions of key customers, as they're influenced by the social Web (e.g., how fast deals close, how fast products come out), and (2), a Social Customer Insights solution that has good sentiment analysis—pick any one from the vendors above, but I'd try to go with something that works on your CRM system. Then, they'd also want to hire a great PR firm to figure out what the messaging would be, so that when the consumers are speaking to the key customers (e.g., Unilever, P&G, etc.) on the brand's behalf, they're saying the "right" thing.

What's the Catch?

Writing the strategy and buying the technology to do Social Pull-Through Marketing isn't the hard part. Having a brand value promise (the value that the brand promises to provide to the consumer) strong enough to make consumers stand behind you is the hard part. Social Pull-Through may be easy if you're making best-in-class organic gluten-free baby food. Not so much, though, if you're selling truck tires or tampons.

Next, we can move on to the fun part—getting out there in the field and closing deals. Some people like sales, some people don't. I really do. For the first three years of my career I sold truckloads of computers and computer software, over the phone.

If you used to be a sales manager, say 10 years ago, the following chapter is going to completely blow your mind, not so much because the new technology is really cool, but because there are so many things that sales professionals used to have to come into work on a Saturday morning to do (e.g., prospecting, sending greeting cards, networking) that can actually happen through different types of social customer management technology and sales-force automation (sometimes called SFA).

6

SOCIAL SALES

There are some Social CRM sales solutions in this chapter that will make you want to go out and start using them tomorrow. The cool thing is, you actually can do that. Take, for example, the Sales 2.0 software InsideView. If you really wanted to use it, you could put down this book right now and start using their 30-day trial. Whereas some of the marketing and customer-support use cases of Social CRM have more of a "slow burn" to their assessment strategy, those concerning sales can quickly show you their effectiveness.

This chapter isn't so much about closing the deal *directly* with the social customer as it is how to use the social Web to generate *opportunities* to get the social customer into the sales funnel. (If you're looking for the first "show me the money" section in the book, this is it.) Granted, most of these social sales use cases will show bigger results on the business-to-business side of a consumer brand (think of our client MBT Footwear selling 10,000 pairs of shoes to FedEx, rather than selling one single pair of shoes to 10,000 individual social customers). I've included the three original use cases from the Altimeter Report (Social Sales Insights, Rapid Social Sales Response, and Proactive Social Lead Generation) and also added a new one: Social Demand Generation. Yup, it's that demand value chain again.

SOCIAL SALES INSIGHTS (NUMBER 7)

What Is It?

This is one of the big ones. Social Sales Insights is how salespeople and brands figure out where their customers hang out online. In the last three years it's been hard for brands (especially consumer brands) to sell in social channels because they've had low budgets or inferior tools. Social Customer Insights provide foundation-level insights, which can then be built upon by Social Sales Insights software. This stuff has two goals: (1) figure out where the prospects and customers are having their conversations, and (2) figure out what their urgent needs and key concerns are.

Here's how it works: it calculates what level of influence a given social channel has, then allows organizations to focus their sales efforts, rather than using what Owyang and Wang call the "shotgun approach"—a little time spent everywhere—which usually yields middling-to-crummy results. They give a good B2B example in their white paper: one of their Fortune 100 financial services clients implemented Social Sales Insights to figure out the "exact right moment" they could be helpful in social channels—four months later their social channel territory sales made up 10 percent of all sales.

There are two different flavors of Social Sales Insights, too: proactive and reactive. Reactive programs like Rapid Social Sales Response (we'll get to that one in a moment) respond to what customers and prospects have already said or done. Proactive ones like Social Sales Insights, Proactive Social Lead Generation, Direct and Distributed Social Commerce, and Dynamic Social Supply Reallocation manage social customer relationships by proactively engaging with social customers to drive sales.

Which Consumer Brands Are Using It?

Oracle's Mark Woollen has a big prediction here: Social Sales Insights is going to become an "everyday" use case for brands.

"You'll see [Social CRM] underneath the umbrella of basically sales performance, improving the performance of the business," he said. "There's a larger reason why companies need to invest in these kinds of things. Social is effectively one of *many* tools. It's, as we've discussed, not necessarily the best-known tool."

But, the holy grail of Social Sales Insights is the cross-channel sale:

> [Social's] certainly not the most mature tool, but it is rapidly growing, and if you look at the revenue derived from cross-channel sales, and how that continues to grow (this doesn't mean online sales, but maybe something that starts by [a customer] doing research from an online community) ... If you're going to be truly cross channel and ride that huge growing wave, it's larger than online sales only already, and growing faster than online sales. You've *got* to be there.

But finding consumer brands that are using Social Sales Insights on a daily basis can be tough, and it's something much more commonly found in B2B brands than in B2C. I'm going to have to downgrade this one to Early Mover for consumer brands, as there's little traction in the space so far.

What Is Market Demand and Tech Maturity?

This one is right in the middle, for our purposes. Although the Altimeter white paper calls this one an Evangelizable—because the technology is about "beta ready" and Social Sales Insights are currently being used "in the wild"—the case studies lean heavily toward B2B brands, rather than B2C or "B2C2C" brands, as Oracle's Woollen calls them. (This means that when your brand sells to consumers, consumers are essentially selling you to other consumers.)

Which Three Vendors Are Doing It Well, for Consumer Brands?

For small business, my pick would be Lithium, since it's simple, cheap, and easy to use. Lithium has owned the low-cost segment of the brand-monitoring space for the last couple of years. Any time you mention Lithium, you're not far from mentioning their competitor, Jive, whose Social Business Suite has some impressive sales applications (as well as a full-fledged application platform), as well as Alterian. Obviously, thinking outside the box and looking at marketing automation platforms like Eloqua and Marketo may be prudent, here, as some of their social campaign tracking use cases are similar to Social Sales Insights, in terms of functionality—the Eloqua Golden State Warriors case study that drove $287,000 in incremental season ticket revenue in the last chapter is definitely worth reexamining here.

What's the Catch?

There aren't a ton of *consumer* brands that have clear success stories here, so planning may require careful handholding from vendors or consultants. B2B companies have clearer success stories here.

RAPID SOCIAL SALES RESPONSE (NUMBER 8)

What Is It?

The key difference between Rapid Social Sales Response and Social Sales Insights is *speed*. Here's a crazy example of how my tiny little consulting firm used Rapid Social Sales Response about a year ago.

I received an e-mail at 9:02 A.M. from InsideView, our social sales solution, informing us that a Colorado-based hotel chain prospect of ours had hired a new director of sales—this was published in an obscure hospitality trade publication that we didn't even follow. By 9:04 A.M. that new hire received his very first e-mail, from my company (a free electronic copy of my first book). Dumbfounded, he replied, "How did you get this e-mail? I just started this morning." That's Rapid Social Sales Response. That hotel company now regularly engages with my company, over e-mail, and attends our online events.

Which Consumer Brands Are Using It?

The consumer-brand list is actually short to nonexistent: I can only think of seeing Joie De Vivre Hotels doing this currently. For B2B brands, however, the list here is fairly long and includes GE, Adobe, Merrill Lynch, and perhaps the software company SuccessFactors.

What Is Market Demand and Tech Maturity?

Near Tipping Point—I agree with Jeremiah and Ray on this one. There are just not enough consumer-brand case studies yet to call this *Evangelizable,* but you can clearly see the use case, say, to the B2B or distribution side of a consumer brand.

Which Three Vendors Are Doing It Well, for Consumer Brands?

The one that has always blown my mind here is InsideView (a former client of mine from their early days). The other one that's pretty cool is called DemandBase—it actually monitors who is browsing your brand's Web site, in real-time (some people would lump this into the next use case, Proactive Social Lead Generation). Lithium Technologies is also solid here, especially if your brand is running its own branded community. Jive is also worth a look, if your company has internal *and* external communities.

What's the Catch?

Once your B2B sales team gets ahold of these technologies, most of the savvier people on the team will be unable to function without them. Some "traditionalists" may also be highly resistant to using these tools, to their own detriment.

PROACTIVE SOCIAL LEAD GENERATION (NUMBER 9)

What Is It?

There are two ways to educate prospects about your brand. You can do it, or your customers can do it. Think about it as a prospective car buyer: would you rather hear about the new Toyota Siena Minivan from the TV commercial, or from your friend Dan at a backyard BBQ? Proactive Social Lead Generation is what happens when your own customers refer leads to you, over the social Web. These are generally the most highly trusted leads, because they come from "customers like me." (If you don't recognize the phrase "someone like me," it's most likely because you haven't been reading the Edelman Trust Barometer surveys—they come out every year, and they measure who consumers trust, and why.[1])

It's simply *not enough* for brands to get cold and warm leads through the social channels the previous two social sales use cases deliver (Rapid Social Sales Response, Social Sales Insights); brands need "feet on the street" referrals from real people; scalability is a key challenge without this. You can only have *so many* people on the sales team, right?

If you're looking for an entry-point to dabble in sales-force automation and marketing-force automation, this one may promise the quickest wins.

Which Consumer Brands Are Using It?

It is difficult to find consumer brands that are mining this vein of Social Customer Relationship Management, but the SBLI Life

Insurance Company is one. First, they performed a social assessment to figure out where their social customers "lived," which is pretty basic, as brands were doing this in 2006 and 2007. But here's the crazy part. They learned that a small subset of their customers (Texas, Tenessee, Virginia, California, and Colorado) were highly social, that their "average friend count" was way higher than the average, by state, when it came to the percentage of customers socially engaged with the company. It would be my strategic recommendation to pursue these leads ahead of other similar leads in less social states, as I think these customers would be more likely to evangelize the brand profitably.

One of the best examples in Jeremiah and Ray's white paper is when a major consumer electronic brand using Proactive Social Lead Generation converted leads to sales adding "immediate profits and reduc[ing] sales channel costs by as much as 33 percent."

Sharebuilder 401(k) is a consumer financial brand that's done some great work with Manticore Technologies, a Proactive Lead Generation and marketing-force automation brand from Austin. Key outputs of their work together were revenue per rep increasing by 9.3 percent, and the increase in inactive leads closing was 250 percent. Sharebuilder's sales cycle also got 12 percent shorter. Although I'm uncertain if Manticore had introduced their social functionality (Jigsaw, LinkedIn, and Facebook, to begin) into the product (it came on-line in September 2009) throughout *all* of their work with Sharebuilder (the relationship goes back to 2006), I'm fairly confident that Sharebuilder will see continued growth with the product, now that the social component is online.

What Is Market Demand and Tech Maturity?

It is totally Evangelizable. In fact this is the *most* mature of the social sales uses cases.

Go for it.

Which Three Vendors Are Doing It Well, for Consumer Brands?

The clear fit for small business here would be Lithium, although some custom coding may be necessary for it to integrate with your CRM system. The Oracle/Buzzient "cocktail"[2] or the Oracle/Radian6 combination would be a solid fit for larger brands, and Manticore Technology is worth a look, as they offer some advanced features at a fairly low price point. If lead scoring and lead nurturing is your primary aim, Manticore could be for you. If you're on a smaller budget, it's likely that the price of Radian6 could decrease, in the coming year.

What's the Catch?

Proactive Lead Generation is not something to be dabbled in; it permanently alters the way your brand's B2B and B2C2C sales pipelines will work. Entry costs are a bit high for tiny brands, but so are the rewards, and will likely result in shorter time-to-close, better qualified leads, and a chance to tell if your sales team is any good.

DIRECT AND DISTRIBUTED SOCIAL COMMERCE (NUMBER 10)

What Is It?

When a brand sells products in a *distributed* manner on the social Web, in the form of branded widgets or content distributed across social channels (as opposed to destination e-commerce, like Gap.com or Vic toriassecret.com), that's direct or distributed social commerce. What it frequently looks like is a series of widgets or pieces of content that may at first look like ads, but they are actually "helper" applications that allow brands to sell product across a series of platforms on the social Web, simultaneously (on mobile apps, on social networks, in many places at once, essentially). The key difference between direct and distributed social commerce is that in the former, the commerce piece (where the user buys the product or service) lives in one place only—on the brand's destination Web site.

Imagine this: you go to WetSeal.com for the first time, and you're asked if you'd like to sign in—once you do, you can create outfits for yourself, then share them with friends on either the Wet Seal Web site or across the social Web. If you or your friends can purchase the outfits only through Wet Seal's Web site, it's direct social commerce. If you and your friends can buy the newly created outfits in many places at once (e.g., widgets or mobile sites), then it's distributed social commerce.

Which Consumer Brands Are Using It?

Although social commerce began with the little guys (small arts-and-crafts makers, independent musicians), the list of big consumer brands using this use case is getting larger. The most notable examples include Delta Airlines, Brooks Brothers, wellness/self-help brand Gaiam (all Facebook), and clothing and cosmetic brands like Avon's Mark program and Wet Seal. Avon's doing well with this type of commerce—Mark's 2009 revenue was $70 million (although this figure included both door-to-door and online sales).

"We thought it would be an innovative way to bring together our direct selling approach with our social media marketing," Annemarie Frank, director of e-commerce, Digital and Strategic Alliances for Avon's Mark brand, said in an interview with *Direct Marketing News*.[3] Delta Airlines launched their pioneering "Ticket Window" on Facebook in August 2010, becoming the first airline brand to engage in direct social commerce, and clothing retailer JCPenney launched an on-Facebook shopping app a few months later. Avon is probably the only cosmetics and beauty brand to approach social commerce head-on (and rather early in the game).

"Our rep is our store owner and our customer," said Claudia Poccia, global president of Avon's Mark, in an interview with WWD.[4] "She has to have a voice and be able to customize her business. Anything short of that is unacceptable." Avon's got their money where their collective mouths are, committing $50 million over the next few years to the program—that's a commitment of nearly $1,000 per rep. If you think about it, the Facebook direct social commerce engagement fights against the one thing that's been plaguing Avon salespeople since the beginning of the company—unanswered doorbells.

To simply reduce the term "social commerce" to brands selling consumer packaged goods and apparel on Facebook would be a *gross* oversimplification. In the last three years, a series of social commerce brands like Payvment, Cartfly, and BeeShopy were launched. Most of these brands specialize in the "widgetization" of consumer-packaged goods and clothing, and most work either only on certain social Web platforms (like Facebook) or on the social Web. Even the bigger payment platform brands have introduced a social commerce aspect, like Amazon and Paypal, but many of their solutions look like afterthoughts, and usage of their social commerce products is not widespread.

What Is Market Demand and Tech Maturity?

I was having coffee with Ray Wang at a hotel bar, and he looked up at me and said, "Adam, *nobody's* really doing social commerce." Since this conversation took place a little after the Delta launch, I was confused by his remark.

My reply was that nobody is really doing it very *well*. I spoke with the second-largest hotel in Los Angeles the other day, and about 5 percent of their online revenue comes from social commerce. That said, Avon practically bet the farm on it—we'll get further into their case study in a later chapter. I'd place both market demand and tech maturity at "early adoptions," which means that by late 2011 we should expect to see direct and distributed social commerce in the Evangelizable quadrant.

Which Three Vendors Are Doing It Well, for Consumer Brands?

If you're looking for a quick get-up-and-go solution to simply test the waters, something small like Cartfly could be a good place to start. Small-to-medium-sized brands may want to look into using Payvment due to its support for multiple vendors, making it akin to a product that allows for an Amazon-type experience on Facebook, for example. The third choice here is a custom solution based on larger CRM and ERP platforms. The larger implementations that I'm seeing in this space are primarily based on Enterprise-class platforms like Oracle Retail.

What's the Catch?

This is still somewhat untested, and if your product isn't "viral" (i.e., "Do your customers *love* to talk about it to other prospective customers?"), in and of itself, social commerce may not be a fit at this time. I'm unsure that social commerce would be a good fit if you're selling, say, snow tires, or rhinoplasty. Then again, if everyone in your neck of the woods needs snow tires, or if you run the best nose-job clinic in West L.A., then maybe this is the way to go.

DYNAMIC SOCIAL SUPPLY REALLOCATION (NUMBER 11)

What Is It?

This is where we begin to explore the notion of the "social supply chain." The idea is that brands will be able to reallocate products that are in the supply chain, dynamically, based on customer conversations on the social Web.

I call it the "blue sweater" problem. Imagine there's a fashion show at an East Coast college outside of Philadelphia. Five hundred college students are there. A fashion brand debuts their new blue cardigans at this event, and the students immediately begin talking about the sweaters on the social Web. Meanwhile, a truck is about to leave a loading dock in New York, filled with purple sweaters for a chain of clothing stores on college campuses—say Urban Outfitters. The social media monitoring software triggers a micro decision to someone at Urban Outfitters who then sees this conversation and decides to reroute the truckload of sweaters (remember Jacob Morgan's diagram of Macro vs. Micro? Human decisions versus robot decisions?), which then sends the purple ones to California, and sends out an alternate truckload of blue sweaters to Pennsylvania colleges, where they're more likely to sell.

A lot of people call this whole supply-chain idea the "Internet of Things," meaning it's very beneficial for the social customer if brands know where all of their products or components are within the supply chain. Most Social CRM vendors get wide-eyed when you mention this scenario and say something like, "This is at least five years off." I say they are entirely incorrect, and I've got a few senior CRM guys who can back me up on it.

"What you're describing [dynamic social supply reallocation]," said Duncan Angove, of Oracle Retail, who we'll chat more with later in the book, "no one's doing exactly [that], but it's *not* science fiction. All of the pieces exist today."

Which Consumer Brands Are Using It?

To the best of my knowledge, nobody. This one is pretty much theoretical. "But the pieces are all there—no one's just put them together in that way," said Angove.

What Is Market Demand and Tech Maturity?

This one sits firmly in the bottom left-hand quadrant. We're looking two years out into the future. It's a prototype, with low market demand. But keep your eyes peeled in 2013.

Which Three Vendors Are Doing It Well, for Consumer Brands?

Any CRM or ERP vendor that has a solid social-media monitoring front end would be a fit here—Buzzient and Radian6 both come to mind. The key is that you need three pieces to do this: social media monitoring, ERP, and CRM. A few combinations I can think of that would work are Buzzient/Radian6/Oracle Retail or Radian6/Glovia/Salesforce (Glovia is an inexpensive ERP platform that works on Salesforce); or for enterprise, Salesforce/Netsuite.

Each time you're doing something like this, you will need four pieces: a social media monitoring tool, a social media management tool, a CRM solution, and some kind of supply-chain management or ERP solution to actually move the inventory around, catering to your customers' wants.

What's the Catch?

You're going into seriously uncharted waters. But it might save your company millions, because you're getting the right product to the right customer at the right time, and replenishing your stock at exactly the right speed. (This is something Wal-mart started going after in a big way in 2010. A 2010 *Wall Street Journal* article showed that when American Apparel rolled out a 2007 radio frequency ID tags [RFID] program on their apparel, stores that participated saw a 15.7 percent increase in sales, which could mean billions for Wal-mart.[5]

SOCIAL DEMAND GENERATION (NUMBER 12)

What Is It?

There is a big difference between lead generation and demand generation, and it's as big as the difference between Paul McCartney's

Wings and the Beatles, even though they sit on the same side of the value chain (the *demand value chain* side of the house). Demand generation uses multiple sales and marketing programs to drive your prospects' awareness of your products and services, and attempts to marry the multiple marketing processes to the structured sales process, or the "funnel." Proactive Lead Generation is usually just a *subset* of demand generation, and it's not always used by all demand generation programs.

"Social Demand Generation is the use of social media *as a channel* to listen to and foster conversations with prospects and customers as a means of creating or *qualifying* revenue opportunities for a company." This is according to my demand generation guru, The Pedowitz Group's Bruce Culbert.

Culbert isn't pretending that demand generation didn't exist before the social customer—it did—but just like much of the volume of customer service and support has "migrated down-channel" to the social Web, demand generation has gone that way, too. Same stuff, different channel, right?

Demand generation is no joke. Big consumer brands that didn't even have someone tasked with demand generation just a year ago now have employees with "Demand Generation" in their title, usually a fairly senior-level marketing person who works as an adjunct to the sales team. In 2009 the big wine and beer brand I mentioned in the last chapter had no one in charge of demand generation. Today they have a Director of Demand Generation on their direct-to-consumer division, and she has an employee who works on demand generation reporting to her.

Demand generation today is probably where lead generation was about 10 years ago, but growing at a rapid pace for consumer brands.

Which Consumer Brands Are Using It?

A bit of growth is occurring in the normally conservative sports segment, including NBA basketball brands like the Miami Heat and the

Portland Trail Blazers, as well as the Golden State Warriors (my home team) and the Cleveland Cavaliers. Eloqua's case study page features some pretty "household" brand names, including Comcast Spectacor (their Philly-based sports/entertainment brand).

The video case study by Comcast Spectacor's Mark DiMaurizo is a cool little story about how his team stopped using the old "spray and pray" methodology (akin to the old "smile and dial" method from the world of public relations), and moved over to a Social Demand Generation solution that allowed them to "shorten [their] sales cycle to work with hotter leads," both on the B2B and B2C2C side. An example of where Comcast Spectacor used Social Demand Generation was in their Season Ticket Renewal Campaign: their online conversion-to-sale for season tickets increased 12 percent.

What Is Market Demand and Tech Maturity?

I'm thinking that 2011 is the year that Social Demand Generation hits the beach. The reason a lot of consumer brands held back in 2009 and 2010 was because this type of work was typically the domain of B2B brands, but the mainstream demand-generation brands are finally getting some consumer-brand case studies together. I'd call this one Near Tipping Point, in terms of consumer-brand readiness. These days it's what I do for B2B and B2C brands all the time—Social Demand Generation.

Which Three Vendors Are Doing It Well, for Consumer Brands?

Eloqua would be the first brand I'd look to in this space, followed by Marketo. Although the Boston-based company primarily works with B2B brands, they've been doing demand-generation for a number of cool consumer brands in the last year or so. Brands on a lower budget may want to check out HubSpot, who also have a very cool Inbound Marketing University (a no-cost 16-hour course) on how to get customers to contact your business, and how to generate leads from the social Web and otherwise.[6] INBOUND

What's the Catch?

While the good news is that this is a fairly well-developed use case, around the social customer, automating demand generation from the social Web is time consuming, and will require some dedicated resources in terms of personnel and budget. A very basic solution, with CRM integration, will set you back nearly $10,000, and some solutions can run more than a good employee. They can, however, yield multimillion dollar results, so don't be scared off.

Okay, so now you've made the sale, or maybe your customers still have questions before they buy something from you. Let's switch gears from the Sales stack of social customer use cases to the Support stack: here are all the things your customer support team can do with the social customer. Once you've sold social customers something, you have to take care of them. If you don't, the whole thing will fall apart.

7

SOCIAL SUPPORT

Let's take a step back in time to 2000, when customer support as we know it today was pretty different. For example, say you received your first cell phone bill, and it was $100 too high. You'd call the phone company's call center, and be put on hold for five minutes. Then you'd complain to the customer care representative, and if they didn't adjust your bill, you'd ask to speak to their supervisor. Hopefully, within a half hour, your bill would be fixed. This method of problem solving was expensive for the telephone company brand in two ways: the customer dissatisfaction caused churn (customers to come and go), and each phone call to the company took a good amount of time to resolve.

These days, our company is beginning to get phone calls from big-name call center brands because their own customers

are beginning to ask them what they should do with the social customer. For example, a 1-800-employee call center brand contacted
us wondering what they should sell their customers, to help monitor the social channels, because the customers are telling them that
a lot of the comments and complaints that their brands are getting
have "migrated down-channel" to the social Web. Hence, social service and support.

Social service and support allow brands to solve customers'
problems a lot faster in a way that's more meaningful to customers and provides them the opportunity to solve one another's problems *because they want to.* You read that right. There are certain
brands where the customers love the brand so damn much that
they're willing to do customer service gratis. I'll give you an easy
example.

Ever use Tide detergent? It's made by Procter & Gamble. They
use a Social Customer Management tool to talk with their customers called GetSatisfaction. You can check it out at community.tide.
com/tide. This social service and support community is there to
serve four functions (Tide keeps it simple): customers can (1) ask a
question, (2) share an idea, (3) report a problem, or (4) give praise.
There's also a spot where customers can give Tide a tip. It's like the
old "write to us" P.O. Box on the back of the detergent box, except
incredibly more transparent. Who knows where those letters were
going, right?

Now, there are some serious conversations going on in these forums, in full view of the public. For example, after the Haitian earthquake in January 2010, a user named Barbara was dissatisfied with
Tide's response to the earthquake, so she asked why Tide wasn't doing more about it. Within a few hours, Mandy, a Tide employee,
revealed that the Tide team was planning something to help the
Haitian earthquake victims, and within a few days Tide clearly explained their plan to work collaboratively with their customers to
raise $250,000 to $500,000 to send to Haiti.

SOCIAL SUPPORT INSIGHTS (NUMBER 13)

What Is It?

You start with basic analysis that comes from Social Customer In-sights: the foundational material that tells you what your custom-ers want you to know about the experience they're having with your brand. Social Support Insights technology can usually automate a few things important to your brand, like how influential a given customer is, whether the customer is "friend or foe," figure out if the customer is associated with any given organization (e.g., trade group or cus-tomer group), and, most important, picking the appropriate response channel—mail, e-mail, social Web, phone, and so on.

So, here's where it gets involved. A B2C consumer, in a social sup-port situation, can actually be a B2B influencer. I read about this case study a couple of years ago where there was an unhappy customer of a phone company who turned out to be the CEO of a huge B2B partner of the phone company. So, frequently, a B2C problem can become a *huge* B2B problem. Turns out the phone company actually upgraded the service *just* in the partner company CEO's neighborhood, as not to put their partnership in jeopardy. Smart, huh?

Without using some sort of Social Support Insights solution, your company might be wasting a ton of money by responding first to nonin-fluential customers, and using the wrong channel to respond to them. Social Support Insights isn't about working hard to satisfy the customer, it's about working smart. In Jeremiah and Ray's white paper, they talk about a utility brand that implemented a social support solution to help their support team figure out which influencers were of key importance, and they saw an 11 percent increase in customer satisfaction.

Which Consumer Brands Are Using It?

The list here is gigantic. Let's start with Pepsi, Coca-Cola, McDonald's, and Eurostar. You can pretty much assume that smaller brands are getting into Social Support Insights, too. One easy-to-wrap-your-head-around example would be Whirlpool Corporation. These guys have been known as being serious about voice-of-the-customer since 1967, when they launched the first toll-free customer support line. They began using Social Support Insights (Attensity was their solution of choice) in 2008, launching their Digital Detectives program. The goal of the program was to identify and *proactively* reach out to distressed customers using social media. Dig that last part: Whirlpool wanted to proactively figure out which customers were having big problems before the customers even called them. When the program first launched, Whirlpool scoured through customers' postings in online forums, and then contacted them by e-mail to take care of the problem.

Fast forward to 2010, when Whirlpool truly decided to put the "social" into their Social Support Insights. They opened up a unique Attensity account for each of their brand extensions (kitchen, laundry room, water filtration), which allowed their Digital Detectives team to follow their social customer support mantra: "respond online, resolve offline." Each customer support team was trained to speak on the social Web in the unique voice of each brand. When a customer posted a distressed "tweet" or lifestyle forum posting, the Digital Detectives followed up with public response, and then with a private phone call once they engaged the customer publicly.

The big difference between the 2008 and the 2010 strategy (essentially, what makes the 2010 strategy Social CRM and the 2008 strategy *not* Social CRM), is that Whirlpool chose to address the problems publicly. Whirlpool, however, isn't running any sort of influencer software to gauge which customers are more influential than others. They're not responding to the Ashton Kutchers of the world (5.9 million Twitter followers as of this writing) any faster than to my Bubby Burnis (yup, my grandmother again), up in Syracuse, New York. And she's not even on the Internet. Now that's social customer democracy-in-action.

On top of the whole Digital Detectives program, the brand units of Whirlpool—like the Whirlpool Institute of Fabric Science—took to the social Web as "laundryologists" in pursuit of customers who have laundry-related questions on Facebook and Twitter. Whirlpool's goal was to build their brands through service (rather than differentiate on, say, price), and they did this by leveraging the social customer. They also utilized a response time metric seen from the consumer's point of view (from the time the first tweet was written until first response), as well as an internal metric (how efficiently the problem gets cascaded and routed, using micro and macro work flows).

One of Lithium's customers, a consumer electronics brand that manages their community on the Lithium platform, reported a deflection of 1.4 million customer support calls, saving the brand an estimated $10 million. Funny, that $100,000 software investment and the $1 million in consulting and training doesn't sound so crazy now, huh?

What Is Market Demand and Tech Maturity?

There's seriously high market demand for Social Support Insights, and by the time you read this, the technology should be very mature: market-ready and swiftly declining in price.

Which Three Vendors Are Doing It Well, for Consumer Brands?

For big brands, Jive Software, which integrated start-up Filtrbox into their Social Business Suite, is worth a look. Attensity's also a pick here, as is Radian6 or Lithium, which are both price-accessible to smaller brands.

What's the Catch?

If you want to derive Social Support Insights for a consumer brand, someone will have to watch the dashboards every few hours, 24/7. That said, it only costs about $7,000 a year to have someone overseas watching your dashboards while you're out of the office if you don't already have non-U.S.-based offices. The customer service savings here could be in the millions.

Also, the level of customers you'll be supporting on the social Web are anecdotally more affluent and influential than those dialing into your call center, but you'd probably want to call up the folks at Right Now to get a study that actually puts that in writing. The study is called Customer Experience Impact: North America 2010 Report.[1] CXI It's a simple report, but it makes a *ton* of sense—it includes all the statistics on why customers leave you. Fact of the matter is, 82 percent of all customers have reported leaving a brand because of a lousy customer experience, *and* most customers are actually willing to pay extra for a great customer experience. (If you have kids and you've ever been to an American Girl store, it will completely validate this finding. Paul Greenberg wrote about the phenomenal soup-to-nuts American Girl customer experience in *CRM at the Speed of Light*.)

RAPID SOCIAL RESPONSE (NUMBER 14)

What Is It?

This one is sort of the customer service "cousin" of Rapid Social Sales Response. If you do one without the other, there's a pretty big risk factor involved: your sales team will appear highly engaged, but the customer service team behind them will seem kind of out-of-it.

Your customers are expecting real-time customer service. If your brand can't respond to customer cases and feedback in real-time, your customer expectations are not being met. Numerous big-name consumer brands like Comcast, Best Buy, and Dell have been able to turn around egregious customer service problems by implementing Rapid Social Response solutions. What happens when a brand doesn't respond to customer feedback on the social Web? Look at the real-world PR disasters created by the social customers who posted "United Breaks Guitars" video[2] or the sleeping Comcast cable guy (who fell asleep at a customer's house).[3]

Which Consumer Brands Are Using It?

Another big list. For starters, you can look at Motorola, Dell, Hilton Hotels, TiVo, Starbucks, and Papa Murphy's Pizza.

What Is Market Demand and Tech Maturity?

Same deal as Social Support Insights, above. This one is ready-to-go. Brands are using it today. Big ones. They're pretty much afraid *not* to.

Which Three Vendors Are Doing It Well, for Consumer Brands?

There's a lot of crossover between the brands that do Rapid Social Response and Social Support Insights, so I'm going to focus here on just the ones that do Rapid Social Response really well, in case you want to only focus on this. Salesforce does a pretty great job on this one, mainly because their customer support engine was already fairly well built out—you can also tell they're pushing further resources into this area, as their Service Cloud is now touted as a core product offering—it's probably the most "mainstream" social customer support solution for small and medium business.

Alterian's SM2 product is also a nice fit here, as is RightNow. (Now we're getting a bit further out there, going from Social Customer Management to the heady world of Customer Experience Management—more about that later in the book.) I was pretty impressed with the Rapid Social Response that I received from Doubletree Hotels, in San Diego, on a recent business trip. Priceline had sold me one room, when I needed two, and when my colleague tried to purchase a second room (unbeknown to us, 60 seconds after the 8:00 P.M. cutoff), he was unable to check out. The hotel manager and Priceline were inflexible, and to make up for the disconnect, after we contacted them on Twitter, Doubletree Corporate (Hilton) not only refunded the difference for my colleague's full-price hotel room, but actually insisted on refunding the *entire* two-room stay.

That's Rapid Social Response. Thanks, Hilton, you'll definitely be seeing me again. (I also donated all of my Hilton points to the Japan earthquake effort, because they were great enough to match customer donations.)

What's the Catch?

Once you start doing Rapid Social Response, if you stop, your customers will become seriously upset. It's the social customer service equivalent of not picking up the phone when it rings.

PEER-TO-PEER UNPAID ARMIES (NUMBER 15)

What Is It?

This one has a bit in common with Social Pull-Through Marketing, because when brands use P2P Unpaid Armies, they're cultivating groups of advocates to "march" on behalf of the brand. Let's face it: these customers and advocates, collectively, know more about the brand than the brand does, and they have more resources to support other customers. It's also a numbers game.

Let's say the brand has 10 employees on the social Web that can work to change global opinion. Well, that brand might also have 100,000 customers who can help do this. I was chatting with BlueKiwi CEO Carlos Diaz once, and he told me about a huge luxury clothing brand that approached him, saying they wanted to reach out and talk directly with the 2 or 3 million customers they had in Europe to get them to evangelize the brand's new fashion line. He politely suggested that they use his software to instead figure out who the most influential 10,000 or 20,000 customers would be, work directly with them, and let those customers speak to the other 2.9 million customers. Makes sense, doesn't it?

Imagine if, say, a customer who had never tried Bare Escentuals new lipstick posted a question on Twitter, asking if the stuff was any good. A special Social CRM tool "pipes" this question to a customer advocate in the Bare Escentuals forum—the advocate answers the question, in the forum, which sends the answer, "Yes, I especially love Amaretto—they have it on Amazon for like nine dollars," and then invites the original customer who asked the question if they want to join Bare Escentuals' online forum. Pretty cool, huh?

Which Consumer Brands Are Using It?

The list isn't too long here, but it does include a few big brands like Nike, Scheels Sports, Best Buy, AT&T, and Sony PlayStation.

What Is Market Demand and Tech Maturity?

This one's not nearly as mature as its two brothers, Rapid Social Response and Social Support Insights. By late 2011, I'm thinking this will be in the Near Tipping Point category—this means the technology should be pretty "baked," but we're not sure if the market's going to have high demand for it.

Which Three Vendors Are Doing It Well, for Consumer Brands?

From what I've seen, the nod here goes to Jive Software (discussed throughout the last few chapters) and Lithium. My criteria for what makes a good vendor for doing a little peer-to-peer army motivation here (training the foot soldiers) is that the software needs to work on both sides of the firewall (inside and outside the company); it needs solid social media management and influence detection, and enterprise-level CRM integration. It's also crucial that the community platform have some sort of rating for social capital—meaning that new members of the community need to be able to tell smart older members of the community apart from members who are just, well, old and out-of-touch.

What's the Catch?

This is *very* time consuming, but unless you want your brand to be able to achieve massive scale, you'll probably need to do it. But the results can be insanely awesome. When Nike used Jive in their customer community, Nike+, they found that 40 percent of the people in the community actually became customers, in real life. Apple's also a Jive customer. Engaging customers, and getting those customers to engage other customers, brought up the bottom line. Peer-to-Peer Unpaid Armies is a good use case for achieving your objectives if your fans are pretty much zealots. If you're selling snow tires, it's time to call the rural sheriffs who depend on your product to get the job done. If they don't go on the social Web and evangelize your product, it's time to bust out the Four Actions Framework, derived from *Blue Ocean Strategy,* that we will discuss in Chapter 13. You can still do Peer-to-Peer Unpaid Armies, but if you don't have the customer evangelists yet, it's going to take a bit of work.

The ability of social service and support to help brands rapidly solve issues facing individual customers is a major leap forward. Not only in regard to the speed at which these problems can be solved, but also as to how they can be handled, and by whom, in a meaningful way to the customers, also providing them the opportunity to solve one another's problems *because they want to.*

Take a quick look back at Figure 4.1 in Chapter 4. As you'll see, now that we've covered the topics of Marketing, Social Sales, and Service/ Support, we're ready to move on to our fourth category of granular use cases of Social CRM: Innovation. We'll start with a discussion of number 15, Innovation Insights.

8

SOCIAL INNOVATION AND PRODUCT DEVELOPMENT

Some would say this is the most "mature" of the Social Customer Management use cases, because, in this one, the brand actually creates products and services *with* their customers. You've got to trust and love your customers to do this. The concept is not really that new. European automotive brands like Volvo and BMW have been doing this since at least 2005. Social innovation makes the product development cycle faster, and more in-tune with the voice of the customer. When I said "mature" earlier in this paragraph, I was implying that this use case resembles a 1993 Screaming Eagle Cabernet (I'll save you the trouble of Googling this one—it is a $3,200 bottle of red wine): it's expensive, but it can be insanely profitable (and pleasurable).

INNOVATION INSIGHTS (NUMBER 16)

What Is It?

If your brand wants to see the innovation trends that are happening right now, in the voice of your customer, you're going to want to take all the good data you've received from Social Customer Insights and turn it into *innovation* insights. If time-to-market is important to your brand, and you want to design products that embody the voice-of-the-customer (think of how Scion just redesigned their Scion TC to attract more young male buyers, or how numerous auto brands went through costly billion-dollar redesigns since 2005 to attract more female car buyers), then this use case is going to be key.

Which Consumer Brands Are Using It?

Starbucks, Kraft's "Innovate With Kraft," BMW's Customer Innovation Lab, and Sara Lee Open Innovation immediately come to mind. Since social innovation software is becoming very affordable, many more small/medium business (SMB) brands are getting involved.

What Is Market Demand and Tech Maturity?

Market demand is still fairly low, but the technology is evolving. This one still sits in the bottom-left quadrant, though: Early Adoption mode.

Which Three Vendors Are Doing It Well, for Consumer Brands?

The key is to look for vendors that have had *successful* product releases with consumer brands. With the other use cases, it might be okay to go with a newer software brand that's only been around for a few years, but because of the amount of money on the line here, you won't want to look at anyone who hasn't been in this game since about 2005 or 2006. The ones I'd stick with include Salesforce (best known for their MyStarbucksIdea job, the one that brought you the green splash sticks that prevent you from getting coffee all over your shirt before the big meeting), or any other product that's already embedded in a major CRM platform, like the CRM component of German software powerhouse SAP's SAP Business Suite.[1]

Small brands that have never deployed a CRM system before may want to check out Spigit's ContestSpigit product or BrightIdea. Brands that do a high volume of Web sales or e-commerce might even want to give BazaarVoice a serious look. One of our clients, a shoe company, MBT, used BazaarVoice to allow their customers to share ratings-and-review feedback with one another and also gain ideas for new products.

"At the point when we were clear that developing a deeper relationship with our current—and many potential future—customers was key to our growth in the U.S.," said former MBT Vice President for Marketing and Retail Development Rebecca Kotch (now a Bay Area marketing consultant), "our traditional marketing activities required an infusion of energy and emotion, [so] we devised a social customer strategy to become the hub of the activities rather than the outlier. MBT is a true 'talking' brand—our customers were beyond fanatical and our social customer strategy enabled them to connect with us on a consistent and meaningful basis—and talk as much as he or she wanted to.

"Specific to my career," Kotch added, "the learning around the strategy and supporting tactics of Social Customer Management has shifted how I approach any other product or services-based project I am involved with."

Kotch's lieutenant, at the time, MBT's Online/Retail Marketing Manager, Vanessa Willson, also found that using an idea innovation strategy via ratings and reviews was highly engaging, and provided a venue not only to make product and marketing-level changes, but to serve another use case: Social Customer Insights.

"We knew we had an audience that *loved* to rave about our shoes and how [the shoes] changed their lives, we just never had an arena for their voices to be heard. The addition of Ratings and Reviews on MBT's site allowed our customers to share their feedback with us as well as provide greater insight to new customers wanting to learn more about MBT," Willson said.

And here's the best part of it: instant customer feedback drove product design.

"For the brand," Willson said, "it allowed us to take the information provided and work to improve our product, from small design changes to the introduction of new styles. Overall, it was an essential tool for our brand to grow in the online world."

In a conversation I had with Oracle's Mark Woollen, he addressed MBT's competitor, Skechers, who are trying to successfully engage with the social customer, across international lines, just like MBT. Although Skechers is a much larger brand than MBT—they touch roughly 15 times more social customers than MBT on a daily basis— both occupy a hugely growing segment of the athletic footwear market.[2] Here's how Woollen would have done Skechers:

> I think what you need to start doing in this case is to begin to have very discreet ownership for certain functions, based upon your business unit, business function, and geography. So, I think if you look at the case of Skechers, there are multiple countries, locales, where they're doing business. The communities in those environments are going to have very different needs, say, from Australia to the U.S. In order to make sure that [their customers] have very authentic engagement, they need to have, at minimum, community managers as part of the local marketing team that own the communities and each of the social media properties they think are key to go after.

Woollen also realizes that many companies can't do what he recommends for Skechers. "This is why [a] bank (whose name I may not mention) that I've spent a lot of time with is very eager but also very cautious," he said. "[This bank] really doesn't know at the end of the day how to do anything beyond a very, very small, local market-specific experimenting space."

What's the Catch?

The downside of an implementation is pretty low. But you've got to prove that you're actually *implementing* customer ideas for this type of strategy to be meaningful. I was speaking with my friend, supply chain and management consultant George Freuhan, and he said, "The last time the customers got exactly what they wanted, they ended up with the Ford Edsel, and you know what happened there."[3]

CROWD-SOURCED R&D (NUMBER 17)

What Is It?

The *difference* between Crowd-Sourced R&D and Innovations Insights is that Crowd-Sourced R&D delivers *real-time* feedback. So, if you're using Innovations Insights, you'll find out what your partners, customers, and industry geeks (analysts, pundits) want, and speed up your prototyping, requirements gathering, and basic demo testing—essentially, they'll help you make a better Swiffer[4] a lot faster. Crowd-Sourced R&D is a trip; in Jeremiah and Ray's white paper, they found that when a large software company began Crowd-Sourced R&D, they were able to employ the same amount of product managers but scope out twice the number of features.

Which Consumer Brands Are Using It?

Kotex's use of the LiveWorld platform, in my opinion, was mind-blowing—I was so impressed by this use of Social CRM that I called up my friend Juan Martinez at *CRM Magazine* to write an article about it.[5] Kotex has created a number of customer communities on the LiveWorld platform, (The Ladies Room, Girlspace), and customer objectives run the gamut from Crowd-Sourced R&D to Social Sales

Insights. Consumer brands are actually a little behind the curve on this one. Tech brands like Microsoft, Google, and Salesforce, however, have been extracting data and support from users for years.

What Is Market Demand and Tech Maturity?

This one's just beginning to cross over into the mainstream, but B2B brands are currently using it more than consumer brands. I'd put this one slightly to the upper right of center in the four quadrants. Whereas market demand is a little low as of this writing, the technology is pretty much baked, and customers are largely responsive when brands use it.

Which Three Vendors Are Doing It Well, for Consumer Brands?

Since this is a highly time-sensitive use case, I'm going to pick the vendors that have the easiest software to learn and use: Jive's Social Business Suite, RightNow, and Lithium.

What's the Catch?

Like Innovations Insights, Crowd-Sourced R&D requires a whole-hearted commitment from the brand to keep up with customer requests, and to innovate at the speed of customer intent and demand.

Social innovation, both in regard to Innovation Insights and crowd-sourcing, leads us nicely into our next topic, Collaboration, where we will discuss three use cases: Collaboration Insights (number 18), Enterprise Collaboration (number 19), and Extended Collaboration (number 20). We'll explore the *new* notion of collaboration, showing how brands collaborate with customers, partners, suppliers, advocates, and sales channels.

You see, sometimes it's just not enough to collaborate with your customers. Sometimes, culturally, collaboration begins at home. Let's look at some great examples of companies you know that did this successfully.

9

COLLABORATION

I f you watch the TV show *Mad Men*, you can see the "old" way companies collaborated with their customers. In one episode Dr. Faye Miller, a consumer psychologist, ushers a group of secretaries into a conference room to discuss makeup and their "beauty routine"; Dr. Miller asks focused questions, and many of the secretaries (the consumers) end up sharing deep, personal responses—a few even begin to cry. The social customer will do this, too, but they'll do it in online forums or on social networks. Each of these social collaboration methods have one thing in common: they're letting the customer or partner inside the enterprise a little bit. This would have been unheard of 10 years ago, let alone 40 years ago, in the *Mad Men* days.

There's a big difference between the following three collaboration use cases in regard to who the collaborating is done with. Collaboration Insights is more of an inside-our-company operation, while the other two extend far beyond the company.

COLLABORATION INSIGHTS (NUMBER 18)

What Is It?

This is a big one for large organizations. If you've got multiple business units, or a huge number of employees, it's pretty amazing how many great ideas can get stuck in tiny little silos, within your company walls, which prevents them from getting out.

Which Brands Are Using It?

Most of the brief case studies you can find on this use case focus on one of two things: (1) how Collaboration Insights made the brand collaborate faster or better, or (2) how Collaboration Insights helped a company tear down the silos. The big example that comes to mind here is Southwest Airlines[1]—they used Spigit to power an employee platform called Idea Runway, and the results were pretty clear. By allowing cross-functional collaboration and giving full transparency, Idea Runway let work groups from all different parts of the company carve out the path for ideas to become products. Nearly 4,000 of Southwest's 35,000 employees—that's 11 percent of the company participating—signed on to Idea Runway, and 98 percent of the ideas submitted received a response from the community.

Here's another (unexpectedly) cool one: the Department of Defense's APAN (All Partners Access Network) used Telligent's platform as their primary platform of information sharing during their response to the 2010 Haitian earthquake. The result was a swift launch that allowed the emergency-response community to leverage unstructured information sharing into fast, actionable response.

What Is Market Demand and Tech Maturity?

This one's right in the middle of the spectrum. It's funny how many companies have adopted Enterprise Collaboration (the next use case) or Extended Collaboration, but both the market demand and technical maturity for Collaboration Insights isn't as high—there are few software vendors that concentrate just on this solution. I disagree with Jeremiah and Ray on this one—I feel that the technology is "baked," but I agree that the market demand is still kind of middling, so I'd put this one in the Near Tipping Points category, and I expect it to move into Evangelizables in the next few years.

"The one that I think is [really taking off is] Enterprise Collaboration," Oracle's Mark Woollen said. "It's not the most fun of the use cases, but I'm seeing this with every customer I talk to. When you get down to it, this is kind of the boring part of the business. . . ."

He added: "At the end of the day, people do use [Oracle's] software, and if you think about your average guy who is working in sales—he's three years out of college—I mean, that guy graduated in 2007!"

Woollen brings up a crucial point here: this 25- or 26-year-old sales rep doesn't even work like the employees of a decade ago:

> How do you think he works in every other capacity of his life? The notion that the software you use inside your job and collaborate with people on your inside sales team and your outside rep and everybody else in the organization, the fact that these solutions aren't today very well structured to facilitate collaboration, they're exceedingly tops-down.

And that, alone, makes the case for Enterprise Collaboration: the fact that you're most likely not leveraging the younger half of your workforce without it.

Which Three Vendors Are Doing It Well, for Companies?

The ones I dig are Oracle, Spigit, the flexible platform Mindtouch, and Telligent—and if you're going outside the company firewall or combining Collaboration Insights with the use case below, Enterprise Collaboration, Jive, or GetSatisfaction are worth a look.

What's the Catch?

Culturally speaking, Collaboration Insights can be a huge shift for any company that's used to a top-down "command and control" mentality.

ENTERPRISE COLLABORATION (NUMBER 19)

What Is It?

My fiancée does Enterprise Collaboration for a living. She helps companies migrate from Microsoft's Office and Exchange products onto Google Apps or Gmail. By working with companies to help them migrate from Microsoft to Google, she's improving the means by which their enterprises collaborate.[2]

Enterprise Collaboration is, quite simply, when a corporation uses a single collaboration tool to cut across nearly the entire company, to optimize process and share ideas. Some of you might say, "Well, that means Enterprise Collaboration has been around since *at least* 2005, since Microsoft's Sharepoint has been around that long—our company's already using it." Well, not exactly.

Sharepoint did *some* things, and allows *some* information to be shared between *some* departments inside your enterprise. But a lot of the newer products—like Salesforce's Chatter, PBWorks, or Yammer—are explicitly meant for fast enterprisewide rollout. Some are stand-alone, and some are a little more sophisticated than the collaboration solutions of years past. Some are even quite simple: Yammer is just a private way of asking people, "What are you working on right now?"—sort of an enterprise version of Twitter. The other thing to remember here is that Microsoft never meant for Sharepoint to replace file servers in the first place, or for it to be a one-size-fits-all solution.

Oracle's Mark Woollen gives us a more concrete idea of what it looks like when an employee is empowered to use Enterprise Collaboration to create ad-hoc communities:

> You'll see the initial things we're doing in this space, everything around activity streams, that both foster internal collaboration, and the other piece of this, of course, is that [people within a given company] should have a certain purview over what [they] deem to be [their] secure communications, so that allows me, as a sales guy or a marketer, to create my own community, my minicommunity, if you will. A container that I can use around this deal, this campaign, this event—[essentially, whatever the employee is working on]. And that can include Company XYZ, a business partner, it can include customers beyond the firewall. That's the other key piece here as well.

Which Consumer Brands Are Using It?

Although this is something you're more likely to find within the walls of a B2B brand, some consumer brands are currently utilizing Enterprise Collaboration. For example, Yammer's clients include Groupon and Nationwide Insurance. Another case study that comes to mind is Papa Murphy's Take N' Bake Pizza. They used Salesforce to get a centralized view of the business, while also letting franchisees have a mobile view of their data. They actually built a franchise management system on top of Salesforce's Force.com software platform. Although this solution was not a 100 percent "open collaboration" model—it honestly sounds more like a collaboration pyramid—it did allow a small enterprise to collaborate in a way that they never could before, solving a huge business pain. Imagine trying to run 1,100 pizza franchises using Microsoft Excel spreadsheets and e-mail.

What Is Market Demand and Tech Maturity?

Totally Evangelizable. This one's really been around for a while.

Which Three Vendors Are Doing It Well, for Consumer Brands?

The vendors that are the most familiar here are Microsoft Sharepoint, IBM Lotuslive,[3] and, to a lesser degree, Salesforce's Chatter.

What's the Catch?

Cultural adoption can be a serious challenge, especially for teams that don't traditionally use collaboration software. Be sure to read Mike Fauscette's tips and Michael Krigsman's Social CRM avoiding-failure tips later in the book to swerve around the potholes in this road.

EXTENDED COLLABORATION (NUMBER 20)

What Is It?

This is when companies collaborate with all of the other folks in their ecosystem to create outcomes for the social customer—channel sales partners, vendors, and suppliers. Oracle's Mark Woollen calls this one the "sleeper hit" of all of the Social CRM use cases. Out of all of the collaboration ones, it's certainly the most mature—I'd completely agree with Jeremiah and Ray on this one, and call it Evangelizable—you can find dozens of case studies on it.

The reason brands started doing this years ago, as soon as the technologies existed, was because it saves a huge amount of money and removes a great deal of friction from important business-to-business relationships. Extended Collaboration differs from Enterprise Collaboration because the latter is almost always *within* the company, and Extended Collaboration goes *outside* the company's walls.

Which Consumer Brands Are Using It?

National Breast Cancer Foundation, Long Realty Company, and the BDA (British Dental Association) have seen success using Telligent, and Salesforce's collaboration customers include Dell and Starbucks.

Numerous case studies can be found on the vendor's Web sites, and the typical results are faster time-to-market on products, quicker close time for sales channel partners, and increased quantity-of-sales. Other brands that have found success here, by collaborating with partners (and even customers), include Microsoft's Office Live product and *Reader's Digest*'s immense Taste of Home recipe finder Web site—both of these brands used Telligent's solution. Microsoft focused on using their community supporting 10,000 questions about their product, so their use case here is sort of a cross between Extended Collaboration and Social Support Insights, which we looked at a few pages back. When you're dealing with Extended Collaboration, you may run into some "combined" use cases like this one.

What Is Market Demand and Tech Maturity?

This one's ready-to-go: Evangelizable.

Which Three Vendors Are Doing It Well, for Consumer Brands?

I'm torn here between the mainstream CRM platforms, which pretty much built Enterprise Collaboration into their products, as a response to businesses' demands, and the guys who just do straight-up Enterprise Collaboration. If you want both, I'd look at Salesforce's Chatter product or Oracle. That said, if you can take your Enterprise Collaboration without the CRM, Pbworks and Jive are great depending on how "deep" or "far out" you want the collaboration to go.

What's the Catch?

You're sharing data with your partners, vendors, suppliers, and sales channel (and sometimes even your customers). If you release the right amount of data, all your partners can help you grow, and, ideally, align their selling cycle perfectly with your buying cycle. The rub is that if your team isn't well-trained on what data should or shouldn't be released into the Enterprise Collaboration system, then you may occasionally release strategic data. That said, security breaches are not something to worry about here; most of this software is highly secure.

Now that we've covered the three specific collaboration use cases, we can move on to our final use case category: Customer Experience (CX). This is a strange field since it's basically a new discipline. Don't get me wrong—there are companies that have built their whole brand around customer experience. (Disney and Apple Computer come to mind as two notable examples.) But, as a total of all the experience a person has with a brand, across every touchpoint it is a fairly new notion—nobody talked about customer experience until about 2000, when two guys named Pine and Gilmore wrote about it in the *Harvard Business Review*. Let's see if we can take their heady *HBR* write-up and turn it into something your social customers will dig.

10

SEAMLESS CUSTOMER
EXPERIENCE

Customer experience can either be small (one single transaction) or big. It can refer to the *entire* customer life cycle, from the beginning stages (awareness, discovery, attraction), to the middle stages (interaction, purchase, use), to the later, most advanced stages (cultivation and, hopefully, advocacy). The whole idea of Customer Experience Management is to take a customer from being a satisfied customer, to a loyal customer, to an advocate.

According to the 2010 Customer Experience report we referred to in Chapter 7, 76 percent of your customers are willing to pay a 5 percent premium—like an extra five bucks out of every $100 they spend with you—for a great customer experience. In fact, 10 percent of your customers are willing to pay a 25 percent surcharge—those are the folks who are probably flying first-class (I highly recommend you take a minute to review the report).

SEAMLESS CUSTOMER EXPERIENCE (NUMBER 21)

What Is It?

In what is probably the best line in Jeremiah and Ray's white paper: "Customers don't care what channel or department you work in." This whole concept of Seamless Customer Experience is all about providing customers with a consistent and seamless experience everytime they touch your brand—from the early stages (awareness, attraction) to the most advanced stages (advocacy).

Brands are facing two big problems about Customer Experience today: (1) they've got a huge proliferation of social channels—every time you look, there's another one, and (2) they've got more *federated* customer data than ever—this means that a huge amount of different flavors of customer data (social and nonsocial) are being mashed together on their end. So I wouldn't be shocked if, in addition to my billing information, my phone company knows my Twitter name, knows that I have a dog, and knows that I get my DSL from someone else other than them.

Which Consumer Brands Are Using It?

The video-game brand Electronic Arts, Nikon, and Overstock.com are all customers of RightNow. Nikon used this Social CRM use case to reduce their call response time by 50 percent and increase their e-mail response time by 70 percent—overall their entire customer satisfaction went up to 95 percent. Overstock was able to accelerate customer agent training times and lower their call handle times as well. These are all measurable data that customers can feel.

What Is Market Demand and Tech Maturity?

This one is just beginning to go mainstream since it has been adopted by a few big brands. In some ways, Dell Computer was an early user of Seamless Customer Experience,[1] as they used social media in 2005 and 2006 to help transform their customers' perception of the Dell brand as anticustomer or uncaring. CXI This one's still in the Early Adoptions quadrant, but it's soon to cross over into Early Movers, once demand for it picks up at little.

Which Three Vendors Are Doing It Well, for Consumer Brands?

RightNow Technologies is probably the only vendor I know of that explicitly specializes in quantifying and improving Customer Experience. On a smaller scale, GetSatisfaction and Helpstream are worth a look for brands that want to dabble in Seamless Customer Experience. One product you may have actually used in the workplace that was designed with Customer Experience in mind is Siebel Systems CRM product, which is now a part of OracleCRM. The product was designed from what Siebel called a customer experience Blueprint; it's a user-centered way of developing products.

What's the Catch?

Like many of the other Social CRM use cases, once you start using it, you can't stop, unless you want to run the risk of losing a large volume of customers you worked hard to obtain.

VIP EXPERIENCE (NUMBER 22)

What Is It?

Maybe you've had bottle service at a nightclub or been upgraded to first class on an international plane flight. Feels good, doesn't it? VIP Experience is all about giving special perks to your best customers. Remember when all of those airline customers freaked out, back in late 2009 and 2010, when airlines like USAir devalued their mileage programs? Well, that's pretty much the *opposite* of the VIP Experience use case. The idea here is to use your Social CRM information to surprise and delight your customers, not anger them. Any brand that has frequent direct customer contact (travel and hospitality and retail come to mind) will want to pay attention to VIP Experience.

Even my favorite airport parking spot, Espresso Parking, at the Oakland Airport, understands VIP Experience. They give their frequent parkers (Big Shot Rewards) big discounts, fast in-and-out, and relevant awards like free parking, free car washes, and the ultimate prize in airport parking—a free car detailing job. Of course, all of their customers get free Peets Coffee, muffins, and a copy of the newspaper on their way to the airport. Part of the way to build a VIP Experience is to treat all of your customers like VIPs.

Which Consumer Brands Are Using It?

From my clients, the big one is Wente Vineyards (a winery and concert venue). While stuck in traffic on the way to their location, I thought of the Wente Twitter Concert Concierge—like a VIP Concierge for their customers who might, say, be held up by traffic on their way to a concert at the venue. I figured that a customer could tweet the Twitter concierge that they're running late, and Hospitality could then set aside an extra plate for them and their dining companion so they wouldn't miss the delicious dinner before the concert.

This program lasted two years, and through a combination of VIP Experience and some of the other Social CRM use cases, Wente Vineyards was able to keep their concert attendance flat in a rough concert economy that was down 8 to 12 percent (2009 and 2010) in the Bay Area.

What Is Market Demand and Tech Maturity?

It's almost Evangelizable. There are enough brands using this now that we can say it's just barely "early mainstream."

Which Three Vendors Are Doing It Well, for Consumer Brands?

This is a tough one. Jeremiah and Ray were unable to find any vendor that specializes in this, even in the hospitality space (where you'd think there would be plenty). I know of VIP features of property management system software, and I've seen it in CRM software, too—mostly Siebel (which is now OracleCRM), but I'm also stumped on a specific vendor. My recommendation is to go with a larger CRM brand like Oracle or Salesforce, or even Microsoft Dynamics (Hard Rock Café uses it), and build a VIP app on *that* platform.

What's the Catch?

Again, like some of the other service and Customer Experience Social CRM use cases, these programs, once started, can't be easily stopped or drastically modified, unless you don't mind a bit of customer churn—just ask USAir. Also, it's important to remember that when everyone's a VIP, nobody's a VIP.

MOBILE-ON-LOCATION (NUMBER 23)

What Is It?

The big difference between Mobile-on-Location and VIP Experience is that the latter is only for a small subset of your customers. Mobile-on-Location Experience is meant to engage the everyman social customer (or the every customer), regardless of how much they spend. There's somewhat of a spectrum of brand experience offered to the social customer in the Mobile-on-Location use case.

On one end of the spectrum is what we'll call Mobile Lite, in which Tex-Mex restaurant chain Chili's is involved. When a user checks in at a restaurant location using Foursquare, they get a free order of chips and salsa. The value to the user is about three bucks. It's as though

Chili's is saying, "We'll pay you, the social customer, two cents for every friend you tell about your brand experience." Notice that the only enhancement to the brand experience here is a free basket of chips. You'd probably get that if the waitress spilled a Diet Coke in your lap. Mobile Lite engagements of the social customer tend to be discount-driven. There's one big problem with Mobile Lite: the brand doesn't get a holistic view of the customer, and the customer may receive a fragmented brand experience.

Most Mobile Lite brands work in conjunction with location-enabled check-in brands like Foursquare, Gowalla, Yelp, and Facebook. Gap's BlackMagic campaign is a super example. It's a fusion of Social Event Management (one of the marketing use cases of Social CRM) and Mobile Lite. They gave shoppers who were able to either speak a Twitter code, show a Foursquare check-in, or print a Facebook coupon, 25 percent off.

On the other end of the spectrum is Mobile-on-Location. This stuff goes *way* beyond walking into a Chili's and "checking in" on Foursquare or Facebook. In Mobile-on-Location, the check-in is the first step in personalizing the experience for the social customer. Oracle Retail writes software that fully integrates the retail store point-of-sale experience.

"We already have some customers that are playing with this," Oracle's Mark Woollen said. "We've got one of our customers, (famous Hong Kong luxury department store chain) Lane Crawford in Asia Pacific that's looking at this notion of check-in very seriously.

"Lane Crawford's been a longtime customer, invested a lot in loyalty management. And what they're doing is providing tablets [i.e., iPads or similar] to their salespeople. When you walk into the store, the customer checks in, the salespeople know you're there, they can pull up your profile, and they can pull up a very, very highly targeted set of offers related to the merchandise in that particular store."

If it isn't clear by now, this Mobile-on-Location technology is no joke.

"This is making the traditional point-of-sale obsolete," Oracle Retail's Senior Director of Technology Strategy, David Dorf, said:

> Try to find a cash register in an Apple store. It's there, but it's hidden because it's not part of the store experience. Paying is a "formality" at the tail end of shopping. Don't think about the cost; think about how the products will enhance the way you live. I think what you're going to see is that this location-based capability, it's not well figured out yet … The customers you know the most about are typically your most loyal ones. You have these loyalty programs in place, like, say, SJ (an Oracle Siebel Loyalty customer, Sweden's public sector rail company that went through deregulation in 2002 and fought its way back from bankruptcy, by 2009).

Which Consumer Brands Are Using It?

Wet Seal (a retailer mentioned earlier that caters to a young, female audience; most of their clothing costs between $3 and $20, per item) is one of the best examples I've ever seen. Its holistic picture of the social customer has been led by their CIO, Jon Kubo. "[Wet Seal] runs all of our stuff—their stores, supply chain, merchandising," Duncan Angove, SVP and general manager of Oracle Retail, said, and it's clear why: the Wet Seal customer, statistically, is nearly 90 percent social. Read that again. Nearly 90 percent of their customers are using social technologies, with a frequency that varies between daily to monthly.

"Seventy percent of their customers are on Facebook, 30 percent on smartphones, and 15 percent of their customers are on iPhone. They have a huge Facebook community, and they've built custom apps, like the My Boutique app," Angove said. To pick out outfits on the Wet Seal Web site, customers can shop using regular clothing categories (tops, intimates, etc.), or they can shop by trend, behaviorally (Back to School, Vintage Army), *or* they can shop using Wet Seal's iRunway app (which exists outside of their mobile Web site shopping app).

"Their thinking," Angove said, "was, 'Why not let our community of teenage girls merchandise the store *for* us? When a girl goes into the store, she can pull up a blouse on her iPhone, and filter on *just* her friends. Here's where the operational piece comes in—that piece is tied into store inventory. [Wet Seal] will not show an outfit that's not in stock."

According to Angove: "Those outfits drive 20 percent of their revenue now—it's the democratization of retail. The customer is empowered."

What really blows my mind is the supply-chain integration involved in this process. If you look on any Wet Seal item price tag, in addition to the bar code, the size, and the price, you'll see a style code, about halfway down the tag. Using Wet Seal's iPhone or iPad app, you can key the code into the app to see other outfits in the same style as the one you're looking at.

Imagine a plus-size teen looking for a prom dress. She sees the Satin Tulip Tube Dress online (or in the store, with her iPhone). She then keys the style number, 43066209, into her iRunway app, and it pulls up the Gold Charm Bracelet, Pearl Three Row Necklace, Lurex Drop Thread Earring, and the Wood Trim Stud Heel to complete the outfit, all for a grand total of $78.50. If the store's out of stock on certain items, she can even buy the missing pieces online, right there.

Other consumer brands that use it include apparel brands (American Eagle, Ann Taylor, Coach, and Diesel). In the last two years Mobile-on-Location has increasingly been explored by hospitality brands. For instance, Morgans Hotel Group (the folks behind San Francisco's hip Clift Hotel and New York's uber-cool Hudson) began providing iPads in every room in September 2010. The iPads were part of a concierge program, and Morgans used a feed technology similar to FlipBoard (a popular iPad app) called FeedMagnet to show guests a curated version of their pick hits from the neighborhood, combined with Facebook and Twitter. If you think about it, it only costs $50,000 to equip 100 hotel rooms with this kind of device—and how many folks who pay $500 to $800 per night are going to run off to JFK with your year-old iPad?

What Is Market Demand and Tech Maturity?

It depends who you want to listen to. In late 2010 even big analyst firms like Forrester were still pooh-pooing Mobile-on-Location, but I call it Evangelizable, just based on the Oracle Retail evidence, and in the hospitality segment I'm going to go as far as to say market-ready.

Which Three Vendors Are Doing It Well, for Consumer Brands?

Unlike the other use cases, this one is actually sort of a tough question. Here's why: there's three breeds of vendors you need to look at: Social CRM, location/social platform, and loyalty. Let's break it down into each flavor, here. Just remember the order to pick them in: (1) loyalty, (2) Social CRM, (3) geolocation platform.

> **Loyalty:** Well, you want to know if the social customer is "checking in" more than once, right? Here's where it gets a little sticky. Most customer loyalty software programs are inherently tough to integrate with Social CRM software. So here's how you do it. Make sure the loyalty program integrates with the Social CRM and *then* pick the geolocation platform, to allow your customers to "check in." Is this a big enough thing to make you possibly consider getting a different loyalty program? Perhaps. This is going to be a huge space going forward. In July 2010, InterContinental Hotels Group (IHG) began rewarding customers with loyalty points for their check-ins on all major location-based services (LBS).
> **Social CRM:** If you're doing Mobile-on-Location, you're going to need a robust Social CRM platform as the backbone of this

system. I'd only be comfortable with one of the full-featured ones, like Oracle CRMonDemand, Salesforce, Microsoft Dynamics, or perhaps even SAP. I could see Simpleview or one of the smaller CRMs working if you're a small brand, but make sure you ask the vendor if they have examples of other clients integrating their API with mobile APIs. (Remember APIs from earlier in the book—they're the connections that allow software to talk to your other software.)

Location/social platform: The key here is to look for two things: (1) integration with your existing customer software platforms, and (2) something that your customers actually like using. The usual way to do this is to do a *social techno-graphic study*—it's pretty cheap and fairly simple. (If you don't know how, just look it up in my first book, *There Is No Secret Sauce*.[2]) SAUCE Most of the vertical market trade publications (e.g., sports, food) have a point of view on this issue, too. I recently read a piece on which location platforms work best in the sports industry.[3] To figure out which one's best for you, I'd ideally do a Google Site Search of your favorite trade publi-cation for an article similar to this one (just type in *geolocation site:yourfavoritetrademagazine.com* and you should do fine). If you're really stuck here, stick with a geolocation platform that has a good and flexible API (Foursquare and Gowalla both have this kind). You can certainly use multiple platforms with one Social CRM—this is especially relevant if you're a multi-national or multiflag brand, or if you just want to hedge your bets, such as IHG.

What's the Catch?

The location/social platforms are going to change over time, so don't lock in too heavily on one platform. Worry about your customers' concept of value first, and the CRM and supply chain components second, while expecting the other tools to change (i.e., who knows:

maybe FourSquare will get acquired and absorbed into Facebook Places, Gowalla might decide to pursue non-U.S. markets—anything could happen[4]).

23 USE CASES WRAP-UP

We pushed the envelope here beyond the original 18 use cases, but not everyone in the Social CRM space agrees that there should be 23 use cases. Lyle Fong, CEO of popular social community platform software brand Lithium, explains:

> We're certainly familiar with the use cases and grateful for the pioneering work that Jeremiah Owyang and others such as yourselves have done on codifying potential use cases for Social CRM. The original publication—I think there were 18 at that point—was a milestone in the history of Social CRM, since no one previously had drawn a definitive line around what is obviously an extremely diverse discipline.

That said, Fong thinks there may be a bit of duplication among the use cases:

> We would probably quibble a bit with some of the use cases around collaboration, since [there are] those duplicate things that are already going on inside the enterprise with no immediate connection to social customers. But, by and large, the use cases are a great blueprint for companies to understand some of the things that they can do in concert with their social customers.

However, in an attempt to be comprehensive and concise, I believe these additional five use cases are essential to a brand's performance in the Social CRM space. Without them, your company might miss out on some major benefits of a fully rounded SCRM plan.

23USESCASES

Now that we've profiled the 23 Use Cases of Social CRM, what's next? Well, since you understand this stuff, you're going to want to go back to Chapter 4, print out that big chart,[5] and pass it out to everyone in the meeting you call.

What I'd do is go through the chart and figure out the top three most urgent use cases. Then I'd see if I could get my team to all agree on them. Next, I'd have everybody vote on which one is the most urgent, and start with that one, combined with the top-level use case, Social Customer Insights. Start small and build on incremental success. And you're going to hear a lot more about how to start, as we get into Chapter 11, "Metrics and Rationale," and Chapter 12, "The Methodology."

11

METRICS
AND RATIONALE

I magine you're back in your senior year of college and it's a chilly Friday night in fall. You're at a raging party. There has to be nearly a hundred people in this house! But all the partygoers are standing around, looking sort of confused. There's a keg of beer in the middle of the living room and everyone's looking for cups, but there are none in the house. Someone goes to the grocery store and comes back 15 minutes later. "There's no cups at the grocery store," he says. People begin to rumble in conversation. Slowly, everyone leaves the party, because there's just no way to drink the beer. People wander off to the bars, leaving the house empty.

This situation, my friends, illustrates the key problem with customer social data. There's tons of data. The data's cheap and good (like all beer seems when you're 21, right?). But just as there is no party without cups for the beer, without somewhere to put the customer social data, there will be no results for your brand.

So, where is all of the customer data supposed to go? From everything I've read about CRM, the folks at Siebel (later, Oracle, when they acquired that brand) were probably the first to put forth the "Single Sources of Truth" theory, which answers that question pretty simply.

What it all boils down to is this: every business essentially reconciles their data to one of three different places:

1. Customer Relationship Management software (CRM)
2. Enterprise Resource Planning software (ERP)
3. Supply Chain Management software (SCM)

It is easy to remember these three by considering how they coincide with *people* (CRM), *projects* (ERP), and *things* (SCM).

Naysayers might ask, "Well, what would you call Human Capital Management software like Success Factors or ADP?" I'd call that ERP, used for the management of human resources. They might also say, "Well, I work at Chili's, and we can't take all of the people posting on our company's Facebook wall and manually put it in our CRM system. That would take forever." This sentiment may hold some truth, but there are many ways that a brand could do "light" Social CRM and stop short of using a real CRM system. The results, however, won't be nearly as assessable.

There are a lot of Social Media Management systems[1] out there like Buddy Media, Context Optional, and Awareness Networks'[2] Social Marketing Hub. Even the small-business e-mail marketing brands like Constant Contact have gotten into the action with their acquisition of small business social media monitoring companies like NutshellMail.[3] iSOCIALEMAIL As small-business e-mail marketing brands (Constant Contact, Vertical Response) see the potential of their involvement with managing social customer data, they've invented products in the Social Event Management space, competing with best-of-breed companies like Eventbrite, in attempts to become one-stop shops for social customer information for small companies.

Regardless of what management system you use, this social customer data all has to go *somewhere*. So, here's how I advocate figuring out *where* it should go.

SOCIAL CUSTOMER PREWORK

It may sound a little cheesy or a little "Stephen Covey," but you have to take *first things first*. The following four steps to routing customer data must be taken *before* you engage in the actual Social CRM strategy. Note, these steps are not the strategic methodology itself, they are only the prework. (Similar to things you need to do before you put on a tuxedo—shower, shave, a little spritz of cologne, perhaps?)

1. **Figure out which systems your brand currently has working around the social customer.** These systems are Social Customer Relationship Management (SCRM), Enterprise Resource Planning (ERP), and Supply Chain Management (SCM).

2. **Decide which ones you absolutely need, and which ones you can live without.** It's entirely possible that your brand is too small for an ERP system. Maybe you're using some legacy HR software that just can't or won't connect to your Social CRM system. This is the part where you're going to have to make tough choices about the social customer.

3. **Decide on the implementation timeline and build the missing systems.** This isn't that simple a recommendation, if your brand lacks, say, a SCRM system. This timeline could reach out 12 to 36 months into the future. You may also want to look at marketing or sales automation or lead nurturing systems here, as an extension of the SCRM (stuff like Eloqua or

Marketo). It's nice to have the customer data, but you need to make it hum.

4. **Simultaneously, begin any and all "listening programs" on the social Web.** These programs, running on a Social Media Monitoring System (SMMS) don't necessarily need to be connected to the three single sources of truth, at this time. You can connect them later. If your organization has no experience with social media monitoring, just spend the first 30 days "listening" before you engage. You may be tempted to jump right in if the social customer is saying bad stuff about your brand, but try not to until your team has become good at listening. How do you know you're good? You feel like you're getting a reading of all of the stuff out there, across all channels. And don't think that the integration between the SMMS and Social CRM systems is automated or perfect. Far from it.

"It's pretty early to be too proscriptive in the work flows that connect social systems together with traditional systems," Lithium's Lyle Fong said.

"There are obviously standard work flows built into our tool set to handle various processes, and we also have escalation points where our systems can message out to other systems using various protocols. But the rapidity and fluidity of change on the social side suggests that it may be a while before everything is standardized, or before organizations can even standardize on a small, fixed set of tools."

That said, everything may be standardized in a year or two.

All of this social customer prework may take six to 18 months. And don't expect the systems that monitor your customers and the systems-of-record to be 100 percent in sync for a few years. But 30 days in you'll likely be using your SMMS to talk with the social customer. Even though all of these systems (SCRM, ERP, and SCM) might not be connected at that point in time, you're going to be much better off than you were in the early stages of the implementation.

To go back to the social customer scenarios we discussed in Chapter 1, you've just moved from Scenario One (No Engagement: No Value to Enterprise) to Scenario Three (Departmental Engagement: Measurable Value to Enterprise). And we all know that it's better to have an incomplete strategy that's on the way to being completed than no strategy at all. (We have one large winery client that's been stuck on step three of that prework for about three years, so it's easier said than done.)

HISTORICAL CONTEXT OF SOCIAL CUSTOMERS ON THE WEB

Before we even get into strategic methodology, let's examine the metrics by which success has been measured, around the social customers on the Web, over time.[4] This bit of historical context will put our metrics in a clear light.

Web 1.0 (1991–99)

What happened and the key metrics. Early Web analytics programs measured Web server logs and turned them into readable reports. Key metrics are Hits, Page Views, Visits/Sessions.

What we should call this wave: reporting. "What Happened?" or "How many hits to our Web site?"

What was wrong with this era, and what the next era tried to solve. Although these early metrics measured basic user interactions, they're now considered rudimentary because they don't show *customer intent*.

Web 1.5 (1999–2004)

What happened and the key metrics. E-commerce reporting grew up. Conversions show which customers committed which actions.

What we should call this wave: analysis. "How many of these people did we turn into buyers?" and "How can we remove barriers to conversion?"

What was wrong with this era, and what the next era tried to solve. Customer intent was not measured. Brands understood some conversion factors, but had an incomplete picture of customer motivation.

Web 2.0 (2004–today)

What happened and the key metrics. Web analytics solutions get slowly woven into mainstream business intelligence (B.I.) solutions, to combine customer's on-Web actions with other information for that same customer. Social media analytics are born. The overflow of qualitative data begins (i.e., "Death by 10,000 tweets"). Key metrics are conversions, mentions, and influence, as well as media-centric social media metrics like fans/followers.

What we should call this wave: action. "We need more than static reports—what is customer intent, and why did this happen and what can we do about it?"

What was wrong with this era, and what the next era tried to solve. Still doesn't provide a holistic view of any one given customer, or a solid picture of customer intent. All social media metrics are immature or evolving.

Social Customer Web (2011–16)

What happened and the key metrics. All mainstream B.I. (business intelligence) solutions feature Web analytics data. Key metrics for social media are evolved and integrated into all mainstream Web analytics solutions. Key metrics here include:

- Number of market-qualified leads (MQLs) derived from social
- Number of sales-accepted leads (SALs) derived from social
- Return-visit velocity to any social collateral created by our company (this is a cross-channel metric)
- Number of monthly active users (MAUs) that touch our brand's social properties

- Total Net Promoter Score®, with the social customer
- Total social customer revenue
- Revenue per social customer

What we should call this wave: intent. Companies are saying, "We need to know why our customers are doing what they're doing, and how we can better anticipate their needs to provide an amazing brand experience, across all touch points."

What was wrong with this era, and what the next era tried to solve. Half of the metrics haven't been invented yet, and there's little consensus among brands about which ones are the best to use.[5]

SOCIAL CUSTOMER AND WEB ANALYTICS

"The idea of measuring social media is becoming widely accepted as a necessary business practice, but many are finding it tough to land on the *exact* metrics they need to measure their specific social media initiatives," Chris Newton, founder of the social media monitoring and engagement brand Radian6 said. Some of Radian6's customers include Pepsi and MolsonCoors, so you know Chris Newton's speaking from an authoritative place. (All of the italics here are mine—sometimes it helps to bring out the key points.)

"Indeed," Newton continued, "there is no *one* way to measure, and the metrics your organization might need to measure the success of a social media campaign could be drastically different from those, even, of your competitors. Ultimately, you want to connect your strategies to exact community member actions, but that is not always an immediate solution."

Okay, so Newton's bringing up a few key points here. You don't need to measure what the next guy is measuring, and if your strategies are not connected to discrete actions that you want your social customers to commit, then it isn't going to go anywhere. This isn't all a bunch of hocus-pocus, though.

"There are methods you can begin to measure relevant awareness, attention, and reach through a combination of social media insights *and* Web analytics," Newton said.

What he's saying is that it's not enough to have just social media or social customer analytics or Web analytics. You've got to use both. If you're not measuring how many social customers you have *and* what they're doing in regard to your *conversion objectives*—the stuff you want them to do or buy—then you won't be able to assess whether you're gaining any traction with the social customer.

Also, notice that he just used a pretty conventional advertising metric in that last line—*reach*. If you don't have an ad background, *reach* is just a measure of the size of an audience. For example, Newton's client Pepsi has a reach of nearly 3 million people, on Facebook alone. Not including all of the other reach they have on the social Web.

"While the path to individual action may be difficult to pinpoint, beginning this process will help identify how your community is interacting with your organization and where the touchpoints are that your organization wants to connect with legacy assessment systems," Newton said. He's talking about legacy assessment systems—those your brand has been using for a long, long time. Maybe it's your Siebel CRM, which your company implemented 12 years ago.

Now that we've discussed the social customer prework to get you prepared, and you have an understanding of the rationale behind the metrics, let's move on to the methodology in Chapter 12. Get ready to roll up your sleeves and get to work.

12

THE METHODOLOGY

The Social CRM methodology all comes down to six letters: l, P, O, S, T, and m. The *m* and *l* are lowercase, but you really can't forget them. That's about it. Charlene Li and Josh Bernoff developed 66 percent of this concept, the POST methodology, in their seminal 2008 book *Groundswell*,[1] which is the root of the overall methodology. *Groundswell* was really the first great book about the enterprise and the social Web.

The term POST was first referenced in Charlene Li's speech at the Forrester Consumer Internet Conference in 2007. In terms of cultural significance, for social customer and social media measurement, I would equate this talk with Jimi Hendrix's performance of "The Star Spangled Banner" at Woodstock. POST was the first time that anyone put a coherent structural vision to the mess of social technologies that has been moving onto the market since 1997. (Yes, people were blogging in 1997.)

POST METHODOLOGY

P Stands for People

When it all comes down to it, Social Customer Relationship Management is all about your company's relationships with people—the people inside it and the people outside it. Chances are, if your company does not have good relationships with the people inside of it, then they won't have good relationships with the people outside of it. You can group the people into four sets (your customers, your employees, prospective customers, everybody else).

To summarize: social is frequently where the conversation starts (or is restarted if the customer hasn't engaged with your brand in quite some time). Then it gets "right-channeled" to where it needs to go.

O Stands for Objectives

These are the things your brand wants to do, with your internal and external stakeholders. When your executive team is combing through the 23 Social CRM use cases, they are generally seeking two to four different assessable measures of success from one (or more) of those use cases. Without objectives there can be no strategy.

S Stands for Strategy

This is the confusing part: the elusive "how." My favorite quote about strategy comes from author and consultant Alan Weiss: "Strategy is vision. Planning is organization. Most people mix the two up, forget about the vision and get bogged down with details."

When it comes to Social CRM strategy, that's the part where not a lot has been written. It's easy to go out and review the tools or profile use cases, and even connect how a brand (e.g., Snapple) got from Point A to Point B (from choosing an objective and a use case to picking a tool), but the strategy part is frequently left out. That's why we're going to spend most of this chapter on it.[2]

T Stands for Tools

In this book alone, you're learning about nearly 100 different tools. The tools are going to change every few months. To write a strategy based on tools ("We need a Facebook strategy!" or "We will use Twitter. That is our strategy") is myopic, and will fail. Any of the 16,000 "social media consultants" on Twitter can tell you that. Any Social CRM platform is a tool. Any Social CRM application, either Web-based or application service provider (ASP), is a tool.

If there's one thing you can count on, it's that the tools will change over time. Take a quick look at Table 12.1, which shows the growth and decline of English-language social network application platforms.

English-Language Social Network Brand	Year It Peaked	Size at Peak (in millions of users)	Size Today, Globally (Unique Users) (in millions of users)
Facebook	2011, (2012, maybe 2013 . . .)	750	750
MySpace	2008	125	65
Friendster	2008	40	115

Table 12.1 English-Language Social Networks and Their Peaks[3]

What you'll notice as you look over this table is the clear trend over the last two or three years for tools and application platforms on the social Web to get bigger or smaller. Picking which one will succeed is rather difficult, unless you have a whole team of analysts studying the space (this is why white papers from social technology analyst firms like Forrester and Gartner still sell, even at a few thousand dollars a pop). Judging by the data in this table, basing your social customer strategy around tools would be foolhardy (and difficult to do effectively).

IPOSTm METHODOLOGY

So now that we have covered the root, the POST methodology, we'll add the two other components that I think are crucial and have led to the lPOSTm Methodology: Listening and Measurement.

Listening

The lowercase *l* stands for listening. Whether or not your company is engaging directly with the social customer, or having an agency or a team help you do it, the listening phase is absolutely critical. If you don't spend two or three weeks figuring out what customers are saying about you, your competitors, and your space, you will lack a baseline of operations. Even the most basic strategy begins with a battlefield survey. Who better to talk to about strategy in listening to your social customer than Chris Newton, the founder of social media monitoring and engagement brand, Radian6?

"Yes, we are familiar with the [23 Social CRM use] cases and believe every company needs to build a comprehensive listening and response mechanism." Right off the bat, Newton's saying that you've got to not just listen, but engage.

I agree with him, to an extent. You should engage, but first it is imperative to develop impeccable listening skills in real-time. Such development might take a month. Here's how he says it should look: "The integration of a listening platform with a CRM system, and a layer of business rules and work flow engine on top of it, is becoming crucial."

Newton's quick to explain how it all fits together, not just with the legacy assessment systems, but with the whole company: "A listening platform will also tie into other business systems and organizations such as PR, sales, and business intelligence to develop a holistic view of the customer across all these systems and silos."

This is where it all falls apart for a lot of brands. For example, I received a call from one of the best hotels in Vegas interested in managing the social customer, but they kept throwing all ownership for the project into the PR department, rather than spreading it holistically. I know what you're thinking: Well, that hotel could have been using the centralized model of Social Customer Management that you talked about early in the book. Potentially, yes, but this particular PR team wanted to completely own the social customer, end-to-end. They didn't want any other departments involved, and the PR lead, who had an advertising background, saw social media as yet another broadcast channel where the brand could increase its reach. This is also the reason why nearly every large ad agency has tried to become a "social media agency" in the last couple of years—they've realized that a majority of the customers they used to help their clients reach on television, radio, and outdoor advertising have migrated to the social Web.

I ended up not writing a proposal to work with this prospective customer, because I thought their viewpoint was strategically flawed, and after numerous attempts at educating them as to why, I was unable to. Newton lays down the "where" of listening to the social customer here: "Organizations must spread 'listening' throughout all business functions and embrace the new reality of *every* employee being tapped into the parts of conversations that are relevant to them."

What does this look like? Well, if you're turning back to the Social Customer Management models, it looks like the holistic model. Companies actually doing this include Zappos and the software company 37signals. The whole concept of "everybody in the company talks with the social customer" must be one huge prerequisite. The company must deeply understand Enterprise Collaboration, while the notion of "we are one big team" must be fundamental to the company's mission.

That said, if this notion of "we're one big team for the social customer" is a physical impossibility, and you just want to see where a "social media manager" (mid-level employee, sort of akin to a marketing manager) would fit in to the traditional organization chart, Edelman Digital's David Armano has a proposal, shown in Figure 12.1.

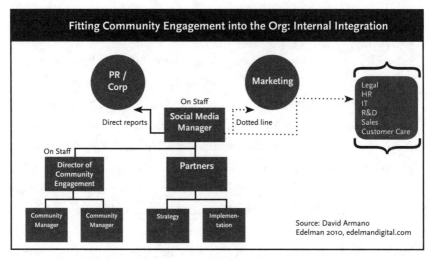

Figure 12.1. Fitting Community Engagement into the Org: Internal Integration

Obviously, there's a bit of a slant to this model, as it's aimed at brands that want to outsource a portion of their Social Customer Management to hybrid PR/ad firms like Edelman Digital. And plenty of big brands do, and there's nothing wrong with doing that, per se. It just depends on which scenario your company culture is currently in around the social customer. If you're stuck in Scenario One, and there seems to be little to no organizational buy-in to get to Scenario Two, this might be the way to go.

Edelman Digital would be the Partners referred to on this org chart. The Community Managers, here, are also external. That said, if the holistic model of Social Customer Management is totally unworkable for your company, this variant on the centralized model of Social CRM might be the only logical fit. This can actually be a good fit if there are a few teams in your organization (usually it's PR and marketing) who want to work with the social customer, but a majority of teams that don't.

Measurement

The lowercase *m* stands for measurement. This is one I added because I didn't think it was clear enough in the initial POST methodology.

This is the part where your team measures their success of executing the tools, in the manner that the *strategy* prescribed, against the *objective* (which is going to require one or more use cases). These measurements will generally be quantitative, but there will also be some qualitative measurements. Here's a breakdown in Table 12.2 of the two types of measurements in Social CRM. We're avoiding media-centric metrics like "fans" and "followers" here because they do not contribute directly to business outcomes.

Qualitative	Quantitative
CEO of your company rates brand as more "in touch" with social customer than last year, citing three pieces of anecdotal evidence.	Average number of minutes to get customer service call to close, when Social CRM solution is used on call intake.
Key customers cite improved customer service and management of expectations through social customer strategy.	Click-throughs from social Web collateral (e.g., Facebook page) to online shopping cart, year-over-year.
Customers on social Web anecdotally state that the brand is fast and responsive, in open-answer survey feedback.	Fewer returned merchandise requests (RMAs) from customers that are in SCRM solution, than the average customer RMA benchmark.
Key partners indicate that their sales team members are able to obtain faster, easier service from your company from the Social CRM assets of the partnership.	Number of members that sign up for loyalty club membership from social Web.

Table 12.2 Two Types of Social CRM Measurements

We'll want to bring Lithium CEO Lyle Fong back in here because measurement is a little subjective, and sometimes it's hard to tell what should be included and what shouldn't.

"It depends on what your business objectives are and what you think constitutes a Social CRM system," Fong said. Sometimes you don't even need to build the connection between existing CRM process and the social Internet.

"Some of our clients who use social media monitoring seek to measure how many conversations they discover and act upon directly, and that number is fairly small, in which case it's possible to tally them up within an existing CRM framework without necessarily building that connection out."

And then there's all of the stuff CRM measurement misses—that's where a lot of brands begin to measure all the wrong things.

"CRM systems are really good at tracking and measuring your direct interactions with your customers," Fong said. "But that's not all—or even most—of what social customer programs are about. It's important to think about a social media monitoring platform enabling you to measure the overall effects of social customer programs on customers you don't interact with directly."

I read another good white paper from the Community Roundtable (Jeremiah Owyang, who worked on the 23 Use Cases of Social CRM had a lot of input here), which contained a solid three-part formula for tying measurement to any given business objective around the social customer.

1. **Response.** Sales, click-throughs, or downloads that come from a given interaction the customer has with your brand. This one's my favorite, as I do most of my work in social demand generation.
2. **Survey.** Measures the extent to which a brand's social community member is willing to take action on behalf of the community or the brand.
3. **Measurement of relationships.** A metric measuring the strength of the bond between either your brand's social customers or between your brand and its social customers.

"If you're building a community and doing other forms of outreach to your social customers, you should be able to see the effects of in buzz, sentiment, and the kinds of feedback you're getting on the social Web," Fong said.

So, again, sometimes you're measuring the qualitative (kinds of feedback), and sometimes you're measuring the quantitative (new customers, new sales, etc.).

Now that I've broken down the methodology and what you'll need to use it, let's take a deep dive into Social CRM Strategy.

13

SOCIAL
CRM STRATEGY

Now that we've covered the basics and discussed the lPOSTm methodology, let's look closer at the importance of the connection between the concept of Social Media Management Systems (SMMS) and the Social CRM system you plan to implement along with the overall strategy.

SMMS AND SOCIAL CRM

A typical first question on the topic is: "How do you kick the data from the Social Media Management System into the Social CRM system?" Chris Newton from Radian6 has an answer for us:

> [We] use integrations in order to automate the Social Media Management System to the Social CRM system when it comes to entering leads and cases, to track all customer conversations automatically, so they may be viewed within the

CRM and not the SMMS, and then contacted through the appropriate account channels."

So why not just cut the SMMS out of the work flow and stick solely
with a CRM system, since that's where the usable information will
be viewed? Let's check in with Kevin Barenblat, the CEO of San Francisco software/advertising company Context Optional, which makes
software that some huge brands use to manage all their social media
and millions of social customers. First off, there's the issue of scale:
what if your brand has multiple properties or multiple compliance
standards (e.g., alcohol)?

"A social marketing platform like Context Optional's Social Marketing Suite addresses a variety of challenges that brand managers face
when trying to manage multiple brand pages, across multiple platforms, with multiple stakeholders and compliance standards," Barenblat said.

Then there's the work flow; if you can't create a routine for this information management process, then how can it scale? Not to mention the fact that this is a 24/7 job, taking place in multiple time zones
and languages all at once.

"Using a work-flow-oriented social marketing platform," Barenblat
said, "gives brands the ability to *efficiently* [italics, mine] and effectively
moderate and analyze their social efforts, assign roles within an organization, escalate issues, publish to multiple time zones and in multiple languages, streamline their brand message, and measure impact
across all of their social presences and the broader open Web."

So, to recap, the benefits to using an SMMS are:

- Scalability
- Efficiency
- Effectiveness
- Impact measurement

At this point you're probably wondering if you can actually remember any big brands that have utilized a social media management system. Barenblat has a few big ones, and a number of firsts, under his company's belt. Chase Community Giving, for example, was the first mass crowd-sourced giving program. Another notable SMMS-driven implementation was the Travel Channel's *Kidnap*, the first branded application to surpass *10 million users*. Einstein's Bagels used Context Optional's SSMS to administer their giveaway, which increased their fan base a thousandfold, to 400,000 fans, over a couple days. It's one thing to say that you've got brand loyalty or to do surveys to get customers to fess up to it, but this is a whole different level.

SMMS's like Context Optional are also behind some of the largest philanthropic efforts ever to have taken place on the social Web. Social CRM brands like Salesforce give free or deeply discounted pricing to nonprofits, and their product also includes a bare-bones SMMS.

Employee Mind-sets

Then there's another thing to remember. Managing the social customer changes your employees' mind-sets, permanently. Remember Vanessa Willson from MBT Footwear, the funky shoe brand that used Social Customer Insights to innovate?

"Professionally, I no longer can look at a marketing plan without having a social strategy in the forefront," Willson said. "In the ever-changing, always-evolving online landscape, a brand's social strategy is an essential piece for their success."

And this is coming from a mid-career marketer who had not touched the social customer prior to March 2009. "Implementing a social strategy was an essential 'piece of the puzzle' for MBT to truly grow as a brand," she said. "Our social strategy was an essential step in order for us to increase brand awareness and loyalty—people simply want their voices to be heard."

"We were lucky, for some time," Willson went on, "to have customers who were truly brand ambassadors, speaking to everyone and anyone about their experiences with our product. What we were never able to do before was to give them an arena to speak to us and share their stories with other consumers." Here, she's talking about using the SMMS to unearth the right customers, and giving the customers the right tools to support your product or service.

COMPONENTS OF THE STRATEGY

So, again here's a quick 1-2-3 to recap how the Social CRM and the SMMS work together, so you can manage your social customers to create outcomes:

1. Something happens on the social Web (e.g., customer complains that they were billed incorrectly, customer says that you make the greatest cheese fries in San Francisco).
2. It's picked up by a Social Media Monitoring System that is integrated with the Social CRM.
3. It's recorded in the Social CRM, and either a macro (automated) work flow is activated, or a micro (human) work flow is activated to solve the problem (by routing it to the right person or department), and the entire incident is recorded for future knowledge around the customer and the problem.

To learn more about the real nuts and bolts of the strategy, let's check in with one of the guys who runs the execution teams for some pretty major brands, including Sony Pictures Television, Hachette Publishing (which published the Twilight series and James Patterson's mystery/suspense novels), and NFL Network, among others. Dave Andrews runs Devious Media and Community102, two Southern California firms known for outsourced community management working with brands that prefer to let a third party manage their (usually very large) communities.

"When working with international [consumer-brand] companies, there is no 'one size fits all strategy.' You have to do the research on each country, their culture, infrastructure, and how they interact with digital media," Andrews said. (We'll fill in the finer points of working with the international social customer in Chapter 21.)

There are a few commonalities, though, Andrews said: "Globally, the vast majority is using Facebook, but there are many social media sites that are specific to the country or region. [Google's social network] Orkut is still very large in Brazil, for example."

One of the first steps in developing the strategy for your own company, or another, is considering who will be interacting with the social customer, and how many staff members are necessary for the job.

Your Social Customer Management Team

When considering the size of the team that will manage the social customer for your brand, there are many factors to take into account, the most immediate being cost. Dave Andrews of Devious Media and Community102 is well-acquainted with this concept. "Depending on the project, our teams are usually one to five people, depending on the social media activity and budget of the client," he said. And these teams are on the small side. I typically assign two to seven people to every project, for enterprise companies, plus the internal team on the client side.

Still, if it takes one to five full-timers to manage the community of social customers around your brand, the human capital investment alone will cost $80,000 to 400,000 annually. You're probably thinking that those numbers are a little high. Well, you just unearthed the next serious problem with who usually gets assigned to manage the social customer. Frequently, it's foisted onto interns or entry-level employees.

"I think the biggest problem is that [companies] choose lower-level employees to do the company's social media management," Andrews said.

"These employees often have 20 other responsibilities and cannot focus on learning and managing the company's social [customers] properly. These employees are often young and do not have the expe-rience or training to interact with your customers. They are just given the task of managing the company's Facebook page and told 'Go!'"

In addition to the advent of new positions like Community Man-ager, previously suggested by David Armano and Jeremiah Owyang, Andrews takes it a step further, but I'm not sure I agree.

"Companies should take social media seriously; I see in the future you will see more senior-level titles for social media like 'Chief Social Media Officer.'"

Realistically, it's viable that we'll see titles like Chief Customer Of-ficer, which would oversee front-office customer operations, inclusive of call center, sales, marketing, finance (customer billing), fulfillment, and post-sale support. This executive would likely report to the CEO. Social media is sure to dominate customer relations and engagement to the point where it is an integral part of the Chief Customer Of-ficer's position, not a separate component ran by a different officer. It's just too narrow a C-Suite position: Chief Social Media Officer. We don't have any Chief Digital Media Officers, do we?

In addition to their pioneering research work on Social CRM, the Al-timeter Group cranked out another great white paper in late 2010, on the role of the Corporate Social Strategist.[1] CAREERPATH (As this report is open research, this chapter, too, is open research.) One of the big-gest things that corporate social strategists complained about, in this white paper, is that their efforts have limited resources and head counts deployed against them, and they seem to be in a permanent "pilot" phase—sort of a corporate purgatory, even when the programs are one, two, or three years old. This is probably the second-biggest problem that enterprise brands face around the social customer. (Number one would be failure-to-engage, but the close second is failure to deploy correct re-sourcing against the social customer.)

In Altimeter's study of 140 strategists in organizations that actu-ally had strategic teams (or strategists) managing their social custom-ers, budgets were painfully small. Nearly 43 percent of the teams had budgets of less than $100,000, with the $100,000 to 500,000 range taking up 34 percent of the social customer budgets. Only 15 percent of the organizations profiled allocated $1 million to $5 million-plus to social media or Social Customer Management.[2]

These small budgets are fine if you're trying to achieve outcomes with values of well under a million dollars, but this book isn't written for brands trying to do anything on that small a scale. (Oddly, 74 percent of the organizations surveyed marked themselves as either "formalized," "mature," or "advanced" on the social media maturity model. This implies that they're fluent in accomplishing small-scale results, something few enterprises would be proud of for long.)

Here's the most prescriptive part of the study: Altimeter found that the amount of staff deployed against real Social CRM engagements (which would only fall into the formalized, mature, or advanced categories) is between eight and 24 people. At an average salary of $75,000 (plus 15 percent for benefits), you're talking about an HR investment of $690,000 to $2 million. You better be sure this first Social CRM program is going to have a $10 million result, in terms of value, *just to make it pay for itself.*

The only companies that the Altimeter report found that had more than 24 people on their social customer programs were tech giants

By Number of Employees in the Company	Average Number of Staff Deployed	By Level of Maturity of the Social Customer Program	Average Number of Staff Deployed
1,000–5,000	3.1	Beginner	1.0
5,000–10,000	5.2	Experimental	3.6
10,000–50,000	5.4	Formalized	8.2
50,000–100,000	23.8	Mature	20
100,000+	20.4	Advanced	24.3

Table 13.1. Two Views: How Many Full-Time Staff Do You Deploy Against Your Social Media Program?

Source: Altimeter Group white paper, 2010 .   © 2010 Altimeter Group and Metz Consulting
Attribution-Noncommercial-Share Alike 3.0 United States

Cisco, Dell, Microsoft, IBM, Intel, and SAP. I have personal knowledge that nearly every one of these programs are at least four or five years old, making these enterprise brands "old hands" at Social CRM (at this point five out of the six of those companies make products used in Social CRM, and the other one makes the hardware the other five run on).

WRITING AND IMPLEMENTING THE STRATEGY

Now that we know the best practices on how a social customer team should be staffed and compensated, (if you're avoiding a Holistic Honeycomb approach, that is, as it evenly distributes Social Customer Management across the entire company), we've got to examine how you actually implement the strategy. Assuming you've followed the lPOSTm methodology (which works regardless of the approach you're taking), you've listened, you've picked the set of people you're working with, and you've vetted the 23 use cases in order to pick your precise objective (or maybe two or three of them).

This is where things get a little tough—you actually have to write the *strategy*. And this is where all of the social media gurus are going to come up short. Because in all the time it took them to tell you you needed to Facebook and tweet your business, they skipped over *The Art of War, The Fifth Discipline,* and W. Chan Kim and Renée Mauborgne's *Blue Ocean Strategy*.[3]

Blue Ocean Strategy doesn't even mention social media or CRM in its 239 pages, but it's all about how to make the competition totally irrelevant (avoiding the battles that create a "bloody red ocean," or Red Ocean strategy, where rivals battle over a shrinking kitty of profits), reach a ton of customers, and do it all at the lowest possible cost.

The idea, in using Value Innovation is to reduce cost (increase scale to reach your customers, actually), and differentiate, like crazy, at the same time. To do so, managers writing the strategy need to look at what's called the Four Actions Framework. The reason you're doing your strategy creation through this lens of questions is because you're trying to break down all of the buyer value elements (the reasons people love you) and create a *brand new* value curve, which is the tool that strategy folks use to tell, visually, whether their strategy works, versus their competitors.

We create social customer strategy around these four questions (based on the Four Actions Framework, introduced in *Blue Ocean Strategy*):

1. **Eliminate.** Which factors that companies in your industry take for granted, around working with the social customer, should be *eliminated?*
2. **Raise.** Which factors of Social Customer Management can or should be raised well above the industry standard?[4]
3. **Reduce.** What can we remove from the social customer relationship? Which factors can be reduced well below the industry standard in working with the social customer?
4. **Create.** Which factors around the social customer can we create, which the industry has never offered before?

All too often in social strategy, brands take the red-ocean strategy route (remember the sharks?), in which they compete head-to-head in a poorly differentiated market, and take similar tacks (and tactics) to manage the all-too-little-available mind share of the social customer. Consider hotel brands. Although Marriott was the first to work with the social customer, and their strategy was certainly Blue Ocean at the time (a 75-year-old hotel CEO blogging in 2007 was *historic*), the competitors that followed in their wake were certainly mostly Red Ocean— (Starwood, IHG, et al.), and even the most Blue Ocean of that bunch, Morgans Hotel Group, which differentiated on high-quality creative, outsourced much of their implementation to an agency (although they're now reeling it in-house[5]).

Here's a clear breakdown of how to tell if your strategy is Red Ocean or Blue Ocean. If you feel like you're competing in the existing market space and channels for social customer attention, it's Red Ocean. If you think you're creating uncontested market space, and a brand new tool set for your social customers, it's Blue Ocean.

Red Ocean is when you try to beat the competition in getting to the social customer. Blue Ocean is when you make the competition totally irrelevant to that same social customer, and create net-new demand.[6] Get the picture?

In the end, remember that you're trying to align your whole company in the simultaneous pursuit of *differentiation* and *high value* and *high profit*—not a crummy choice of one of those three.

Here are five more questions to determine whether you're cool blue or bloody red around the social customer:

1. Is your brand forced to advertise in order to reach the social customer, yet you feel like the marginal impact of every additional dollar you spend on this type of advertising is decreasing?
2. List your competitive factors with the social customer. Then list your competitors'. Is this list the same? Uh-oh.
3. Are people talking about having either college-age interns or people overseas manage your social customers as the only way to be or stay competitive?
4. Organizationally, is it easier to get funding to copy what the competitor did with the social customer than to get funding to start a brand-new initiative?
5. Are people internally blaming your company's slow growth with the social customer on your market conditions?

If you answered yes to all five, then you're bloody red. *Time for a new strategy.*

The Strategy Canvas

You're still going to need a backdrop to cast your entire strategic action plan against. That's where the Strategy Canvas comes in (you can Google this term to try it out). It's the picture of how your company touches the social (non)customers in all of the factors that your industry competes in for their fractional attention.

You need to look at the canvas to understand how to assess where your competitors are going with the social customer and how you can go in a different direction. There's a lot happening with the Strategy Canvas. You'll see the value curve of your industry, and for your brand to own the social customer, you have to have the *best* value curve, and that comes from the right focus and from divergence from your competitors. CREATEWARE

So there are two big reasons you need to use the Strategy Canvas:[7]

1. You need to figure out what the "current state of play" is in your market space, around the social customer. This will show you (a) who's investing where, and (b) the factors your industry competes on, in terms of social customer relationships.
2. You need to change your focus. Focusing on your competitors is going to cause you to lose with the social customer. (Remember Richard Laermer from Punk Marketing's story about what happened to that TAG Body Spray?) You can't focus on competitors. You've got to focus on alternatives. You can't focus on customers of the industry. You've got to focus on noncustomers.

Before we move on to the picking-the-tools part of strategy, let's discuss this concept of the noncustomer. Even seasoned executives, while understanding the definition, have trouble with this term.

Three Levels of Noncustomers

One more key concept from *Blue Ocean*: there are three levels of noncustomers, and they've got to be "unlocked." I know even veteran marketing executives who have big problems with the term "noncustomer," so understand that a noncustomer is either someone who is not currently buying from your company, or it could even be someone who is currently a customer, but is about to "leave."

Below, I present the three tiers of social noncustomers based on Kim and Mauborgne's classifications. After reviewing these tiers, you may want to reconsider the P (people) part of your lPOSTm approach to the social customer. Rather than narrow-casting to find a niche of social customers that's so exact (and so infinitesimally small) that you nail a meaningless target (or a meaninglessly small set of profitable relationships), instead focus on social noncustomers.

The way that the tiers of social noncustomers are set up is based on their distance from your market.

First Tier: Soon-to-Be Social Noncustomers

These noncustomers are on the edge of your market waiting to jump ship. For example, James is a 22-year-old male who prefers to drive his old gas guzzler, small Chevy for big trips to Costco, rather than paying $24 to rent a Zipcar for three hours to run the same trip, faster, in a GMC Sierra hybrid pickup truck. James posts on Facebook: "Drove Zipcar out to Costco . . . must have cost $20 in gas just to get there and back LOL . . . maybe it wasn't such a great idea."

These are the folks who minimally purchase and minimally engage with brands in your market, and do so out of necessity. They mentally consider themselves noncustomers of your industry, and want to leave your industry. That said, if there were a tremendous leap in value or their level of engagement with your industry, they would stay. This would increase the frequency of their purchases and generate what Kim and Mauborgne call "latent demand." James spent that money with Zipcar, and evangelized the brand to all of his friends who have, you guessed it, "latent demand" for their hourly car rentals. But he didn't really identify as a proud customer. It sounds like he might be in danger of ending his relationship with the company.

Second Tier: Refusing Social Noncustomers

These are potential customers who consciously choose *against* your market, refusing to use your industry's offerings. They've evaluated it as a choice, have chosen against it, and have socially shared this choice. Think of Tanya, a 23-year-old who posts: "Never mind rental car companies. I ain't payin' $25/day more to rent a car from the airport when I can have my cousin pick me up and take me to a cheaper car rental instead."

Third Tier: Unexplored Social Noncustomers

They are in markets distant from yours. They are social noncustomers who have never even thought your market would be an option. Imagine Bob, a 22-year-old who had to sell his motorcycle when he moved away to college. He didn't even know he could rent a motorcycle by hopping a 1-hour train ride to Newark, New Jersey, when he landed at JFK, rather than go to the car rental he didn't want to go to. Bob posted: "At lame car rental place—long lines—bored and tired. Miss my bike."

There is almost no data on brands that have unlocked the three tiers of social noncustomers as a specific strategic move. But there are nearly a hundred big-name companies that have specifically used this strategy. My favorite examples here include Gillette[8] and Yellow Tail Wines. GILLETTE (Yikes! Talk about a consumer market in an undercapitalized industry where differentiation among social customers is harder than the wine industry.)

Case Study: Gillette

I can't think of a product that's so useful yet so hard to differentiate as razors or razor blades. Everybody needs them, but how is a razor company supposed to achieve value innovation?

In Mauborgne and Kim's case study, the existing Gillette customers in the early 1900s were medium/high-income white-collar workers (and barbers), and the noncustomers were the "occasional shavers," regular folks who couldn't afford to shave often, because forged razor blades were expensive and difficult to use. The full set of noncustomers included occasional shavers (first-tier noncustomers), low-income folks (second tier), and women (third tier). In a brilliant strategic move, Gillette first pursued the 66 million Americans who lived in nonmetropolitan areas who couldn't easily get to a barbershop—at that time, only one in three Americans lived in a city where there was one. Gillette's low-investment safety razor gave birth to a new industry, broke the cost-value trade-off, and took their blade sales from $14,000 in 1903, to $1.1 million in 1909, and $6 million in 1915.

Case Study: Yellow Tail

Out of all of the vertical industries I've worked in, the toughest one to differentiate in is probably the mature, undercapitalized wine industry. Just think about walking down the red wine aisle at your supermarket or liquor store; there are so many different wines priced between $7 and $20. How does one of them stand out?

In 2001, in an overcrowded wine industry, Australia's Casella Winery tried to do so in the U.S. market, with a goal of selling 25,000 cases in their first year. Four years later Yellow Tail's sales were moving at 25 million cases per year. To create the best-selling imported red wine in the United States, Yellow Tail used a Blue Ocean strategy, designing the wine to appeal to the 85 percent of nonwine drinkers without alienating the 15 percent of the population who do drink wine. The Red Ocean here, in the words of Mike Veseth, professor of International Political Economy at the University of Puget Sound, was "the market for wine, and the Blue Ocean is the market for wine that doesn't taste like wine."[9]

Now that you've seen how the Blue Ocean strategy works, and how it applies to the social customer, let's take a look at some key misunderstandings and failures that companies have had, applying social customer strategy.

14

MISUNDERSTANDINGS AND FAILURES IN SOCIAL CRM

Before leading the troops into battle a general has to be thoroughly prepared. The difference between strategy and planning must be fully understood. To completely ensure that your strategy is sound, pay careful attention to the big misunderstandings about Social CRM and the social customer. There will almost certainly be executives in your organization who will espouse some of these beliefs; take it from me and some of the best-known writers in the space—they're not true.

SEVEN BIG MISUNDERSTANDINGS ABOUT SOCIAL CRM

Most books written about CRM are bone-dry, but Francis Buttle wrote a book, *Customer Relationship Management*,[1] about seven years ago, containing critical data points of how to make a CRM implementation a success, from a technical and organizational perspective. I've adapted the five big misunderstandings about CRM, from Buttle's book, and then added two more, specifically on Social CRM and what executives keep missing out on. This knowledge is necessary before writing the check for the software, and allocating 10,000 worker-hours (a million bucks worth of labor) to having a team implement your strategy.

1. CRM Is Database Marketing

Database marketing is what happens when a brand compiles customer data with the hopes of sending them targeted offers. You can do this with or without a CRM. Over the last 30 years companies have grown larger and farther from the customers they serve—the social Web has only served to exaggerate this situation. When you're doing social, strategic, or operational CRM, however, you're going *way* beyond database marketing.

2. CRM Is a Marketing Process

If you think CRM equals Customer Relationship Marketing, then sure, CRM *sounds* like a marketing process. But it is not, although that's what a lot of people believed this wicked acronym meant during the late '80s and '90s, before the social Web. CRM platforms have many nonmarketing applications: operations, customer acquisition (sales), customer development (cross-sells, upsells), and opportunity management are just a few. At its core, CRM serves to take the voice-of-the-customer and weave it into the fabric of the business, to convert it from the *corporate ecosystem* to the *customer ecosystem*. That isn't marketing—that's your *whole business*.

3. CRM Is an I.T. Issue

This concept is becoming more false every day. I sat on call with a Social CRM vendor the other day that has a pretty neat product—it's a company called Nimble, and they make something that looks more like Facebook than the CRM platforms from days of old. Nothing in this product would require the knowledge of an I.T. department, unless your company still prevents people from using sites like LinkedIn or Facebook, in the office. Even the more robust Web-based Social CRM platforms like Salesforce or Oracle (plus Buzzient) don't require any input from the I.T. department, unless you're doing rather complex work flows and automation that involve the company's e-mail servers, or ties to other legacy databases. (That said, CRM *can* involve I.T., if you're performing complex tasks, or integrating it with legacy databases.)

Most of the Social CRM platforms I know of would need little to nothing from the average I.T. department, aside from maybe an e-mail letting them know they might want to increase the company's Internet bandwidth slightly, if at all, because Web-based application usage may be increasing. The fact that most Social CRMs don't need much involvement from I.T. has actually been central to the sales pitch of most of the big CRM brands, like Salesforce.

4. CRM Is About Loyalty Programs

Don't get me wrong; loyalty programs are important. They have been popular in travel, hospitality, automotive repair, and many other industries in the past decade. In recent years loyalty programs have popped up in more unexpected places (fast food, clothing retail, e-commerce). They provide a base of data for increasing a brand's information about their customers, and they're put in place to get customers (acquisition), keep them (retention), and make them buy more of a product or service (development). They also put something important in place—exit barriers. It would be hard for me to stop flying Southwest if I have two and a half free flights due to my frequent flier miles—that kind of thing makes you want to get that last free flight, and to do that you may have to fly from San Francisco to Los Angeles about six more times. Loyalty programs may be some of the

MISUNDERSTANDINGS AND FAILURES

fuel for getting data about your customers, but to say that CRM equals loyalty programs is a gross oversimplification.

5. CRM Can Be Implemented by *Any* Company

This concept is not at all true, and it may explain the high rate of failures in CRM implementations. Frequently, it's because when a company implements CRM (or Social CRM) they don't know *which* approach they're taking, or why.

We should take a brief detour here. There are three different levels of CRM: *strategic, operational,* and *analytical.*[2] In this book we're mainly dealing with strategic and operational CRM, and you'll see why in a second. The one problem I have with traditional CRM books, like Buttle's book, is that a lot of the writing, while on-target and direct, is frequently hard to remember. You can't really implement what you can't remember, right? So here's a quick breakdown, in which I compare each of the levels of Customer Relationship Management to rock bands, to make them easier to remember.

- **Strategic CRM** (Fugazi CRM). Talk about bands that had a strategic directive. Fugazi was a Washington, D.C., punk band (1986–2002) that never did interviews, kept their show ticket prices under $10 (to this day), and, to the best of my knowledge, never printed merchandise, like bumper stickers or T-shirts. Strategic CRM is the *top-down* perspective on CRM, which views CRM as the *numero uno* customer-centric business strategy. The goal here is to win and *keep* profitable customers. And Fugazi made a career out of their ethos, and they always kept the customer. Fugazi was a band that you could not and did not outgrow.[3] When done right, strategic CRM really works.
- **Operational CRM** (Bob Seger CRM). When you think of meat-and-potatoes (and Chevy commercials), you think of Bob Seger. Seriously, if you've never heard his pre-"Beautiful

Loser" albums, you're really missing out. Bob Seger was one no-nonsense dude from Detroit, back in the day. Operational CRM focuses on automating *everything*, and turning the company into a well-oiled machine. We're talking service automation, sales force automation, and marketing automation. Like a rock, baby.

- **Analytical CRM** (Grateful Dead CRM). Love them or hate them, the Grateful Dead changed music, and changed the way brands talk with their customers. Their whole idea of "tribal leadership" has folks like Seth Godin writing books about it, 40 years after the Dead were doing it. Their bottom-up perspective on the brand-customer relationship is brilliant. Analytical CRM takes a bottom-up approach, taking customer data and letting brands use it for strategic and/or tactical purposes. If the Dead weren't strategic *and* tactical, then I don't know who is.

So now that you know the three approaches to CRM, let's think of these as lenses through which we're crafting our strategy. The majority of the work we do, going forward, will be a mix of strategic CRM (Fugazi CRM) and operational CRM (Bob Seger CRM)

It's generally accepted that strategic CRM can be implemented by any company that wants to become more customer-centric. If top executives set a vision that the organization is going to become more customer-centric, and then convince the rest of the team to get in line with that vision, this can and does happen. Beginning in the mid-'90s, the banking industry was able to successfully do this. The other two types of CRM are not quite as easy to implement.

Let's say you want to implement operational Social CRM, because you want to speed up your sales team's time-to-close, and make the deal-creation process more "social." You can go ahead and add social applications to your existing CRM solution, and you can automate the key parts of the selling process (lead management and contact management processes). But frequently, operational CRM is not as successful as it can or should be, because it's not properly supported by analytical CRM. Here's an example: your company is selling motorcycles to two distinctly different customer groups (two different types of motorcycle dealerships: a rural one that caters to 40- to 60-year-old men, and another, an urban dealership that primarily sells to 20- to 35-year-old women). Without the analytical CRM approach to support distinctly different selling processes, the operational CRM approach could run into a wall.

This whole analytical CRM (Grateful Dead CRM) approach relies on one thing only: solid customer data, to make decisions. You're always trying to figure out one thing in analytical CRM—which customers are going to create the most value, in the future. Thus, the guiding question for analytical Social CRM is: *which customers (that we think will build value in the future) can we build our enterprise and business around?*

This means that analytical Social CRM would need to contain what a lot of software geeks call the "full stream"—the *complete* social stream of everything the customer is saying, the public stuff they say on Facebook, LinkedIn, the public postings they may make in discussion forums, maybe even their Twitter, if they're using that. A few Social CRM products feature this—Nimble does, and Salesforce can be configured to do this with a bit of work, too. Granted, the examples above are aimed at an English-speaking Western Social Customer, but you can certainly extrapolate how this would fit around your customer.

6. Social CRM *Is* Social Media

Though we've mentioned this one earlier in the book, I want to reiterate the point. Here's why: Imagine you were on a team of famous heart surgeons and a journalist walked into your medical practice and said, "Heart surgeons are really only good at preventing people from throwing up, having digestive disturbances and shortness of breath." You know that's not the truth. Heart surgeons prevent people from having cardiac arrest, and dying of heart attacks or heart disease. When you call Social CRM social media, you're only talking about the *symptoms*, or the pieces of content customers create, not the outcomes they're intended to generate, or the business outcomes companies hope to achieve by working with the social customer. To confuse the two is to confuse the things that lead to the fulfillment of your business objectives (social media outcomes) with the business objectives actually being met (the data in your Social CRM that ties media-centric outcomes like fans and followers and content postings to real business outcomes like sales).

7. Social CRM Should Be Owned by the Marketing and PR Teams

Remember this one? Social Customer Scenario Number Two? Everybody knows that when something that's supposed to be owned cross-functionally gets swallowed up by one team, other teams don't get input, and buy-in across the company is pretty low.

PR and Marketing may argue, in this case, that other departments are either "too busy" or "too unskilled" to deal with the social customer, when in reality no one ever explained to them how the social customer impacted their department. I mean, who in your company sat down with the purchasing department when Facebook hit its 500 millionth user and said, "Listen guys, we need to talk about this development, because it impacts you." Here's who it *should* be owned by: Social CRM, on the front end, should be owned by anyone who touches the social customer, and that includes marketing, sales, human resources, and customer service. The Social CRM should be connected to the other systems-of-record around the social customer so that the other departments (purchasing/procurement, etc.) can drive insight from the social customer's actions.

WHY DO THESE IMPLEMENTATIONS FAIL?

When Social CRM programs fail, they fail big. When a CRM implementation goes down, it usually takes more than a few consultants with it. The problem with looking up anecdotes of failed CRM implementations is that no one who's had a real turkey wants to talk much about it. I was able to get one brave soul to speak up, though, and he's a VP-level exec at a major training and development firm. I can't even tell you where to find this guy—he was referred to me by the CRM Witness Protection Program. We'll call him "Dan."

"CRM makes so much *intuitive* sense *but* it requires changes in people's behaviors," Dan said. "Getting the tool is the easy part, gaining adoption is a different story. [Our company] failed dismally, our salespeople were used to acting independently and felt threatened by sharing 'their' information. 'Professionals' felt that other things were a priority. As long as [CRM] is an extra task added on top it will fail. To adopt it, CRM must be integral to the way individuals work, get paid, and operate as teams."

So, right there, we know that successful CRM implementations are a result of teams having the right incentives and behavioral motivations, and deep support by key executives. Let's step aside for a moment to talk with one of the best business analysts out there, IDC's Mike Fauscette. Fauscette is the leader of IDC's Software Business Solutions Group—one of the best enterprise software research teams in the world.

How to Succeed in Social CRM Implementation

Here's Fauscette's quick rundown of how *not to fail* in a big Social CRM implementation. He was kind enough to answer a number of my questions on the subject.

What is it that causes new technology implementations to fail in small, medium, and enterprise businesses?

> In general, I think the biggest cause of project failure is not devoting enough time up front to clearly define what outcomes you want from the project and exactly how you will get to those outcomes. That results in something I call "requirements mismatch," where the outcomes don't solve the real needs of the business.
>
> There's a simple and successful method to use for planning and executing a successful project: (1) define factors driving the need for the project; (2) define the overall business strategy, goals, and objectives, (3) define the current business state and the future state of what the business should look like after the implementation. This is a basic needs assessment and is critical to building a successful implementation plan.

Right here Fauscette sets up a critical 1-2-3 sequence, in terms of how not to fail. It's so simple, yet so often missed, that it bears repeating:

1. Define the factors driving the need for the project. If you don't have urgent need, you don't have a project.
2. Define the overall business strategy, goals, and objectives.
3. Define the current business state and the future state of what the business should look like after the implementation. We got our Stephen Covey here, again: "Begin with the end in mind."

Okay, so that's enough about failure. What about the stuff that's needed to actually make the Social CRM implementation succeed? How about the three key factors in ensuring success in a new social technology launch? Fauscette says:

1. Get executive and management buy-in to the project early, and check in often to make sure they stay supportive. This is most likely going to be a C-level executive. With every rung you descend the chain-of-command, you lower your odds of success.

2. Clearly define what the end state should look like. Stephen Covey's "Begin with the end in mind" concept. The reason he sold 30 million books is because that simple piece of advice usually works.

3. Start small and build on success in incremental phases. If you can't get adoption from the 20-person sales team or the five-person marketing team, imagine what would happen if you rolled out the solution to, say, 20,000 users. Train wreck.

Ah, but you're probably thinking, Our company is different—you don't understand! Well, Fauscette thought of that. So, let's examine, politically speaking, the real "silent killers" to watch out for. Fauscette:

> Be careful of managers who feel threatened by the project and work behind the scenes to kill it off. Change is hard, and often people are very resistant to change. Employees say they will "participate" but in reality they drag and resist at every turn. Starting small and building on successes can help with adoption. Finding and promoting champions of the new technology can also help.

When you're talking about drinking whiskey and playing guitar, you want to talk with Keith Richards, right? And when you're looking for enterprise software success tips, you talk to Mike Fauscette. Well, I have to say that when you're talking about gigantic multimillion dollar (and even billion dollar) technology failures, Asuret's Michael Krigsman is your man,[4] and the only guy qualified to put in the *last word* on Social CRM failure. Krigsman, covers I.T. failures for ZDNET.[5] Here's what he had to say on the specific reasons why not just a CRM implementation, but a *Social* CRM implementation, might fail:

> Social CRM offers a *different* set of challenges from those associated with ordinary I.T. or CRM projects. To achieve

success, Social CRM practitioners should understand these differences and the impact for their own organization.

The meaning of Social CRM goes far beyond technology to genuinely engaging, and communicating substantively, with customers. Although technology provides enabling platforms and channels through which this engagement can occur, successfully cultivating relationships with customers is not a technology issue.

Here are three primary reasons that social CRM projects fail:

1. **Poor strategy.** Success always requires specific plans, goals, and objectives. If you don't have a clear direction in mind, then achieving success becomes a hit-or-miss proposition. Before starting any Social CRM initiative, define the end state you hope to reach; then realistically consider plans and activities that will take you in the right direction.

2. **Overfocus on technology.** The technology part of Social CRM is relatively easy: buy software, install it, and use it. Unfortunately, as many companies have discovered, merely putting up collaboration forums, for example, is meaningless unless accompanied by significant efforts to engage users.

3. **Minimizing culture.** Ultimately, Social CRM represents a long-term process of change leading to greater commitment and engagement with customers. Such changes require organizational leadership to support, and actively champion, customer-oriented goals inside the company. This frequently

requires a culture shift that takes time to develop; changing an organization's cultural DNA does not happen overnight.

During [a] conversation with the "Accidental Social CRM group"—a community of thought leaders and practitioners—I asked for feedback on the topic of failure. Overwhelmingly, the group pointed out that developing a customer-aware culture is distinct from any particular technology or tools.

The key to Social CRM success lies in planting seeds and cultivating positive change over time. From this perspective, traditional I.T. (including CRM) projects are relatively self-contained events, with crisp boundaries and resources. Social CRM represents a broader lifestyle change for many organizations.

As with any lifestyle improvement regime, Social CRM success depends on determining goals, stepping forward on the path, and maintaining the persistence needed to achieve consistent results. Of course, the steps may be simple, but traversing the path requires time, patience, and overcoming obstacles.

So, when you're bringing this strategy to the team, make it clear to everyone that you've accounted for all of the cultural and strategic factors brought up by Fauscette and Krigsman (either of whom, I'm sure, would be happy to get on the phone with your team for an hour). Being able to name-check the two biggest CRM failure experts is a sure way to prove to the rest of the executive team that you've vetted your strategy thoroughly before sending the troops (mid-level managers) into battle.

15

THE 98 PERCENT
CUSTOMER MANAGEMENT
MODEL

With a maximum amount of effectiveness, you're going to be able to take care of 98 percent of the social customer data you need. You can try for that last 2 percent, but it's really not worth the time. Consider a brand like Apple, which we profiled thoroughly in Chapter 1, as being a "social object"—they use the 98 percent Customer Management Model. They're not afraid to do things that absolutely thrill 98 percent of their customers, and they're fully aware they are going to encounter deep resistance from 2 percent of their customer base. We're talking about 50,000 to 100,000 people flipping out, on the Internet, every time Apple makes a product announcement, but Apple is entirely comfortable with this arrangement.

We need a frame for organizing customer data, so we need to think in terms of distilling the data into a "single source of truth"—a term you'll hear a lot in enterprise software going back nearly a decade—whether you're dealing with data about an organization's bulldozers or its customers. What's complex about getting a single source of truth around the social customer is that you typically need a half-dozen to a dozen software solutions to work with the customer. So, which one's the right one?

What you're hoping for when you purchase one of those pieces, like a community management solution for example, is twofold: visibility and health. First, you want to make sure that the solution allows you to see what's happening in all of your communities, in real-time, so the brand can react quickly. Second, you need to be able to dynamically measure the health of these communities. (Lithium actually wrote a good white paper about a year ago, "Measuring Community Health for Online Communities," and this one would be pretty useful, if you're thinking of doing your own branded community.) [1]

Monitoring a brand's health across *multiple* branded communities (both internal "white label" ones as well as public ones like Twitter and "walled garden" communities like Facebook) is a lot harder, but brands like Lithium and Jive Software (who call this whole category SBS—social business software) are trying to own this hard-to-capture space with products like Lithium Community for Facebook and Jive SBS 5. In case you're wondering, Lithium and Jive are the two big players in this space, but you'll need to read the big white papers if you go shopping for this kind of software. For instance, Gartner's "Magic Quadrant for Social CRM, Externally-Facing Social Software Magic Quadrant," and their "Social Software for the Workplace" reports; as well as Forrester's less current "2009 Wave: Community Platforms" report). Either vendor is happy to hook you up with a free copy.

If the social community data is not analyzed properly on your platform, then your team can't make sensible micro and macro decisions on what to do, in response to events and actions in your social communities, or from your social customers in general. If you don't remember the difference between micro (human) and macro (robot/work flow) decisions, flip back to that figure from Chess Media Group in Chapter 2. Essentially, if you don't have something that can structure all of this unstructured data about your customers, you might be wasting hundreds of thousands of dollars on software, and 10 times that on labor.

I know, it sounds like the Social Analytics engine and the Community Management piece have a bit of overlap. The reason for this is because social business software brands like Jive and Lithium are trying to write unified pieces of software (similar to a Microsoft Office for the social enterprise), and sometimes that means the "layers" of Social CRM bleed together a bit, which is not necessarily a bad thing.

SUPPLY CHAIN MANAGEMENT

Supply Chain Management (SCM) has come a *long* way since I graduated college in 1999. I remember my first job, at CDW, when our customers were able to log on to the then-new CDW extranet. The extranet allowed my customers to buy computers and software at their preferred corporate pricing (and largely check our stock) over the Internet, in a secure environment. At the time, it was a revolutionary development—that consumers could see, roughly, where the inventory was, at any given point in time.

From where the vendors are coming from, Social CRM and the supply chain (and human capital, and enterprise resources...) are deeply connected. Just ask Oracle's Mark Woollen:

> We have a variety of different application containers or contextual environments, in which that capability is consumed—CRM being one, HR and Talent being another, Supply Chain and what-not being another.

And by the way, since all these apps [Social CRM, Human Capital Management, Supply Chain] share a common data model, what you can do is, depending on your role, like you may be a salesperson, and you're concerned with CRM, but you're also concerned with incentive compensation, you're also concerned with your channel's sales partners—so PRM (Partner Relationship Management), CRM, Finance, all of that is actually very unique to your role. Now you have this [one] activity stream capability facilitating enterprise collaboration across all entities. It's not just for that one app, it's for everything.

Such comments highlight why the Facebook news-feed approach to the enterprise begins to make sense.

Here's how the supply chain became social: when the consumer clicked on the IBM laptop on CDW's Web site, and, instead of showing a price, the item said "CALL," it meant the laptop was at an Ingram Micro warehouse (distribution) somewhere, and not in CDW's warehouse. That was the first big shift in how the supply chain got "socialized," or exposed to the social customer. This was a big deal for the I.T. guy, who was used to calling up a Compaq rep, back in 1985, just to find out when they could ship him some new computers (see Supply Chain 0.0 below).

Here's a history of supply chain and the social customer in three sentences. First, we got big, expensive computers and entered all of the supply chain people and things into them. Next, the Internet let the customer see some of the data in our computer systems, on a need-to-know basis. As the plain old customer became the social customer, businesses began opening up, and allowing the social customer to see a ton of information and guide brands' decisions about what to do with the supply chain. The discussion below breaks it down more clearly, with some help from the guys who wrote one of the defining modern supply chain books.

Where social touches the supply chain can most easily be seen in the Wet Seal example we saw in Chapter 6. The fact that you can walk into a store, today, and look at (1) the items your peers and friends have bought based on (2) what is in stock, at the present time, is mind-blowing.

Here's a little fantasy example: Imagine being on vacation in Oakland, California, for the first time, and walking into my favorite restaurant, the 1920's Art Deco–style eclectic American restaurant Flora. Instead of a menu, let's say the waiter handed you an iPad or an inexpensive tablet computer with the daily specials on it. By signing into the menu with your Facebook login, you get free bread and sparkling water at your table. And when you swipe your finger down the menu, you see that two of your friends have tried the burger, one has tried the Wild Coho Salmon, and everyone in your Facebook network loves the caramel pudding with rock salt. You're only being shown your friends' opinions on the dishes the kitchen has in stock tonight. Pretty amazing, huh? Well, this technology exists, is for sale today, and you don't need to use something as huge as Oracle Retail to participate. There's nothing preventing your brand from using the technology with the social customer.

As we move on to Chapter 16, we'll be looking at figuring out the complex assessment piece around the social customer, and we'll be breaking down the dashboards your brand can use. But first let's take a quick look at supply chain milestones so you can see things from the view of your social customers.[1]

SUPPLY CHAIN MILESTONES IN RELATION TO THE SOCIAL CUSTOMER

Supply Chain 0.0

Milestone: Supply chain information goes into big computers—a little oversimplistic, maybe, but seriously, such material was in manila file folders previously, which is still how some companies operate.

When: 1960s to 1982.

What: In the 1980s manufacturing organizations began to develop and change products to meet customer needs. The term SCM was born in the early '80s.

How It's Social: Everyone from end-users to suppliers were interviewed to see how these processes should be constructed. When users have a problem, they either complain to their vendors or suppliers.

Supply Chain 1.0

Milestone: E-business, in which customers can actually see if what they want is in stock on the Web (ERP-SCM integration).

When: Sometime between 1997 and 2002, depending on whether you are considering consumer goods (e.g., Amazon), technology (e.g., CDW), or corporate supply chain.

What: The consumer can tell, by looking at your Web site, whether what they want is in your warehouse, or, if not, roughly where it might be right now. Customer awareness of supply chain, 24/7/365, is a key innovation here. Service and sales processes improved, and operational, production, and inventory costs began to decrease.

How It's Social: Customers could e-mail and tell their friends and colleagues if they had any chance of getting their Nintendo Game Boy by Christmas 2001. Technically speaking, a customer could blog about supply chain events, but crossover between SCM and social technologies was very low at this point.

Supply Chain 1.5

Milestone: Supply chains begin to transform into integrated "value systems," but feel the weight of e-businesses' complications.

When: 2000 to 2001.

What: The key transformation between Supply Chain 1.0 and Supply Chain 1.5 is the new layer of complexity that emerged with e-business innovations (e.g., security, government regulation, reliability, fault tol-

erance), and the time to integrate legacy systems with e-business supply chain.

How It's Social: The brands are finally beginning to catch up with the
Internet customer (the Cro-Magnon man antecedent to the modern
man, the social customer).

Supply Chain 2.0 (Post-9/11 Supply Chain)

Milestone: A catastrophic event creates a hard look at costs, while social technologies simultaneously enhance transparency and visibility
across supply chain.

When: 2001 to 2010.

What: The impact of 9/11 caused managers to face the fact that the
Supply Chain 1.5 model was broken and supply chain performance
and transparency had to be improved. Cost reduction, across supply
chain, went into effect.

How It's Social: The only choice, to reduce costs, is to "'step on the
gas' in a collaborative manner," to quote Handfield and Nichols (*Supply Chain Redesign*).[2] Companies collaborate with partners to reduce
costs, while slowly opening up the flow of information to the bur-
geoning social customer.

Supply Chain 3.0

Milestone: The social enterprise—supply chain is manually and dynamically allocated in response to the social customer (signaling the
beginning of the *Internet of Things*).

When: 2010 to 2020.

What: The social customer, en masse, can cause massive supply chain
entities (like 17 trucks containing 34,000 blue sweaters) to be reallo-
cated, or even produced, based on a combination of their aggregate
conversation and micro/macro decisions. Social customer can see how
supply is allocated, in real-time. RFID slowly becomes ubiquitous.

How It's Social: Social conversation and social customer actions dictate inputs for supply chain events, in real-time. This is not fiction—

Oracle Retail's Duncan Angove (one of the real machers[3] on the social supply chain) states that these technologies currently exist, although no vendor has strung together all of the pieces.

Managing Your Customer Base

Managing for 98 percent of your customer base is completely possible as long as you account for the fact that different customers will touch your brand in different ways (mobile, Internet, direct mail, retail), and your CRM platform or single-source-of-truth around the social customer facilitates interaction with them, the supply chain as they see it, the supply chain as your company sees it, and you.

16

SOCIAL CUSTOMER ANALYTICS: HOW TO TELL IF YOUR TEAM'S DOING IT RIGHT

I tend to see things as just about the sum of their parts, no more, no less. Thinking of all of these Social CRM systems as one "holistic" model for me doesn't totally add up. In assessment, the sum of the parts is just that. This chapter diagrams the five core dashboards (and corresponding variables) of the book's methodology.

NET PROMOTER DASHBOARD

Net Promoter® can be a crucial dashboard for monitoring your customers. This management tool (based on asking customers how likely they are to recommend your brand, then grouping responses along a 0 to 10 scale) was invented by Fred Reichheld, a Bain & Company consultant, who joined forces with Satmetrix to measure the loyalty of customers. Reichheld and teams at Bain combined a methodology focused on very short surveys and customer follow-up with a wealth of data from Satmetrix on how customers rate various brands. It came about in 2002 and 2003 (there's a *Harvard Business Review* article, "The One Number You Need to Grow," that's worth looking at).

"Net Promoter is the most operational market research a brand can do," said John Abraham, the general manager of Net Promoter Programs, Satmetrix. "Word of mouth from your customers all starts with their experience. So you need an operational system to make sure companies know how they are doing, and which experiences drive loyalty and recommendation." Your customers will basically fall into one of three categories: *promoters* (rating 9 or 10), *passives* (7 or 8), and *detractors* (0 to 6). The goal of the approach is to cultivate promoters of the brand, reduce the number of detractors, and track the Net Promoter Score™ or NPS® over time,[1] to get a picture of where the health of your brand is headed with the social customer.

"Indeed, the Net Promoter Score has gained rapid adoption because it solves three fundamental problems," said Stephan Sorger, partner at OnDemand Advisors, a strategic consultant firm focused on increasing revenue, and marketing instructor at the San Francisco extension of UC Berkeley.

"With Net Promoter, (1) businesses can gather customer feedback at low cost (previous customer research efforts proved very expensive); (2) gather feedback quickly (previous research methods could take months to complete); and (3) be confident in the approach, knowing that independent research found NPS to drive growth through repurchase and word-of-mouth advocacy."

What Belongs in This Dashboard?

In the Net Promoter Dashboard, you're trying to get not only a picture of the NPS, but to have it on a relatively frequent basis for decision making. Think about it: if you're doing 35,000 customer transactions a day, you might want to get daily metrics. How frequent depends on your operations, but it should be like monitoring the health of the business, and thus requires at least a quarterly measure.

"Using Net Promoter goes way beyond the metric; it's got to connect to specific activities in the company, and allow you to *take action* on the feedback and improve customer outcomes," Abraham said. He continues:

> If the developers of NPS hadn't thought carefully about word of mouth, they could have come up with different results. If all you're looking at is spending, there are other questions like "the customer's intention to continue buying," which can perform pretty well, but they're usually not as reliable an indicator of loyalty. What happens if a customer is trapped or if it's hard to switch? They may continue buying, but they may in fact be detractors of the brand, and that shows up in the word of mouth. A lot of companies confuse trapped customers with loyal customers.

And since you've read a bit of *Blue Ocean Strategy* by now, you won't make that same mistake.

Figure 16.1 from Satmetrix[2] shows how promoters differ from detractors among consumers who have bought computer hardware. The promoters don't just spend more. Because they refer more often, they actually generate new revenue for the manufacturer as some percentage of their referrals convert into new purchases. The opposite happens with detractors. They sometimes share negative experiences and advise their friends against buying, which makes them look a lot less valuable once the word of mouth is taken into account.

Which System-of-Record Should NPS Live In?

The Net Promoter method and Satmetrix software can be integrated with Social CRM platforms such as Salesforce, OracleCRM, Microsoft

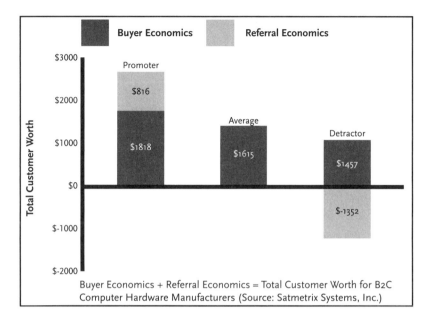

Figure 16.1. Net Promoter and Word-of-Mouth Economics

Outlook, and Web services. Ideally, the customer data should live in the CRM, and the Net Promoter feedback tools can be programmed to use that data, even if the connection doesn't currently exist.

"But to put in place all the processes around it for the follow-up," Abraham explains, "that's where you really want to have not just a dashboard for tracking one number, but a system that supports the customer follow-up process and analytics to understand the things that matter most for the customer."

What Are the Levels of Using NPS?

There are three different ways that NPS can be gradually utilized, with increasing levels of sophistication:

1. **Level One** (Awareness): figuring out your NPS score as a one-time exercise. Think of this as testing out the waters.
2. **Level Two** (Measurement/Research): thinking of NPS as a research exercise, with regular readouts but no follow-up, and

integrating it with a dashboard, with no follow-up. Not best
practice, but often where things head next.

3. **Level Three** (Day-to-Day Use): This is when you really get into
loyalty-directed social customer management, by taking NPS
and feedback data and causing customer-centered decisions
to be made. "You want to get the right information to the right
people in your company," Abraham says, "so they can follow
up with the customer, and do analytics on the feedback to set
strategy. We call that closing the loop—you need to close the
loop one-on-one with the customer, and on the broad themes
that will help you create more brand promoters."

BRAND REPUTATION DASHBOARD

In my interview with Stephan Sorger, an instructor with the University
of California, Berkeley Extension, we discussed how brands are engaging in conversations on social Web sites such as blogs, forums, Facebook fan pages, Twitter feeds, YouTube videos, and mainstream news
sites (e.g., the *New York Times*). Companies need to track critical aspects
of these conversations or risk damage to their hard-won brand reputa-
tions. That said, this is the dashboard that's probably going to change
the most over time.

What Functions Should Be Measured and What Belongs in This Dashboard?

"While every company situation is different, it is useful to include
three categories of metrics in the dashboard," Stephan Sorger said:

- The first is *Company,* which includes information specifically
related to an organization (i.e., yours). Examples include company and product names and variations thereof (e.g., monitoring how "Apple" is mentioned on the social Web), names

of key employees (e.g., monitoring "Steve Jobs"), names of associated partners and organizations (e.g., monitoring "AT&T"), and topical references (such as "Antennagate" for the Apple iPhone 4).

- The second category is *Competition,* which includes similar information about your competitors (e.g., company and product names, etc.).

- The third category is *Industry,* including consumer sentiment about the industry in general (e.g., how poor airline experiences could affect multiple airline brands), industry trends (e.g., how rising gas prices could affect multiple petroleum brands), topical issues (think "BP"), and trade associations (e.g., strikes by union leaders could affect brand reputation).

Which System-of-Record Should It Live In?

According to Sorger, "enterprise-class social media monitoring tools with brand reputation functionality typically offer several integration options to interoperate with multiple systems, making it possible to gather different insights from the different systems." For example:

> Radian6 (www.radian6.com), a market-leading social media monitoring and engagement tool, ties into your Salesforce. com database to enable users to create contacts, leads, and support cases from brand monitoring through the social Web. The system also integrates with [Web and mobile analytics solutions like] Google Analytics, WebTrends, and Omniture to view the social Web results through the lens of Web-based statistics.

Even though there may be a few different pieces of software involved, here, Sorger is suggesting a fairly holistic dashboard.

SOCIAL COLLATERAL ENGAGEMENT DASHBOARD

How should engagement with pieces of social collateral created by the brand be measured? Sorger and I discussed current trends in measuring social collateral engagement. Social collateral, which consists of brand-based or brand-created content presented on social media sites (or in their own members-only social channels), can stimulate conversations with influential prospects and other important parties. By creating content that encourages discussion, organizations move from a "broadcast" model to a "conversation" model.

What Belongs in This Dashboard?

"To accurately gauge the effectiveness of your social collateral, measure both quantitative and qualitative aspects of social media interaction," Sorger said.

Here's the good stuff, according to Sorger: "*Quantitative* aspects include easy-to-measure metrics such as reach (number of users reading the content), *quantity of conversations* (by brand, by product, by day of week, etc.), *influence level of commenters* (such as the number of followers of a commenter), *level of engagement* (passive reading, to 'follow me,' to 'retweets' or 'reposts'), and the *sentiment of the comments* (percentages of positive/ neutral/ negative comments)."

And here, Sorger noted is the tricky part: "Qualitative feedback, while more difficult to measure, can be *more valuable*. Examples include amount of detail in posts (more detail about product benefits/ problems can indicate deeper relationships with the brand), mentions of competing brands (your known competitive 'rivals' as well as other companies your customers feel compete with you), and mentions by brand advocates. In particular, mentions by brand advocates can be powerful because they can be used (with permission) in marketing collateral. Definitely leverage quantitative and qualitative feedback to constantly improve the quality and relevancy of your social collateral."[3]

Which System Should It Live In?

"Mechanisms to measure social collateral engagement will typically live in social media listening platforms," Sorger said, "which provide a variety of tools to quickly and easily measure social engagement."

For example, Cymfony (cymfony.com) offers its Cymfony Maestro Dashboard for in-depth social media listening, analysis, and engagement. Cymfony also offers complementary widgets to deliver metrics right to the desktops of busy executives who need to monitor social media engagement but don't want to access Maestro directly.[4]

SOCIAL ECOSYSTEM HEALTH DASHBOARD

For branded social communities, this is a major question: "How should the brand monitor the health of a branded social network?" In Social CRM there are few dashboards as clearly outlined as this one. Social software brand Lithium, which supplies the social platform to big consumer brands like Barnes & Noble, Home Depot, Sephora, and Best Buy, as well as consumer tech brands like AT&T and Linksys/Cisco, wrote a clear and concise white paper on this subject in 2009. To monitor such information, it will cost your brand around $1 million to $5 million to build up and staff.

What Belongs in This Dashboard?

The Community Health Index, devised by Lithium, is what they hope will become an industry standard. I hope so, too, because I haven't seen anything better yet. This is a critical dashboard because it derives business outcomes from the one thing every brand seems to want to do: build a branded community. These community members are financially important—a *Harvard Business Review* study of an online auction brand stated that members of the brand's community drove an average of 56 percent more in sales than the customers that didn't belong to the community. Until recently, this space didn't have a single-industry standard, like a FICO score or the BMI (body-mass-index) that your personal trainer might use.[5]

Here's the deal: if your Community Health Index is low, your company needs to change the way they're managing the community. The six-point index that the Community Health Index (on a scale of 1 to 1,000) should be graded on is:

1. **Members:** Growing = members. A healthy community continues to grow after its initial launch. Even though an older community's growth rate may slow, growth should still continue on pace with the brand's customer acquisition. If someone registers, they're a member. If they don't, then they're not.

2. **Content:** Useful = content. When you have a ton of good content, it attracts visitors. If you've got a support community for social customers, content solves their problems. If you've got an engagement community, where your brand is marketing or giving brand enthusiasts a place to congregate, content is what attracts members. If it's a listening community, where you're allowing your customers to create, content is the barometer of how much good input you're getting from your customers.

3. **Traffic:** Popular = traffic. The number of page views (or time-on-site, if your community is not page-drive), eyes on your content, is an important statistic of community health. Obviously, you'll want to dilute your analytics to account for the robot crawlers that hit your pages. Ask a good Web analyst for the right formula here.

4. **Liveliness:** This one may seem hard to measure, and even your community members might find it difficult to measure, but people return to communities that they perceive as vibrant. Perhaps you could have an engagement threshold

minimum that a certain portion of the community meets, to quantify liveliness. This is a hard one, I know—it's like, if 35 percent of the people at your party are slam-dancing and one person's sick in the bathroom, does that make it a quantifiably lively party?

5. **Interaction:** Interactive = topic interaction. If the people in your community aren't interacting with one another, then you're missing a crucial pillar of engagement. Thread depth is the key metrics here—how deep are community discussions going?

6. **Responsiveness:** How fast is your brand responding to community members? How fast are community members responding to one another's posts? If conversation response times drop off, then members will begin looking elsewhere to have their needs met.

Which System Should It Live In?

It lives in the community management software, or perhaps on the Social CRM, if those two are built on the same platform (rare, but possible). Ask your community platform vendor if there's a way to truck in external community data (i.e., Facebook, etc.) for communities that surround your brand but don't explicitly live on your brand's platform.

"We are definitely working on new metrics," Lithium CEO Lyle Fong said. "We have some internal metrics that are really good indicators of future health of a community, but when we built the Community Health Index, we *purposely* didn't include those in it because we want to create a standard that non-Lithium organizations could understand. But based on data that we have, we can do things like understand in advance who is going to be an influential user, and we think the presence of 'future stars' is a good leading indicator of health."

Although Lithium's original white paper doesn't speak directly to "future stars," their six-point prescription for community health measurement is pretty easy to follow. But there's one catch: the 2009 white paper, as thorough as it was at the time, doesn't account for multichannel assessment. (But that's sort of like complaining because the Beatles only recorded *Abbey Road* on a eight-track recording unit—it was the best technology available at the time.)

"In the broader realm," Fong said, "we're looking at ways to measure the social health of a brand across multiple channels, and its readiness, based on those factors, to work with social customers toward particular business objectives. For example, if you're Sephora and you've got a pool of people out there who love to talk about what products people should buy, then that's a great signal that you should be doing something in social commerce. We think that a lot of things like that can be measured, and that those measurements can be a great way of helping companies to prioritize the use cases or solutions they want to roll out."

SOCIAL COMMERCE INDEX DASHBOARD

This one isn't an optional dashboard, unless you don't care about making money. It focuses on how your brand should measure the success of its social commerce and social media affiliate marketing engagements. There have been a crop of new social e-commerce vendors popping up, like Taurad, and it's worth looking at multivendor shopping carts like Payvment, which give users an Amazonlike experience (multiple vendors, one single checkout). This system should only be used if you're involved in social commerce, which is growing popular among apparel, travel/hospitality, and software brands.

What Belongs in This Dashboard?

- **Sales, by social platform.** This is pretty cut and dry; it breaks down your brand's sales, per social platform that the brand is doing business on.

- **Sales, by affiliate.** Breaks down which are the most influential social media affiliates, so you can deploy sales support most effectively.
- **Reach, by affiliate.** Breaks down which social affiliates have the widest reach, so you can deploy sales support resources against the ones that have big reach but low sales.
- **Group marketing efforts.** If you're doing any Groupon-like offers for your customer base, you'll want to track somewhere, on a day-to-day basis, whether the customers are biting, or at least have real-time verification of whether your offers need to be modified or revised.

Which System Should It Live In?

This data will typically live in an e-commerce system, and this will vary widely, depending on what e-commerce platform your business uses. Also, if social commerce is based on a widget platform (i.e., Gigya), then you may choose instead to run reports on this platform, and truck it back to your Social CRM platform by using the widget platform's API.

If you're thinking there's a lot of technical stuff in this chapter that's mainly aimed at companies pretty far along in Social Customer Management, you're right. If you're lacking mission-to-metrics dashboards, you're never going to achieve the mission. And if you remember one sentence from Peter Drucker: "You can't manage what you can't measure." So, put in the keys and light up the dashboard. Next up: setting up the work flows to make it all hum.

17

WORK FLOWS AND
ESCALATION PATHS

The point of including an entire chapter on work flows is to explain not only the "order of operations" (what to do at each point in the engagement), but also to explain *which* dashboards should be monitored at which time, and how indices (groups of blended metrics that compose indexes) should be composed. We learned one big thing from our talks with Radian6's Chris Newton: your metrics and dashboards will not necessarily be the same as your competitors.

WORK FLOWS

A work flow is the combination of *replicable* behaviors (meaning you can repeat them over and over) that your company executes to have relationships with the social customer. Some are proactive, some are reactive. Some are macro (meaning they're automated) and some are micro (they can only be executed by a living, breathing human).

If your social media monitoring and engagement products don't have their own work flows, or at least a way to link to what will activate work flows in your Social CRM system, your team will need to do a lot of manual work. One thing to consider here is that vendors like Radian6 and Lithium actually use their own product to sell itself.

"Yes, Radian6 has precisely designed processes to deal with customers throughout the sales decision-making cycle," Newton said. "Leads and prospects are dealt with by certain members of our organization while customers are pushed through to support teams designed specifically to deal with customers."[1] R6PLAYBOOK

It should be clear that one of the hallmarks of using work flow is to divide customer needs into business-function-specific response teams. This division may sound pretty basic, but you'd be shocked at how many companies assign a college intern to this "social media stuff" and attempt to let a 19-year-old solve most of their problems initially. Before the San Francisco Travel Association, one of our clients, purchased a monitoring and engagement solution, monitoring their Facebook page alone had become a full-time job. When you have 700 to 1,000 responses to everything your brand says, there's a great deal of information to consider. So, how do you keep track of all of the responses, comments, feelings, and criticisms, while making sure you are maintaining an appropriate response time?

"All interactions with customers are tracked and recorded to ensure that a certain response time is maintained across the board, while also logging any repeat issues, so that issues can be identified and certain customers given further action," Newton said. "These processes are not automated, but dictated through a customizable engagement playbook."

Wow, there are four gems Newton brings up here that should be highlighted in your social customer listening program:

1. Log everything
2. Monitor response time to maintain consistency
3. Log repeat issues

4. Use micro (not automated) responses from your customizable engagement playbook

What it boils down to is one huge question on social customer
work flows: *what's the most important work flow?*

"Let's focus on what I think is perhaps the most important work
flow rule," Lithium's Lyle Fong said. "*When does the company intervene?* As we talk to clients who are involved in social customer
projects, we see a variety of answers to this question—but most organizations will face a scalability problem if they attempt to intervene in
every mention in every venue."

Fong gives fairly prescriptive advice on combating this immense
scalability problem, and its remedy, the social customer itself:

> So, savvy companies develop a set of rules to prioritize when
> they are going to react. And they focus on giving the right
> people the right tools to make that initial determination.
>
> They also cultivate a situation in which other people [i.e.,
> reference customers] can react on their behalf and help di-
> rect them toward the most important things that are going
> on in their social world. And that often means *not* reacting
> right away, and letting others act first. The most scalable way
> to deal with the volume of conversations on the social Web
> is with social customers. Successful companies will figure out
> how to work with social customers to scale out their social
> media efforts.

If you're still having trouble envisioning what this looks like, think
of a huge brand like Best Buy. They sell tons of products that are a little
tough to configure—like the Cisco Linksys routers. Let's say you were
having a problem with your router. When you go to their community

forums at forums.bestbuy.com and type "Cisco Linksys" in the search box, you can see customers (and a few Best Buy employees who are volunteering off the clock) troubleshooting one another's problems in the Computers and Home Networking category of the forums. Now, message boards have existed on the Internet for over 30 years, but never have so many customers of so many consumer brands been "managed" by other customers just like them.

You don't have to use the Radian6 or the Lithium playbook, but if you're not going to, you need to make a playbook of your own. I saw one on David Armano's blog on Edelman Digital that was pretty basic but should give you an idea of what the whole micro-versus-macro relationship might look like for your company.

We have recreated the work flow in Figure 17.1. It's a pretty basic business process diagram and you don't need an MBA to understand it. If you look across the top of Armano's graphic you'll see that this is a Social Customer Insights work flow, with four phases: Listen, Assess, Engage, and Repeat. The stakeholders here include the community managers (usually six to 20 employees for a larger brand) and the community itself. You'll notice that the notion of "right channeling" comes up here clearly, on the border of the Listen and Assess phases. Before you respond to a customer comment, tweet (or anything), you really need to know the customer's preferred response channel.

Can all of these factors be codified so they can go into a CRM system as a work flow? Sometimes. It just depends on how granular the decision points are. You may look at your company's business process and decide that it's too nuanced to have the actual work flow automation go into your Social CRM. That said, you still may want to use the Social CRM as a system-of-record.

How will these work flows evolve over time to provide your brand with a valuable portrait of your social customer? Lithium's Lyle Fong

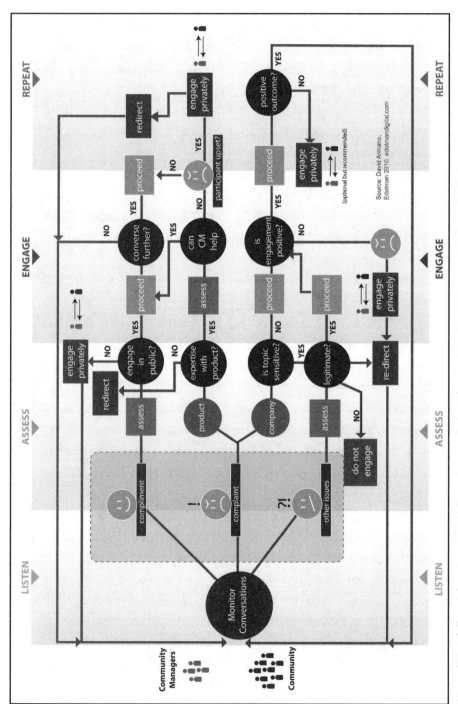

Figure 17.1. A full social customer workflow diagram (micro / macro) by David Armano, Edelman Digital.

has a good forecast about what Social CRM brands are going to develop around work flow in the coming years:

> The most important thing [in work flow] is to be able to help brands make decisions about what social customer issues to deal with first, based on job function and the level of service that you've decided to provide organizationally. We are working on different ways to prioritize and create rules around making that determination.

If you look back at Figure 17.1, you'll notice that the key touchpoint is the borderline between Listen and Assess. Fong agrees that this is the most important spot in the work flow. But Armano's work flow is missing something really important: the presence of existing customers (i.e., the peer-to-peer armies of reference customers) in that touchpoint.

"The next really important thing," Fong said, "is to make sure there's a strong connection between monitoring and response—but not just the company responding. To scale social media programs, companies need to foster conversations so their best customers are more visible and more present in more venues."

Let's get one thing straight: even the leaders in the Social CRM community are a little freaked out about this whole work flow automation thing when it comes to the social customer.

The reference customer issue "is one reason we blanch a little bit at the word 'automation,'" Fong said. "Of course, we want to provide our customers technologies that make social interaction more scalable, but 'social customer automation' is a bit of an oxymoron. You can't automate social. Social interaction is never credible with a machine, and it's not always entirely credible from a brand. It's highly credible from a peer, and even more credible from a friend. Our job is to make that kind of interaction available as often as possible."

In the above quote, Fong provides us with a hierarchy of trust for work flow automation. Here it is again, from most trustworthy to least trustworthy, so design any and all automation with this scale in mind:

1. Customer's friend
2. Customer's peer
3. Your brand
4. Some kind of auto response from your brand

Most of the CRM platforms are a little bit vague (and, really, non-committal), as far as making promises of how CRM platforms will automatically help companies react to customer events on the social Web. That is why a lot of companies are taking matters into their own hands, and writing lots of custom code and custom work flows to make this stuff happen, and why they mimic their existing business processes in sales, marketing, and customer service.

Robin Daniels, Director of Product Management, for Salesforce. com: "Salesforce.com's vision of Cloud 2 is a world where computing is in the cloud, real-time, social, and available anywhere, on any device. But it all has to tie back to ensuring that our customers are succeeding with salesforce.com. With that commitment, we'll review our road map on a regular and frequent basis to ensure we're meeting the needs of our customers."

Daniels works directly on Chatter, the Facebook-like social collaboration product that Salesforce launched in 2010—many companies use it for the Enterprise Collaboration use case. Keep in mind he made that quote a few months before Salesforce made the big decision to acquire social media monitoring product Radian6, and incorporate it into their product.

Also, uses of products initially intended for Social CRM, like Chatter, are beginning to get into Enterprise Resource Planning. Social CRM solutions can trigger non-CRM work flows—this is important to remember, as it can save your team tons of time and money.

"One good example is Durham's [North Carolina] Counter Culture

Coffee," Daniels said. "[They] use Chatter to track inventory of their beans and kick off work flows to order more if needed."

HOW BIG SHOULD THE SOCIAL CUSTOMER TEAM BE?

Although we initially addressed this in Chapter 13, we should check back on the table where we had our first "sizing" recommendations around the social customer. Flip back to Table 13.1, Two Views: How Many Full-Time Staff Do You Deploy Against Your Social Media Program. *Ignoring this table could cost your company millions.*

I don't know exactly how many employees are in your company, but you can look at the table and see right off the bat, that your number will be somewhere between one and 25 team members (unless you are following the Holistic Honeycomb approach, where the whole company's going to participate, but that likelihood is *very* low). Let's consider a few scenarios for brands that are in the "formalized" stage; maybe they've been dabbling in social media and Social CRM for the last two years but are now ready to make it an everyday business strategy, cross-functionally:

- **Small company.** One thousand people. A small company like Virgin Airlines could get away with a team of three to eight full-time employees (FTEs) internally, stretched over about three or four departments, plus agency partners, working in a coordinated approach.
- **Medium company.** Sixteen thousand people. Hallmark Cards is a good example here. I'm thinking five to eight FTEs, stretched over nearly as many departments, in a coordinated or hub-and-spoke approach (the latter if you're on the larger side), plus agency partners.
- **Large company.** Eighty thousand people. You're a Microsoft-

sized software company. I'm thinking eight to 20 FTEs, stretched across about eight front- and back-office departments in a coordinated or hub-and-spoke approach, plus agency partners.

If you don't remember what these approaches (coordinated, hub-and-spoke) look like, just turn back to Chapter 2 for a quick refresher.

WHAT SHOULD ESCALATION PATHS LOOK LIKE?

Escalation paths are an important part of your brand's work flow around the social customer, because they answer a tough question: *who does this need to go to, if the first responder doesn't know how to help the customer?* None of your social customers want to hear, "Let me go get your waiter," to paraphrase Seth Godin. Here's how to avoid that problem.

This is truly one of the toughest questions in the book, and the answer here depends on one thing: do escalations and work flows need to cross the firewall to your partner companies or supply chain? If the answer to that question is yes, then you have a number of things to take into consideration. If the escalation paths stay within the walls of your company, then the answer's a lot simpler. Most work flow in a Social CRM outputs to one of four things:

1. E-mail alert sent to someone
2. Task assigned to someone in a system-of-record
3. Creation of something: a "case" for customer service, a "lead" for marketing or sales
4. Field update on a record, in response to something the customer does, either by phone, mail, the Web, or mobile

One critical concept to keep in mind when developing work flows around the social customer is the "last interesting moment." I'm not sure if this was developed by marketing-force automation brand Marketo, but I've seen it most prominently displayed in their software, and it's a great phrase. What it means is: *what is the last interesting touchpoint this customer had with your brand?* That touchpoint could be across any medium—mobile, Web, mail, retail, or even in-person. This may be a little spooky, but if your customer is using the *New York Times* iPad app, and they just clicked on your ad in that app, maybe you *should* know. Each brand will have to make decisions on what level of data is appropriate.

To determine who needs to be a part of each work flow, here are the recommended questions I'd put each work flow through:

1. Who are the external stakeholders on this issue?
2. Who are the internal stakeholders on this issue?
3. Does this work flow account for each of the three types of social noncustomers?
4. If not, how should it be enlarged or restructured?
5. Does the work flow create any additional steps that will annoy or anger the customer?
6. Does the work flow incorporate all necessary social metadata?
7. How does this work flow leverage the "last interesting moment" of the social customer?
8. What are the "exceptions to the rule"?
9. Does this work flow need to "cross the firewall"? If so, is partner response time sufficient?

If your brand's suppliers and partners use the same Social CRM platform as your company, that's great. Most of the bigger SCRM platforms (Salesforce, Oracle) offer a sort of shared instance, or the availability to share certain data types (e.g., just customer service, or delegating leads down-channel once they reach a certain level of maturity). That said, this usually isn't going to be the case.

We need to get technical here, and talk about Web services for a moment. That's why most of the Social CRM platforms (even the smaller ones) have some sort of partially open API, and most are based on a protocol specification called Simple Object Access Protocol. SOAP is the foundation of the house on which all Web services between you and, say, your biggest supplier can be built. This way, coordinating work flow over two drastically different CRMs (like your company's Salesforce and your supplier's SAP) need not be a total nightmare.

You've seen references to mobile all over this chapter, as it's going to be critical to your brand's work flows. In the next chapter we'll explore all of the technologies that will be peripheral to your Social CRM strategy: mobile, social advertising, and social retail.

18

SOCIAL ADVERTISING, THE SOCIAL/MOBILE PLATFORM, AND INTEGRATION WITH RETAIL

As the social customer begins to dictate how advertising works, the advertising industry—which is usually thought of as a Madison Avenue institution—has begun to geographically spread out to places like Silicon Valley and Hollywood. If you had told Mad Men's Don Draper, in 1965, that there would have been a 200-person advertising network in Los Angeles, and ad agencies beginning to recognize Cupertino and Palo Alto, California as important destinations in the advertising world, he probably would have laughed at you. A lot has changed in 40-odd years.

Now that you understand the scenarios, the models, and the metrics, you need to figure out how to advertise to and reach the social customer at *every* touchpoint. Let's haul *Punk Marketing*'s Richard Laermer back on what social advertising *should* be:

> Sidle up to the customer, and tell them something they never heard before about you. Give the guys and gals *content*. Have a great time with them. Make them laugh till their guts spill out. Shock them. But don't think a slogan that you repeat—or the dreaded tag—will sell anything these days, except out of desperation. I've seen the words "So Good" being used as a tagline for five companies this year . . . and it makes me realize how little anyone thinks of the customer.
>
> That has to change quickly. Today, and tomorrow, and the next day, customers will find more ways to get what they want, contentwise, without ever looking at another ad or marketing ploy. Get used to it. And do something clever/smart/unique/compelling/weird before the person who replaces you does it for you.

Ouch! If you work in or with advertising, it sounds like it's time to choose whether you want to be the hammer or the nail with the social customer.

THE SOCIAL ADVERTISING SPACE

Before we go too deep into any one technology, let's step back and consider the size of the whole social advertising space, bringing back Kevin Barenblat, the CEO of that supercool social media management and marketing company, Context Optional (remember, the ones who make the product that lets you manage your million-fan Facebook page and sync it with your Social CRM). Barenblat's company's software helps big brands manage social, across hundreds of thousands of customer mobile devices, at once.

Let's look at where we're starting from, in terms of what brands are spending.

"Analyst firms like Forrester suggest that one-third of marketers spent more on social marketing in 2010 than 2009, and an additional 30 percent will invest in it over the next year," Barenblat said. So it's obvious that social ad and social marketing space is growing, fast.

"Data clearly demonstrates that [social marketing and advertising] is a category that will continue to grow aggressively," he said. "While nearly every brand out there is partaking in some form of social media, many are still new to the technologies that enable enterprise-level social marketing. By 2015 we'll be seeing this category mature and more brands having significant, work-flow-oriented social marketing platforms in place," Barenblat said.

The brands that are just dipping their toes into the water, and seeing the first fruits of success in 2010 and 2011, will be orchestrating those micro and macro work flows, around the social customer, just like Jacob Morgan suggested back in Chapter 2. The whole "Web goes social" concept, however, is going to be confusing for a lot of brands.

"The Web itself will become more social overall, making delineating online marketing from social marketing difficult," Barenblat said. And then there's the show-stopper: "The social ad market could exceed $20 billion by 2015."

That's about the size of the current Internet ad market today, according to the recent revenue estimates announced by the IAB and PwC US. (In late 2010 Internet ad revenues hovered around $21 billion to $24 billion, for the previous three years.)

Going Mobile

In the 2010 holiday shopping season, consumers using mobile devices accounted for 5.6 percent of the visits to retail Web sites, according to Coremetrics—a 50-fold increase from 2009.[1] Something is brewing on mobile. You want any of this revenue?

"More and more people live on their mobile devices," Barenblat said, "and tying social with mobile allows brands to create more personal and targeted connections with customers who expect a seamless experience."

Okay, so we've nailed down the basic value proposition: (1) a tighter connection with your customers and (2) a more seamless customer experience. Then there's the big one: geolocation. We're going to hear *way* more about that from Ian Schafer, from Deep Focus, later in the chapter.

"The two [having a tighter connection and seamless customer experience] complement each other in significant ways: from allowing brands to target customers with messages and discounts when they're at a specific location, to giving them an opportunity to 'check in' to locations for instant rewards. Social is inherently about sharing, and it's something that more and more people do not from their desk, but on the go," Schafer said.

Maybe mobile Social Customer Management is all about giving your customers something to do while they're waiting in line for that bagel, walking around in your store, or standing on line for that concert your company's putting on. Mobile social lets your brand leverage the tiny little bits and bobs of time. The reason it is going to be so huge in the next few years is due to three factors: (1) mobile devices like the iPad 2 and recent Android tablets are extremely capable and cheap, (2) nearly 75 percent of your customers are on the social Web, and (3) more and more of them are buying smartphones and tablets every day.

Group Social Marketing

Some people might call this Groupon-ing,[2] because that one brand has become such a ubiquitous name in the space, but there are plenty more. Group Social Marketing is a popular form of social event management or social campaign management. Each member of a group gets either a deeper discount to attend an event together, like a concert or a Statue of Liberty boat ride, or the discount does not exist until a certain number of people purchase the discount.

For example, a café could use Groupon by placing a minimum of 1,000 buyers on their $10 gift certificates. Once 1,000 consumers are reached, they and any additional customers involved with the promotion can purchase a $10 gift certificate for $5 (usually with stringent or time-sensitive redemption restrictions). The café makes, say, $20,000, and builds some serious brand awareness in the process. (This is serious business: group-couponing has a market cap in the 11-figure range. Google even tried to buy Groupon for about $6 billion in late 2010.) Today, there are three major players in the group social commerce space: Groupon, Living Social (which received a huge funding round from Amazon), and fashion/home brand Gilt Groupe.

SOCIAL CUSTOMER MANAGEMENT AND RETAIL

Duncan Angove is *the guy* who's standing at the intersection of Social Customer Management and big retail. When Angove's company, Retek, was acquired by Oracle in 2005 he organically came to run the business unit that was the company. Their mission: "to deliver innovative solutions that streamline and integrate all aspects of retail businesses."

"Here's how the social customer is going to integrate with retail," said Angove. "The first thing you have to look at is what the social customer sees on the shop floor. You can't put out the mix of products that the social customer wants without monitoring what the social customer is saying."

"We have a social data stream that we're able to pull off, in terms of what the social networks are saying." But the social network data isn't enough. You need to get down to what consumers are saying on a product-by-product level. "I'd throw another data set in there, BazaarVoice, for ratings and reviews."

If you remember BazaarVoice, this was the reviews-and-ratings solution used by my client, MBT Footwear, along with big consumer brands like Epson, Dell, and Petco—which reduced their product *return* rate 20 percent with this solution; talk about an outside-the-box Social CRM solution!

"Sometimes retailers build custom apps to get what they want," Angove said. Oracle customer Westfield Group (the folks who developed dozens of high-end American shopping malls) is a great example. "That social data helps them form merchandising decisions—it's social merchandising."

So, what does the retail of the future look and feel like? Well, for starters, there are lots of flat-screen monitors, and the edges of the shelves where products are kept are covered in QR codes little black-and-white boxes that look like television snow—if you live in a major city, you'll likely see them on transit billboards for clothing brands).

"[We have a] mock prototype of a store that merges social and mobile," Angove said.

When he walked into the store prototype, he connected his Facebook account with the store's loyalty application, and "it automatically checked me in. It knows my loyalty data and my Facebook data, because I've opted in." You read that right: the customer opts in, prior to even going to the store. Certain stores (those the customer likes) get access to this social data.

"Whenever I walk up to a shelf," Angove said, "instead of shelf-edge labels, there are QR codes—it gives me the shelf-edge label on my phone. It gives me more information than what would fit on my label. Because it knows my loyalty card, there may be personalized promotions that I can opt into as well. The challenge of bricks-and-mortar [shopping] is how to personalize it, but sussing out [customer] intent is very difficult."

Here we are, getting back to one of the central points of Paul Greenberg's *CRM at the Speed of Light*. The retail store of the future is a critical building block of the customer-intent-driven enterprise. And here's how it's done.

"Once people start interacting with shelves and products, they begin communicating intent. From [customer] loyalty data, we know past purchasing behavior," Angove said.

Oracle Retail has also partnered with a company that does near-field communication technology. Newsflash: the next generation iPhones and other smartphones will be Near Field Communication enabled. Sometimes referred to as NFC, Near Field Communication is a wireless technology (a little bit like the Bluetooth, which connects headsets to cell phones) that enables devices about four inches apart to communicate with one another. For example, the flat screens above the shelves turn into a customer dashboard that shows things the customer's friends have bought in the store.

"In a social world, you think about customers," Angove said. "They're deciding what their product assortment should be—it's based on what their friends like, or their friends' reviews.

"The biggest trend is 'how do you empower the customer.'" Angove is getting back to one of the six foundational premises of Social CRM: *if you help people control their own lives and fulfill their own agendas,* and *you're nonobtrusive and valuable* and *provide memorable experiences, they will like you.*

He highlights four best practices for working with the social customer at retail:

1. **Customer empowerment.** You have to give customers the tools to empower them. Giving lip service to the social customer (e.g., a low-value branded mobile application) is not customer empowerment.
2. **Social.** Customers have to be able to leverage their social graph of choice into your brand.
3. **Personalization of mobile.** Angove says, "Mobile is the fourth channel"—the other three are physical stores, Web sites, and catalogues (remember them?). Oracle isn't the only one that feels this way. Tech brand Cisco, which makes a lot of the hardware infrastructure Oracle's software runs on, has been pushing this line for a couple of years.[3]
4. **Transparency.** Complete data transparency between merchants and customers is paramount. You can't fool the social customer.

And here's where we get back to the use case of Dynamic Social Supply Chain reallocation. The combination of two factors—(1) the rise of the social customer and (2) the evolution of the supply chain—have caused permanent changes in certain industries, like apparel.

"All of the fashions that you would see on the catwalks of Milan—now it's available within *weeks*," Angove said.

Then, retail must understand the key customer touchpoint: experience—what customers see and feel when they walk into the store. The biggest one is in merchandising. The guiding question here is: "How do we allow the customer and the community to make merchandising decisions?"

"We're seeing retail undergoing a huge transformation," Angove said, "the shift to 'share-of-wallet,' and retailers shifting to a strategy called New Brand Experiences. The best example for us is what we've done with Disney Stores."

Disney originally had a successful retail store chain in U.S. and European malls in the late 1980s, but the success eventually slowed, and costs increased. Disney decided to turn the stores into a licensed operation.

"The key there was when Disney bought back their Disney Stores from Children's Place, a few years ago, and Disney also bought Pixar. Steve Jobs was involved—he wanted to bring the same thinking to the Disney Stores—they should be the *box office*, but they're not," Angove said.

The question that Disney and Oracle asked themselves was: "How do we make a visit to a Disney Store the *best* 30 minutes in a child's day?" They found the answer by focusing on—you guessed it—customer empowerment.

"They built, like, a theme park in the new one," Angove said. "It's all iPhone-driven—you can control media—the customer's in charge of the experience." From a technical perspective, it's pretty brilliant, and it's all Oracle in the back end—the iPhone taps into the store's point-of-sale and inventory systems. Oracle is currently at work doing the same thing with Victoria's Secret.[4]

Integration

The next big challenge for big retailers, around the social customer, is integration—putting all of the pieces together. Generally, big social retail platforms like Oracle Retail have a whole set of APIs (the pieces that allow the retail software to connect to other systems), and the companies manufacturing them have a huge incentive to keep them as open as possible.

"The approach we're taking," Angove said, "is 'how do we make our product as open as possible,' in order to support innovation. The key is intersecting that data with customer purchases and customer clusters, and having APIs [down to] the store [level], so it'll be actionable."

Here's a real-life example: Oracle has customers using their point-of-sale applications on the iPod Touch. But the actual application on the iTouch isn't an Oracle app. Oracle's customers built these iPod applications, based on Oracle's business logic.

There's another big, tricky integration question. If a retail brand is already using an existing Social CRM, why would they additionally want to deploy a retail solution like Oracle Retail or Salesforce Retail, which has big customers like Starbucks, Häagen-Dazs, and Papa Murphy's Pizza?

"CRM passed retail by on the first go-round," Angove said. "Retailers don't really use Salesforce or sales force automation—they don't need those systems. They don't even use traditional CRM for much besides a call center."

The most Siebel CRM systems we sell in retail are for loyalty (i.e., Starbucks uses it for loyalty, eBay uses it for a call center).

"The key, really, is that retailers have to reinvent themselves, and if they have a legacy point-of-sale system, it won't be able to adopt these innovations or capabilities. The key question is: 'How do you intersect the three Venn diagrams—customer data/transactions, social (open APIs), product—and then manifest it while the customer is shopping?'"

And the reason why? Profit.

In Oracle's case studies, they've established a link between profitability and the use of Oracle Retail. ("Retailers running Oracle are 48 percent more profitable than their peers.") That said, there hasn't been any conclusive link between the use of Oracle's Social CRM products and profitability. Angove is quick to explain why:

> Remember when e-commerce came out? It's the same stuff. Anyone asking for ROI right now is *missing the point*. Retail is so desperately in need of reinnvocation—bad economy, so much change in so little time ... the solution *used to be* to just open more stores. But now, online, social and mobile are growing, and the customer dynamic is changing—it's the perfect storm. We'll look back on retail in 10 years and see this as a huge inflection point.

Besides the rise of the social customer, there's another reason everything's changing in retail: a big shake-up in the hardware.

"In the old world, point-of-sale systems were tied to hardware,"

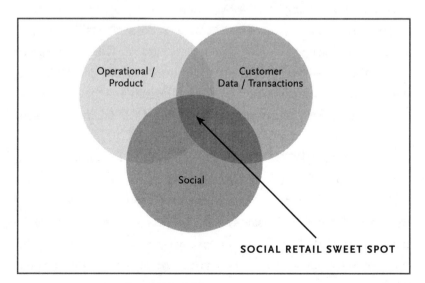

Figure 18.1. Social Retail Sweet Spot

Angove explains. And that hardware was expensive and locked-down, and run on platforms that brands could not innovate on. If new types of software like Oracle Retail (and their competitors) hadn't come along, even if retail brands had wanted to work with the social customer, *they wouldn't have been able to.* Angove joked:

"The guy who ran the CRM group said to me," Angove said, "'They should have called CRM 1.0 Customer Transaction Management.' It actually had nothing to do with *relationship* management. The irony is that the next generation of [retail] CRM is all about relationships, merchandising and supply chain. There are three circles in the Venn diagram (social, operational, customer), and that sweet spot [Figure 18.1] is in the middle."[5] QRCODE

QR CODES

Let's take a quick side road to one of the technologies tying consumer brands increasingly closer to customers that may not be 100 percent social, per se, for the last few years mentioned earlier in the chapter: QR codes.

We've all seen them on bus stops and advertisements: the small black-and-white graphics consumers can use as a special mobile application to photograph on their mobile phone. The small photo of the code then links them to a mobile microsite for the product. Previously, these codes were restricted largely to big brands—they started mainly with European fashion brands like H&M around 2007, and slowly worked their way into American automotive ads in the last few years. Lately, bigger brands like eBay have been using them in transit advertising.

I was intrigued when I received a press kit in the mail from a company called Paperlinks, which is aiming to embed QR codes in just about anything—party invitations, direct mail, you name it. Their idea is to make QR codes accessible to small businesses, or just about any

business, and to all levels of customers—social customers and nonsocial customers.

"Today, consumers experience content across a variety of platforms,"
said Paperlinks founder/CEO Hamilton Chan. "While digital replaces
offline media in newspapers, magazines, and even books, people continue to value the printed invitation, card, or announcement as a me-
mento of important life events. With Paperlinks you have the best of
both worlds: a beautiful, tangible keepsake and the convenience of digital communication."

Now, this isn't so much an outright endorsement of Paperlinks as
of creative technologies like QR codes, which bridge existing customer
collateral your brand has with the social Web, and to slowly persuade
nonsocial customers that there may be some value in getting them on a
slightly social (or at least mobile) platform.

GEOLOCATION

Facebook Places, Foursquare, and Gowalla have changed the way consumer brands work with their customers and prospects in 2010, and beyond, by allowing them to "check in to" stores, and even experiences (i.e.,
a circus, a football game). A few advertising companies, like New York's
Deep Focus, are leading the charge into this new space of geographically
enabled mobile Social Customer Management. Deep Focus calls this
division their "geofocus practice." You might know Deep Focus's work
if you've seen the social strategy in using the popular MadMenYourself
promotion in 2009, if you saw the social strategy for search engine Bing
or the popular game Farmville. Founder and CEO Ian Schafer explains:

> This [geolocation] practice was designed to give the agency
> ample opportunity to be leaders by example in the location
> space. Since we're an integrated agency, that means finding
> new ways to apply location information to improve experi-

ences consumers are having through any form of digital engagement, whether it be mobile, social networking, gaming, anywhere.

If your ad agency or your marketing team isn't experimenting yet with managing your customers on a location basis, it doesn't mean they're incompetent, but it sure means that they're not leaders. So, how do you make solid geolocation strategy? Understand what the data is there for.

"Regardless of the platform," Schafer said, "brands need to understand what they can do with location data. It can be used to actually add value for consumers—the 'distraction' method (commercials, display ads) is less effective than ever. And it's the key to unlocking mobile opportunities and leveraging digital media to move people physically."

When he says "move people physically," he means to move people to make a purchase right there. But how do you do that? You must add value *without* distracting the customer.

"Making the consumer the *center* of your marketing strategy," Schafer said, "changes the way you not only market, but the way you behave," referring back to the idea of the customer ecosystem that started this book. Making great geolocated experiences for the customer isn't simple, and it requires thinking across the enterprise.

"Those [geolocated customer] experiences are a result of location-informed strategic thinking emanating from every discipline (including media planning and buying, communications, creative and technology)," Schafer said. "We keep centralized repositories of information, and collaborate on experiences to maintain a silo-less environment."

But just because Schafer runs an agency known for creative work in Social CRM doesn't mean he advocates having external teams own the customer:

We actually don't advocate outsourcing customer management. We feel that it is best handled using internal resources. Instead, we recommend working with a firm like Deep Focus as

> a strategic advisor and tactical analyzer to build platforms for
> communications that result in the highest degree of quality en-
> gagement and contribute to the achievement of your business
> objectives—either directly, or through clearly defined proxies
> (or key performance indicators).

You've seen key performance indicators (KPIs) before in this book—the entire dashboards chapter focuses on what KPIs you should use, across all technologies that evaluate your relationships with your social customers. Schafer's forecast on where the intersection of advertising and the Social CRM space will go is no surprise; it rests on the promise of ROI.

"In order for Social CRM to break out, we need to be able to track the lifetime value of a consumer throughout social media—including Facebook," Schafer said.

"Right now, many issues (including privacy) are preventing marketers from truly understanding what social behaviors mean to their business objectives—in most cases, sales. If it becomes easier to track behavior, then the market will grow exponentially."

But Schafer is also a realist, knowing that big walled-garden social networks like Facebook won't open up and sell their data anytime soon (or cheaply, if they ever do).

"Waiting for Facebook to open their systems up is not very likely," he noted. "What's more likely is that we'll begin to use Facebook as the CRM measurement platform (as they develop it)—with third-party plug-ins providing ancillary data. There's no turning back from social influence, shopping, and transactions. I'm looking at the space growing to $5 billion and $7 billion in 2014 and 2015—these are fairly arbitrary guesses, but it's going to be huge."

Location-Based Services

We'd be totally remiss to leave this chapter without checking in with

Gowalla's Josh Williams. When you think about one of the coolest types of Social CRM (and social demand generation) to come out in the last few years, you're probably thinking of location-based services. We talked about this example a little earlier, when we referred to how customers can now use their mobile phones to "check in" on a social network when they arrive at your place of business or company. This is kind of an implicit endorsement of your brand.

"Although we cannot estimate the total amount of money brands have invested in location-based services at this time," Williams said, "a large number of brands have recognized the value such services present for marketing in the past year, and we will see an increasing number of brands investing in GPS-enabled applications like Gowalla in 2011 and beyond."

Well, even though that answer's a little vague, Facebook copied most of Gowalla's basic features to create their Facebook Places offering in September 2010. Brands that have done location-based Social CRM promotions with Gowalla include Disney, Toms Shoes, rock band Weezer, Sundance, and publishers like the Associated Press, the *Washington Post*, and *National Geographic*.

Disney, in particular, used a number of the Social CRM use cases, including Social Marketing Insights and VIP Experience. Here's how it worked: in November 2010, Gowalla partnered with Disney to provide a location-based experience at Walt Disney World and Disneyland Resorts. Hundreds of park locations featured custom stamps created by Gowalla. Visitors collected the stamps on their mobile devices in a virtual scrapbook. Park visitors also discovered and collected pins as a special reward for visiting featured spots, and virtual items were distributed throughout the park. One particularly creative way that Disney allowed customers to explore the park was by creating Gowalla trip "bundles," grouping attractions in the park by age or interest.

For example, their "For the Little Ones (under 44 inches)" is a track for small children at Disney's Magic Kingdom, in Florida, which includes tyke check-in spots like Peter Pan's Flight, Dumbo the Flying Elephant, and Mickey's Philharmagic. Step out of the Disney box, for a moment, and imagine what a suite of affiliated software companies could do with this at a trade show providing the right incentives.

BEST PRACTICES

Let's go over the basic best practices you need to account for when it comes to social retail, social mobile, and geolocation. Ask the following questions of your company or brand in developing your Social CRM plan:

Retail

1. How does social fit into the overall retail experience?
2. How does the retail experience address each of the three levels of social noncustomers?
3. How can you leverage your customers' devices for mobile-on-location? Does it allow for VIP experience, at retail?
4. How does retail holistically integrate with all other touchpoints your brand has with the social customer?
5. If you have multiple sales channels, or you don't have retail that your brand directs, how are you empowering your channel sales partners to have profitable relationships with your social customers?

Mobile

1. What are the integration touchpoints, on your Social CRM, for mobile?
2. Are customers specifically asking for branded mobile apps?
3. If not, do you have a thorough list of the mobile platforms customers are using, from your Web analytics?
4. How are you leveraging QR codes or similar paper-to-digital

technologies to account for the less technologically savvy members of your social customer community when they're on-the-go?

Geolocation

NOTE: for geolocation, before you even bother looking at solutions like Gowalla, FourSquare, or Facebook Places, these are critical questions to answer.

1. Do your social customers have any reason to use geolocation with your brand? (Saying that the competition is doing it isn't a good reason.) Does it fit your Four Actions framework?
2. What ways of enhancing on-premise personalization through geolocation can you think of?
3. If there's a resale channel, is there any way your brand can strengthen its resellers' relationships with customers via location-based services?
4. Does your geolocation technology of choice reconcile to your Social CRM system? If not, why?

This chapter should have helped clarify how most of the moving parts work that are not at the dead center of your Social CRM strategy—mobile, social, and retail are three critical extensions of this strategy. They enable the brand to be ubiquitous and receive sufficient touches to be meaningful to your customers. In the next two chapters we will cover legal and business development concepts. And trust me, you're not going to need to get to the business development and strategic alliance bits until you shush up your legal team. Good thing I brought in a good lawyer to help you.

19

THE SOCIAL CUSTOMER
AND THE LAW

You don't need to know, legally, the finer points of what you can and can't do with the social customer until you've actually picked your use cases and gotten the thumbs-up from a few senior execs, if you're not a senior exec yourself. (If you haven't done this, seriously turn back to Chapters 3, 4, and 5 and pick them, otherwise this chapter won't be too useful.)

Not a lot is written in the legal space on the subject of social customer legislation, so you have to pick through a number of legal journals and white papers to compile the appropriate information. I have attempted to break down the key U.S. legal decisions that affect the social customer without turning this into a painfully boring law book.

If you're going to approach lawyers, you have to think of it on their terms: *they just want legal proof that nothing your social customer initiative is doing is violating state or federal law,* or in the case of certain industries like financial services or pharmaceuticals, regulatory compliance.

The "social media policy" issue could also be raised by the legal department. They may ask "'Where is the social media policy'? We refuse to hear any of this until we've read your social media policy." But you don't even need to go there with the legal team. I'll give you a social media policy that's used by a $62 billion software company, Microsoft. Hopefully it's a big enough point of comparison to your company. Their six-year-old policy can be written on a cocktail napkin: "Don't be stupid."

There's definitely one piece of a legal journal that you'll want to print out before marching into their office. In 2008 a Santa Clara University law professor wrote a 26-pager called "Online Word of Mouth and Its Implications for Trademark Law." We'll quote it sparingly here, but it contains most of what you'll need to convince the legal team that your customers and prospects are not going to infringe upon your brand.[1] TRADEMARK

It's worth noting that the Wikipedia page on computer law[2] is comprehensive here as well, if you need a solid reference point, and it has many links to real legal journals that your brand's lawyers will like. (Don't tell them that you did any research in Wikipedia, even though it's been proven to be more accurate than nearly all encyclopedias— lawyers hate Wikipedia.)

MANAGING LEGAL RISKS

If your legal department's already freaking out about what the social customer means to them, don't worry, you can provide them with the information that follows along with a presentation that I highly suggest you review and adapt. Check out this presentation from social media law expert Glenn Manishin, *Managing Legal Risks in Social Media.*[3] MANISHIN (This deck packs more into 15 slides than I've seen in most legal white papers, and it's current. Seriously, if you don't have time to put together your own presentation, give this one, but make sure you give Glenn all the credit—the level of detail and insight are amazing.) Here are some highlights Manishin hits upon in his presentation:

- The adaptation of legacy rules applies. What has been done before will effect what is currently considered legal.
- While there have been plenty of defamation and trade libel cases on the social Web, there haven't been any "false light" case precedents.
- In the case of user-generated content, possession is *not* nine-tenths of the law. Manishin points out that there is "no present consensus on what is protected, what is public domain, and what is between (i.e., owned by Facebook)." This may trouble your legal team.
- Your brand's terms-of-service cannot create legal rights, and Twitter does not claim that copyright is not dispositive, because copyright ownership of content requires an original expression and not facts or opinion, which in 140 characters is difficult to satisfy.
- Genericide is a trademark or a brand name that has become the generic description for a product or service (Escalator, Aspirin, Xerox). The legal team perhaps may have even brought this up before the presentation, as dilution and user name infringement are hot topics today—just ask BP, which fought a fake and hilarious Twitter account after their fatal oil spill in early 2010.
- ECPA and CFAA laws may protect nonconsensual intrusion into third-party employee accounts. So the company can limit employee social media activities that are either work-related or use corporate I.T. assets, but in all likelihood *cannot law-*

fully hack into or otherwise gain nonauthorized access to employ-ees' social media accounts.

- Online privacy data is minimal, though Boucher-Stearns is working on a draft "discussion" version of the privacy bill. But as the House of Representatives has shifted and Representative Boucher lost his reelection bid, the dynamics of these bills are dubious at best. I swear, for every piece of good news you'll give the legal team, there's a piece of bad news. You might want to let them know this up front.

- HR postings and practices with social customers who are prospective employees can create Equal Employment Opportunity Commission (EEOC) and Title VII issues.

- All sponsored posts and content are subject to FTC regula-tion, state regulation, Lanham (Trademark) Act and tort ex-posure. It's a best practice to disclose everything, *even if that's not the law.*

- There are few judicial precedents around the social customer. In the "cauldron of litigation" it is likely that large social me-dia platforms will fare better than corporate GCs. Also, the ownership of social customer user-generated content is going to be a significant IP and human resources issue.

- How your company uses personally identifiable informa-tion—names, DOBs, phone numbers, etc., known as person-ally identifiable information (PII)—is imperative. Any time you hear of a company that did something very bad with PII, a large lawsuit is usually involved. Just remember what PII is, in case they ask.

For an additional supplement, here's a link to Manishin's entire collection of essays on the laws of social media and Social Customer Management.[4] They may cry when they see this stuff, but I'm unsure whether they'll be tears of joy or frustration. Like they say in the bald-ness cure commercials, your results may vary.

User-Generated Content

In regard to user-generated content, let's check in with lawyer Curtis Smolar, who discussed the topic in *VentureBeat*.[5] "A broad answer is that you own it and, most likely, the service upon which you post it owns it, too," Smolar wrote. "The key question is: what terms of use does that service require?"

Smolar provides a brilliant example of real-life dispute. The graffiti artist known as Banksy painted a mural on the side of an abandoned Packard plant. Banksy's people and the Packard plant owners disputed ownership of the mural (worth hundreds of thousands of dollars). Smolar asks two tough questions.

"Obviously, Banksy didn't own the Packard plant, but did the owners of the Packard plant own Bansky's copyrighted work? Could the Packard plant owners reprint the mural on other media platforms?" These questions open up a huge problem in U.S. copyright law, because the law protects any idea fixed in a tangible means of expression, but that is not how it works with online user content.

What the situation all boils down to is "the company can use, reproduce, and change anything you submit. It can also create subsequent versions, for any reason—and not pay you any money for the content's use. In return, you get the opportunity to use the company's Web site," Smolar said. Yes, you read that right. If the customer submits user-generated content to your Web site (or Facebook), your brand can do whatever you want with it (or Facebook can, or whoever the user signed the agreement with can), but *only* if the user signed some sort of terms-of-service agreement with you. (Most of the time the user just scrolls down to the bottom of all the legal mumbo-jumbo and clicks "I agree.")

International Law Around the Social Customer

Before moving on, let's take a quick look on what Manishin has to say on the subject of international legislation:

> "International legislation" may not be the right term, as [we] are referring to national laws and policies, rather than treaties, but in any event, there are many examples of both repressive and democratic regimes blocking [social customer destinations like] Facebook and Twitter, especially after the so-called 2009 "Green Revolution" in Iran. In France, Australia, and the UK, it's the "three strikes" model of banning file-sharing downloaders from Internet access and putting in place countrywide Web porn filters.

"These do not directly interfere in corporate marketing, but the effect of blocking off parts of the social Web is the same," Manishin said.[6] "See also the Venezuelan 'social responsibility' law just enacted,[7]" he added, referring to the bill that gives the government jurisdiction to create a government-run Internet hub, which could theoretically be used to censor Internet traffic.

MAJOR LAWS

The four pieces of law that we'll now explore are largely U.S. law, but international laws that compare are included.

1. Children's Online Privacy Protection Act

What is it? COPPA is a law that has been on the books since the early 2000s. It governs how brands collect personal information about anyone under the age of 13.

Who's broken it recently? Mrs. Fields Cookies and Hershey Foods are notable violations, but that occurred in the early 2000s, when these brands were likely unfamiliar with digital law.[8] In 2006 the social network Xanga had to pay a $1 million fine for violating this law—that's the biggest wrist-slap I know of here.[9]

How do we not break it? If you're collecting information from children under the age of 13, follow the guidelines written in the FTC's 1999 PDF.[10]

What's the international scope? This American law applies to foreign-owned or operated Web sites if they are "directed to children in the U.S. or knowingly collect information from children in the U.S." Australia has a similar law, and it's safe to assume that EU nations will likely pass similar legislation in the future.

2. Digital Millenium Copyright Act

What is it? DMCA is a new update to an old law, the Copyright Act of 1976, for the digital world. It makes it easy for copyright owners, like your brand, to challenge any Web site owner (or social customer) to remove or take down any content that is infringing. This law is pretty controversial because it has been proven to be used by businesses against competing businesses. Further, most times, when a social customer receives a takedown notice from a big brand, the platform that hosts it (e.g., YouTube or Facebook) is going to remove the content, *whether it's infringing or not.* The reason for this policy is because removing the content renders the platform without liability.

Who's broken it recently? There have been thousands of violations, the most notable in 2007 by Stephanie Lenz, a Gallitzin, Pennsylvania, writer and editor who posted a home video of her 13-month-old son dancing to Prince's "Let's Go Crazy" on YouTube. Universal Music Group, which owns the copyright to the song, asked YouTube to take it down. Lenz then did something unexpected; she claimed "fair use" and sued Universal Music. A U.S. District judge eventually ruled that copyright holders can't order deletion of social customer content (like this video) without determining whether the posting was "fair use."

How do we not break it? Do your homework before sending a takedown notice to the social customer. Make sure they read this quick article, "Fair use in a nutshell."[11]

What's the international scope? This law hasn't literally gone international, but the first part of DMCA is called the WIPO Copyright and Performances and Phonograms Treaties Implementation Act. This amends the U.S. law so it is in line with international law, the WIPO Copyright Treaty, and the WIPO Performances and Phonograms Treaty. The legal team will need to keep their eyes open, but it's fair to assume that DMCA laws will hold true in most of the 184 UN-member nations.

3. Section 230 of the Communications Decency Act

What is it? Also known as Title V of the Telecommunications Act of 1996, this law makes brands providing all the social platforms not liable for what people say on them. It also protects the social customers who "pass on" erroneous information from other social customers.

Who's broken it recently? Most of the platforms you know (America Online, Craigslist, MySpace, Google) have been *accused* of breaking it, but most of the time the platform gets off the hook, whether they're accused of presenting false information, sharing sexually explicit content with minors, or threatened with presenting discriminatory housing ads.

How do we not break it? It's not something your brand has to worry about breaking; rather, worry about enforcing protection for the brand against any social customers who don't fit each of the three criteria for immunity: (1) they're users of an "interactive computer service" (e.g., Facebook, Craigslist); (2) the information must be "provided by another information content provider," meaning that your customer wasn't the original person who said it; and (3) the cause of action asserted by your brand must "treat" the defendant "as the "publisher or speaker" of the harmful information at issue.

What's the international scope? It's really all over the place. You'll want to provide them with a link to the Wikipedia page that monitors this.[12] Keeping up on this one is a pain.

4. FTC Guidelines Regarding Endorsements

What is it? If you want to Google this, it's FTC File No. P034520. These are revisions to the 1980s laws regarding consumer endorsements that were modified by the FTC in late 2009. The 1980s version of the law didn't explicitly state that people who endorse your brand, as well as advertisers, could be liable for false or unsubstantiated claims. This means that any consumer or blogger who is incentivized (given money) to talk about your brand on the social Web is subject to the same FTC regulations as advertisers, regarding puffery and disclosure. Although it's been *rumored* that violations can go into the $11,000 fine range, the FTC guidelines never explicitly state this; penalties are to be assessed by the courts, not the FTC.[13]

Who's broken it recently? Obviously, the Interactive Advertising Bureau (IAB) is completely up-in-arms about this, as it's fairly disruptive to their revenue stream. I don't know of any notable violations.

How do we not break it? Print out a copy of "Social Media & the FTC, What Businesses Need to Know," by Dallas Lawrence, from Mashable,[14] for your legal team. It contains a great 1-2-3-4 compliance guide that's in plain English. The key points are: (1) realize that the legal enforcement environment has completely changed; (2) do a level-set with all of your online endorsers to let them know what tools they'll need to maintain FTC compliance; (3) monitor, on a moment-to-moment basis, what the endorsers are saying about the brand, using a robust social media monitoring system;[15] and (4) engage *against* your endorsers on an as-needed basis. If your brand sees an endorser posting misinformation or nondisclosing on the social Web, then you've got to get out there and regulate.

What's the international scope? Check by region; the United States appears to be leading the charge here.

In addition to understanding and explaining these four laws, print out a copy of the *Online Word of Mouth and its Implications for Trademark Law* PDF, by Eric Goldman, for your legal team. This is the number one reference for everything not covered in the above laws. One blog you will want the legal team to follow concerning the social customer is Goldman's Technology & Marketing Law Blog (http://blog.ericgoldman.org/). His opening sums it up: "Trademark law is wrestling with cybersquatting/domainers[16] the sale of keyword-triggered ads and other high-profile trademark disputes, but I believe that 'online word of mouth' poses the most important challenge to Internet trademark law."

The reason word-of-mouth (i.e., the natural habit of the social customer) worries the legal team is because, as Goldman says, "the broad reach of online word of mouth gives customers tremendous power to influence brand perceptions, and this has put doctrinal pressure on trademark law." Lawyers are fundamentally stumped because the social customer will not fit into one of the two neat little boxes of trademark law—commercial or noncommercial activity. What's happening now is that the courts are making often inconsistent rulings when applying trademark law to things the social customer does. When lawyers are confused, they typically err on the side of caution, saying, "Don't do it."

One thing that I also love about Goldman's white paper is that it proves the use (but not necessarily the legal legitimacy of the) whole pay-to-play concept, with stats showing that over 50 percent of senior marketing execs have paid for editorial coverage.

The crux of what you'll want to show the legal team is one of Goldman's tables, which clearly break down your brand's risk factors around the social customer (see Table 19.1). Trust me, they will love this one.

Do some competitive research (any basic social media monitoring solution, or even a few good Google searches, will work) to find out if any of your competitors have run into legal trouble around the social customer. Make a minicase study out of it, and indicate which law the competitor broke. Then write up three best practices on how your company will not make the same mistake.

BEHAVIORAL TARGETING

Your legal team will likely be concerned with behavioral targeting and consumer privacy, considering companies like Rapleaf, Kindsight, and Phorm. (The latter two are best known for what's called "deep packet inspection," and were well-profiled in the *Wall Street Journal* in 2010.[17]) Rapleaf and its recent fracas regarding behavioral targeting is worth understanding.

Basically, Rapleaf is just a database of consumer information that helps companies segment customers, infer consumer behavior across different types of social media, and find influential customers for or from their CRM systems. This database can even help companies with fraud investigations. There are definitely positive aspects here.

But in late 2010, Rapleaf was caught transmitting personally identifiable information, including MySpace and Facebook IDs, and scraping Facebook data for their database. Facebook banned them, and Rapleaf agreed to delete all of this type of data. If you want to learn the finer points of how behavioral targeting brands like Rapleaf work and still stay legally compliant, there was a great *Wall Street Journal* article about them.[18]

OTHER CASE LAWS AND LEGISLATION

There are also a few more pieces of case law worth noting when talking about the social customer, but you'll want to look at them on a case-by-case basis before putting them in front of your legal team.

"We can apply basic principles to predict what courts will do," Glenn Manishin said, "but so far there are few instances of reported decisions that say anything at all about social media."

Here are the three worth noting, especially as they apply to internal social customers (i.e., your employees):

Brand Perception Influences	Effect on Brand Perception	Trademark Owner Control
Product experiences	Significant	High
Trademark owner's advertising	Potentially significant	High
Third-party advertising	Often indirect	Low
Retail Interactions	Significant	Shared between retailers and trademark owners
Editorial publication	Significant	Low in theory, nontrivial in practice
Consumer word of mouth	Significant in aggre-gate, but each per-son's influence may be low	Low

Table 19.1. Goldman's Branded Content Risk Factors

Source: *Online Word of Mouth and Its Implications for Trademark* by Eric Goldman

- FDA citation of Novartis:[19] The FDA is also set to release so-cial media "guidance" for pharmaceuticals, scheduled for Q1 2011.

- The NLRB's assertion of jurisdiction over "protected activ-ity" of employees[20] on Facebook, *even where the company is not unionized.*

- The New Jersey Supreme Court's decision in *Stengart* v. *Loving Care Agency, Inc.*, reversing an older rule that employ-ees have no privacy interests in employer-provided e-mail sys-tems.[21]

We'll also want to fast-forward to the present, and get Glenn Man-ishin's take on how our current Congress will barely legislate around the social customer:

> I expect *nothing* of substance regarding social media to come out of our national legislature. They will continue to wrangle over Internet privacy and data breach notification

bills that have gone nowhere for nearly a decade. Despite its disclaimer of penalties, I suspect the FTC will, by default, start enforcing its sponsored post guidelines. Other than that, cyberbullying is the politically correct social networking issue for 2011. Congress may or may not give the FTC authority to implement its "Do Not Track" proposal.

Though some of the laws and legal issues surrounding the social customer may seem ambiguous, there are obviously many standard rules and regulations currently in place. It is imperative for your legal team to be familiar with the major publications, presentations, and laws discussed in this chapter, not only to keep your brand out of hot water, but also so they will not hassle you with trivialities that have already been resolved in regard to interacting with the social customer.

20

CONSUMER TRUST
AND ETHICS

I've seen hundreds of tweets like this one, from Andy Sernovitz, author of *Word of Mouth Marketing*: "Ethics alert: PR firm busted for social media deception http://bit.ly/de8D2a."

The link profiled Reverb Communications, a video game PR firm based out of Twain Harte, California, who had to settle with the FTC, in August 2010, for engaging in deceptive advertising "by having employees pose as ordinary consumers posting game reviews at the online iTunes store, and not disclosing that the reviews came from paid employees working on behalf of the developers," according to an FTC press release.[1]

"Companies, including public relations firms involved in online marketing, need to abide by long-held principles of truth in advertising," said Mary Engle, director of the

FTC's Division of Advertising Practices. "Advertisers should not pass themselves off as ordinary consumers touting a product, and endorsers should make it clear when they have financial connections to sellers." Back in the medicine shows of the 1800s, these types of customers were called "shills."

When I studied under Ivan Preston at UW Madison, in the late '90s,—he's the nation's foremost expert on puffery, basically "opinion statements" that brands make about themselves, like "Trojan: America's #1 condom" or "The best part of waking up is Folger's in your cup"—the Internet was just getting used to puffery. By 2011 it's probable that your brand *and* your customers will be engaging in puffery. Hey, it's still legal, right?[2] At this point you have no excuse for not only knowing the ethical best practices, but also the law around your social customers. **PUFFERY**

ETHICAL BEST PRACTICES

"Folks, if you lie in social media, you will get caught," Sernovitz said in a 2010 blog post.

In addition to reviewing internal policies, he recommends sitting down with your agencies (ad agencies, recruiters, and anyone else working on behalf of the brand) and giving them an in-depth social customer ethics training. Sernovitz's company, GasPedal (which put on a great best practices seminar series, BlogWell), is partnered with the nonprofit Social Media Business Council (McDonald's, Starbucks, Wal-mart, and other big brands are members), and they've put together a Disclosure Best Practices Toolkit. I'm not saying you must use this kit verbatim, but it's a great place to start[3] when putting together your ethics policies around the social customer. Here are three other tips from Sernovitz, and while they may sound a little scary, they're dead on:

1. The FTC enforcement campaign is just beginning.
2. Truthfulness and disclosure are the law, not an option.
3. You are legally responsible if your agency or any outsourced team does something sleazy in your name.

"You can't start an honest or open program of communications by lying to people or tricking people," Sernovitz said, in a September 2009 keynote.[4] (The video is a great and easily understandable primer of the 2009-10 FTC regulations.) If you work in the world of content (e.g., publishing, radio, TV), a good place to start would be the National Public Radio (NPR) social customer guidelines. It's a single page, and fairly clear.[5]

If your team protests about why the company needs to follow these precautions (besides citing legal liability—that one never fails), you can actually cite your company's existing ethics policy, and this quote, from Social Media Explorer's Jason Falls, the guy behind Makers' Mark's pioneering social customer program:

> Professional ethics and personal ethics are intrinsically tied together. You can't have professional ethics without a heavy dose of personal ones. And neither can be turned on or off. If you have them, others can tell because you are true to your word. You try hard to fulfill your responsibilities and obligations.

Also, Sernovitz's points mean that, legally, your "social media agency" or any agency to which you outsource customer relationship management creates liabilities for you.

Let's look at this from a different angle. What if you manufactured superhero capes, and your ad agency put ads on TV showing how children could fly wearing your capes, and then a child broke both of his legs jumping from a second-story window, wearing one? Would your brand be liable? Of course, the same goes for false advertising on the social Web.

"We live in a world where three out of four peers look to their friends for advice before they make a decision about their health, or a major purchase, or any other important issue," said Bob Pearson, CTO and media officer for WeissComm Group, a PR and strategy firm that works with big medical brands like Genentech and Alsius, in E-Commerce Times.

"Companies don't have the bully pulpit anymore. Rather, we have to earn our way into the conversation, and we accomplish this by being respectful, building trust and, essentially, behaving like a trusted peer. When clarity emerges, your reputation will be right in the center. It's worth wondering whether your board of directors would be proud of how you promoted and protected your brand. Think ahead a year or two and imagine this scenario."

And the ethics practices go all the way down the chain, into social commerce. "If your store doesn't live up to your company brand, then you don't get the chance to harness the power of your own satisfied customers," said Shel Horowitz, author of *Principled Profit: Marketing that Puts People First*, in an interview with *CRM Magazine*.

Horowitz says that automated responses to customer queries are ethically wrong-headed, as they don't provide the human experience. It reminds me of a post I saw on Andy Sernovitz's blog once. He grabbed a single sentence from the Whole Foods Web site and pasted it on his blog: "Many issues can be resolved with a quick phone call. This store can be reached directly at 512-476-1206." Mind-blowing. It's like the brand actually *wants* to help their customers. That's good Social CRM—printing your phone number on your Web site, and actually asking customers to call because you want to help them.

CONSUMER BRAND ETHICS

You don't need to be a statistics genius to know that feedback for any kind of customer interaction (e.g., surveys) is tainted by any incentives you provide them. When you're working with the social customer, if you want to incentivize them, that's fine, but not only does your brand have to be crystal-clear with the general public about who's being incentivized, but your customers need to know that if they evangelize the brand after being incentivized, without revealing this big, important fact, they could be liable for fines. So, let's review five rules for keeping your ethics straight with the social customer, while thrilling the legal team and keeping your PR team happy as well:

1. **Social customer policy.** It needs to be in plain English, and every employee needs to read and sign it upon being hired. It shouldn't be longer than a page. If your company doesn't have a social customer ethics policy, now is the time to draw one up, pronto.

2. **PII policy and security.** Your brand needs a clear statement of what you will and won't do with social customer PII (personally identifiable information), and what your partners can and cannot do with this information. There may already be some sort of customer data policy that just needs to be modified here.

3. **Agency partner agreement.** Like item one above, it should be signed by any third-party that touches your social customers—PR firms, marketing agencies, etc.

4. **Transparency and disclaimers.** Be transparent at all times, and indicate to your customers what they need to disclose— promos, freebies, beta testers, and loaners especially fall under this label.

5. **Every time the competition screws up here, reverse-engineer it.** Seriously, it could have been you. Figure out what they did wrong, and how you could have prevented the social customer foul-up from happening.

Consumer Brand Strategic Alliances

Let's take a moment to outline the strategic alliances that are key for companies to have a successful social customer strategy: You don't necessarily have to think of this as an all-inclusive checklist, but if you're going to skip one of these partnerships, you should probably have a good reason before presenting your social customer strategy to the rest of the company, because someone's going to ask why it's missing. Pay attention to where each of these entities need to touch your Social CRM.

1. **Customer relationship management brands.** Sometimes your Social CRM can be built on your existing CRM platform, sometimes it cannot.

2. **Enterprise resource planning** (sometimes). The relationship between Social CRM and enterprise resource planning can be fuzzy, but often (say, if you're an Oracle customer) those two systems may live on the same vendor platform. Investigate whether your Social CRM vendor has an ERP offering; having both on the same platform gives certain conveniences (possibly lower software and service costs), but brings other headaches (few vendors are great at both Social CRM and ERP).

3. **Search.** This has a bit more to do with your Web analytics than it would seem. If your search engine marketing team doesn't know the critical keywords that are bringing social customers to your brand (especially customers engaging in any branded communities), then the ROI from those searches will be inaccurate. Now that Yahoo's beginning to slide away, Microsoft's Bing offering is cemented as a minority player, and Google and Microsoft are embedding Social into search in 2011 (the key players in Social search are fairly clear).

4. **Monitoring.** As we saw from reading about the social media

monitoring systems (SMMS), this vendor relationship is absolutely critical. That's why I wouldn't be comfortable doing business with a brand of this type that won't be in business a year from now. Here's what I'd look for in a monitoring brand: connectivity, profitability, great usability, and solid leadership. I'm fairly certain that three of the bigger players—Radian6, Jive, and Lithium—have all four. Connectivity with the public-facing areas of all major social networks is now a table-stakes feature.

5. **Web analytics.** Any brand doing over $1 million per year in e-commerce revenue needs a real e-commerce solution, and probably a real Web analytics solution (unless you've got some crazy Google Analytics ninja, but even that's a stretch on millions in e-commerce, as companies with revenues of less than $10 million are beginning to hire senior Web analysts). The obvious name that comes to mind is Omniture, but Webtrends and Coremetrics still come up.

6. **Social network platforms.** There are the branded ones like Lithium, Jive, and their ilk (which sometimes refer to themselves as "Social CRM in a box"), and then there are the big ones you have no control over (Facebook, Twitter, etc.).

7. **Mobile app platforms.** This question isn't as simple as iPhone or iPad or Android; you want to think about what infrastructure is going to support all of your various mobile platforms, and, from a technical perspective, how it will reconcile to the CRM. Consulting teams may be helpful here, if your brand has limited mobile experience.

8. **Widget platforms.** One thing to remember here is that your brand's widget platform may be driving better analytics than your regular Web analytics if you have some popular widgets (just ask the Discovery Channel—I'm guessing their widgets on the social Web for certain shows may have become more

popular than their entire Web site). Figure out a way to integrate those analytics platforms, if possible, to give your team a holistic view of the analytics.

9. **Social commerce and social advertising platforms.** This is where you want to look at your current advertising and e-commerce platforms, and figure out a way to avoid having components siloed away from them. The last thing you want to do is create a second demand chain, from the social Web, especially if your brand works in an area that's hot in social commerce right now (e.g., apparel, travel/hospitality).

SOCIAL CRM PARTNERS

There's also something else that's crucial to remember: the critical difference between strategic alliances and vendor-client relationships on the social Web. If you've never done Social CRM before, you'll notice that a huge majority of the technology vendors are going to truly approach their clients as partners, as they recognize that this is a new space, and they're very eager to help your company evangelize your successes in the space.

As we begin to wrap up and review Social CRM practices internationally, this may be a good time to begin envisioning your company's multinational Social CRM use cases and top-level strategy for social noncustomers, with a local flair—because that's what the next chapter is going to help you do.

21

INTERNATIONAL FEEL

M ost business owners, and certainly most multinational businesses, understand that international expansion is going to be a key growth area between 2011 and 2020. Even niche *small business* publications like *Inc.* are publishing articles like "10 Steps to Start a Business in China."[1] The tricky part is that the social customer in each part of the world acts in substantially different ways.

"People in the U.S. have a tendency [to think] that 'if it worked in the U.S. it will work anywhere,' and that is not always the case," said Devious Media's Dave Andrews. "Think globally with social media since there are no borders with the Internet. Plan locally if you are seriously thinking about entering an international market."

Then there's another yellow flag on your international social customers: unrealistic budgets.

"Part of the challenge of working with international companies is their budgets in the digital space," Andrews said. "The digital ad dollars internationally are nowhere near that of the United States. These regions are trying to mimic what the United States is doing in the digital space with less resources, budget, and experience. This often leaves the project with too many priorities and not enough people."

So, what works for the social customer in El Paso, Texas, may not even work, one mile away, in Juarez, Mexico. That's why I hauled in a team of experts in each of these international areas to highlight the differences. Also, the BBC News published a pretty mind-blowing chart on the growth of Internet adoption from 1998 to 2008.[2] You'll want to consult this chart before planning anything. We're going to start by heading south from the U.S. border.

LATIN AMERICA AND SOUTH AMERICA

The *first* person I thought of to discuss international Social CRM was Jesus Hoyos, from Solvis Consulting—he's a sharp CRM consultant who lives outside of Miami, Florida, and he's probably been responsible for bringing Social CRM to hundreds of companies south of the border. His expertise lies specifically in Latin America and South America. You just can't get insight like this from someone who doesn't know the territory.

Here's how he first breaks it down; you have to take a four-zone approach, which takes mobile into account in a major way:

> You probably want to divide Latin America in four areas: Mexico, Andean countries, Argentina (South Cone), and Brazil. Focusing just in Mexico and Argentina (South Cone) you see the difference of social customers in two aspects: (1) e-commerce and (2) browsing.
>
> I would say that Argentina is more into e-commerce and

Mexico more into browsing. However, both countries like to create conversations on forums and dedicated sites such as www.apestan.com [apestan means "Your company stinks"].

In terms of being a "social" customer, I think it is a global trend: in Latin America we can search in both Spanish and English in order to find the content needed. And it does not matter which country; all social media places are growing, from Facebook in Argentina to Twitter in Mexico. But keep in mind that, in the end, the Latin American social customer is more active on the Net with a mobile versus a PC. Mobile is everything in Latin America.

Hoyos takes it one step further, explaining how the Latin American business climate is not fundamentally different from the U.S. business climate, in terms of how you work with this type of social customer. Do you need to do things differently for the Latin American customer? Not necessarily, but Hoyos clearly states that you need to give them equal priority with your North American customers. And their numbers are huge. As of 2006, Brazil had as many Internet users as the UK.

It is not different. But you need to act locally, and think globally. Whatever Best Buy or Ford are doing in social media, it is reflected in the Latin American markets. I would say that small business and local multinationals need to start creating communities for their consumers. ASAP.

If not, the Latin American consumers will go elsewhere to find this content. Keeping in mind that control of the content is something many local companies—especially family owned companies—don't want to let go. In Argentina and Mexico, many consumers are already native Internet users—where the executives from these companies are not.

Then there's the whole governmental regulation issue. Here's what Hoyos says you need to know:

> Countries are now presenting new legislative projects to protect the consumers on the Internet—from data collection to data security—[they're] going after everybody on the Internet chain of data—ISP, Telco, content providers, data hosting, etc. . . . the hybrid cloud will help ease these concerns, but [it] remains to be seen what changes these new laws will bring. It could take years in Latin America.

There's one last note. Social CRM customer care use cases and Social Demand Generation use cases are on the rise in Latin and South America:

> I see a tendency in Mexico to relate social media with demand generation, and in Argentina with customer service—specially setting up social media agents in call centers. I have been speaking to consumer-packaged goods and electronics companies, and all they want to do is generate sales via a cross-channel strategy using social media—this is the case in Mexico. But in Argentina it is all about customer service—[for example, people have] been able to drop your phone line via Twitter with all the checks and balances of doing this in the billing system.

So, to break down all of the best practices for the Latin American and South American social customer, here's what we can take away from Jesus Hoyos':

1. Take a four-zone approach to Latin/South American social customer strategy, because technological adaptations will differ by region.

2. When it comes to the sales use cases (Social Sales Insights, etc.), some nations are more adaptive than others (e.g., Argentina's ahead of Mexico).

3. Treat Latin and South American customers just as well as you'd treat North American customers; they're going to want their own branded communities, too.

4. Watch for some of the funkier use cases in Latin America and South America, including Social Demand Generation and Social Support Insights.

CANADA

The Social CRM situation in Canada may come as somewhat of a surprise. From all of the stats I've read, Canadians are actually *almost* as highly adoptive of social technologies as U.S. customers. It's kind of a surprise, given what we know of the number of tech companies in Canada, and the fact that the Internet infrastructure arrived later there than it did in the United States. (These Canadians are obviously pretty smart, as they did give us Rush and Neil Young, right?)

The eMarketer Daily Newsletter published a paid study in late 2010, called *Canada Social Media Marketing*,[3] and although the report itself focuses on the marketing use cases, the abstract features some key stats on the growth and projected growth of the number of Canadian social customers. Here's where we are today: the American average, from the Forrester Social Technographics Tool,[4] is that 73 percent of your customers in the United States are "social." That said, the Canadian average, from the eMarketer study, is 59 percent (the Forrester study says 64 person)—either way, at the present, it lags behind the U.S. percentage.

But the projections are what you need to pay attention to. By 2014, eMarketer researcher Mike Froggatt predicts Canadians will be at 68 percent adoption; which puts them *right up there* at U.S. levels. If you haven't begun strategic planning around U.S. or Canadian customers, you can essentially assume that they're similarly using social technologies. Here's a little color commentary from Froggatt: "Canadians readily adopt social network activities, often at rates higher than users in the United States, but gaining the trust of users on a social network is a brand manager's biggest obstacle."

EUROPE

Although Europe has historically been known, socially, for being more conservative than the United States, Canada, and Asia, 60 percent of European Internet users are social customers. Given the population of Internet users in the region (use varies dramatically between lows of 29 percent in Georgia and highs of nearly 95 percent in Sweden), there's likely an Internet user base of 475 million[5] people and 285 million social customers. European mobile social usage is rather similar to the United States, and the top four platforms in Europe (Facebook, YouTube, MSN/Bing, Twitter) bear a similarity to the top four platforms in the United States (Facebook, MySpace, YouTube, Twitter), so distribution among mainstream social channels is surprisingly similar on mobile, according to ComScore.[6]

The European population bears *very* serious consideration, and in the UK, Germany, Iceland, and Scandinavian, among others, social customer strategy will be critical. Although accounting for local language considerations may necessitate somewhat of a narrow-cast strategy, technographic adoption in this region is so high that it can't be omitted.

MIDDLE EAST

The Middle East is a region that has been growing fast, especially since 2010. Geolocation trends arrived in late 2009, as Foursquare expanded to the region.[7] Although Internet use was probably at 11 to 20 percent of the general population during the first decade of 2000, by 2011 those numbers are closer to 20 to 40 percent, according to a ITU[8] study.

As far as social customer percentages go for the Middle East, I'd expect that adoption parallels the most high-Internet-use countries in the region (Turkey, Iran, Israel), and that it's followed by Egypt, Syria, and Jordan. Before deploying serious financial resources in this region, I'd encourage you to check with a large social research/analyst firm like Forrester or Gartner to see if more current data is available.

ASIA

Metropolitan China, Japan, and South Korea have the highest level of adoption to social technologies of all of the nations profiled—it varies between 77 and 99 percent of the general population. This is where I anticipate levels to be in the United States by about 2014 or 2015. Socially, East Asia is actually about five years ahead of the United States. According to recent ComScore numbers, Japanese social customers were the most connected, with 75 percent of customers accessing mobile media in a given month (June 2010), and more than half of that group using mobile applications. Usage of these platforms was comparatively lower in the United States and Europe, at 43.7 and 38.5 percent, respectively.

Sadly, we have scant specific data on Southeast Asia (Vietnam, Thailand), but quite a bit of data exists on social technographic adoption in the Philippines. If you're wondering where the once famous social network Friendster still gets most of its user base, that would be the Philippines and Indonesia. Universal McCann put out a series of three studies, since 2007, and in a profile in the most recent study, noted that Filipinos were among the most highly adopted social customers, with 83 percent of respondents claiming that they're social customers. That said, there's one key stat to remember: only 10 percent of the population of the Philippines (91 million) are actually on the Internet. So, the social customer population of the Philippines is actually closer to the social customer population of, well, Michigan or Ohio.

One complication you're going to have with the Asian social customer, in nations like Vietnam and China, is Internet censorship. Although in the last two years the Chinese government has blocked many popular social platforms (Twitter, Flickr, numerous search engines, Wordpress, YouTube, and Blogger), numerous alternative platforms have been launched, including Tencent QQ[9] (sort of a cross between an instant messaging platform and Facebook/Zynga), RenRen (literally, "everyone network, and the eighty-fifth most trafficked site on the Internet), and these call for serious consideration. Of course, the political climate in China has to be monitored carefully before deploying serious resources against Chinese social customers[10] The Chinese government actually did launch a Twitterlike service called Red Microblog, to encourage local governments to master social media, in late 2010.[11]

AUSTRALIA AND NEW ZEALAND

Australian and New Zealand Internet adoption has always mirrored U.S. use, and Australian social customer usage is now nearly as high as in China and South Korea. Approach this area with some of the cultural and economic values of the European market, but with the technological bent used to approach Asian nations.

One cultural note: the Australian government has taken major issue with some of Google's practices, and like the U.S. government, are beginning to tangle with Facebook. Australia's communications minister Stephen Conroy has called Facebook a "corporate giant who is answerable to no one and motivated solely by profit."[12]

INDIA

The Indian subcontinent requires an *altogether different* approach. India is similar to the Philippines in that only a small percentage of the population is on the Internet. Out of 1.1 billion, Internet use is 81 million, only 7 percent. (About 7 million of this 81 million have access to broadband, so the stat implies that there's a very large mobile Internet infrastructure.)

The best study I've found on the Indian social customer was published by Blogworks/NM Incite (Nielsen McKinsey).[13] The biggest news that connected India to the rest of global social media platforms was Twitter's 2009 announcement of full SMS capability, which linked 110 million potential new users to the service (a majority of Twitter accounts are held outside the U.S.).[14] Usage on the service, in India, has increased more than 100 percent since the beginning of 2010, due to the use of Twitter by Indian politicians like parliamentarian/author Shashi Tharoor and Bollywood stars like Sharukh Khan, Priyanka Chopra, and Abhishek Batchan.[15]

According to this study, most in-India social customer management is B2C, and program ownership typically lives in marketing or sales silos. Channel usage seems to mimic top platforms in the United States, including Facebook, Twitter, and LinkedIn.

Again, to form a solid strategy for Asia, the Asian subcontinent, and Australia, you need to look very closely at how regional technographic adoption and cultural values are aligned against your brand's business objectives. Keep in mind that what works well in Barcelona, Spain, might be a disastrous failure 728 miles away, in Rabat, Morocco.

A December 2010 Mashable article by Jolie Odell profiles a current perspective of the Chinese government's take on the Internet: "China's attitude toward the Web comes across as simultaneously paranoid and confident—paranoid that freedom of information, be that Web pages with politically delicate keywords or images of government buildings, would only be used negatively; confident that the Internet can and will be controlled by the Chinese government."[16]

AFRICA

The data is a little scant for Africa, but mobile is critically important. Although the population of Africa is 1 billion, this is where the world's least adopted social customers live. In fact, there are a number of African nations where wired Internet infrastructure was never built, and the most common way for a new social customer to come online would be on their mobile device. Here's an example of how it works, from a 2007 *Business Week* article, "Upwardly Mobile in Africa":

> The 134 million citizens of Nigeria, Africa's most populous country, had just 500,000 telephone lines in 2001, when the government began encouraging competition in telecommunications. Now Nigeria has more than 30 million cellular subscribers.

According to Mashable freelancer Gregory Ferenstein, more than 33 percent of the African population now has a mobile plan—it's not clear whether they have Internet, but SMS and phone service, yes.[17]

There are also serious governmental Internet restrictions in northern Africa (Sudan, Nigeria, Ethiopia[18]), and few nations even have what is known as "pervasive censorship," which can be classified as "extreme censorship"—Egypt, Tunisia, and Libya. In a case of bizarre timing, the 2011 revolutions in Egypt and Tunisia lowered this level of "extreme censorship" to "moderate censorship," by that study's standards, mere weeks after I initially wrote that sentence!

That said, it's important to remember that Internet censorship also affects many developing and developed nations, including Australia and Malaysia. Writing social customer strategy for these nations will be very challenging.

Regarding South Africa, it's not too tough to form a cogent strategy around the social customer. There are 6 million[19] Internet users, so what you're dealing with is a social customer population similar to what you'd find in a large American metropolitan region, like the Bay Area or the Boston Metro area. Recent growth has been driven by the installation of a $600 million Seacom cable (under the sea) between Europe and South Africa. It looks like the blog index to pay attention to is Afrigator (sort of the South African Technorati), and Facebook and Twitter have sufficient traffic in South Africa (5 million and 570,000, respectively). The Facebook segment also mimics U.S. trends in that the user base is mostly female and over the age of 26. The other social network to look out for is MXIt, a mobile messaging and social networking client. According to their stats, they reach 40 percent of the South African population (though I find that hard to believe). One thing I've learned from personal interaction (my assistant Janine lives outside of Cape Town, South Africa)—their Internet, like much of Brazil, can be a bit spotty. Expect this to improve by 2016.

"If you are entering into a market," Devious Media's Dave Andrews says, "you need to find out how those users are going to interact with your brand in the social media space. If you are using social media in South Africa, you want to make sure it focuses around the mobile device. The users in South Africa are primarily using mobile devices to get on the Net and interact with one another."

Here are my best practices for working with the African social customer:

1. Regionalize into three segments (pervasive censorship, developing infrastructure, developed infrastructure).
2. Map out languages needed, per segment.
3. Pick a separate social customer use case (and platform) for each segment; it's likely that only an SMS-based strategy may be effective for the pervasive censorship category, if at all.
4. Evaluate quarterly, to see if levels of customer interaction are proportionate to other global strategies.

REGIONAL DIFFERENCES

As you can tell by now, regional differences among the social customer are tremendous. When planning internationally, it might be helpful to pretend that your company is not your company, per se, but to take a Coca-Cola-like customer outreach tack, and pretend your company consists of 15 different social customer agencies *representing* your company.

When assessing how to reach the social customer in each global region, you'll need to consider a few factors that are going to be drastically different, by region, including:

1. **Adoption.** Social technographic adoption. (How many of the population are social customers?)
2. **Mobile.** Prevalence of mobile and geolocation technologies.
3. **Culture.** What cultural differences do you have to account for, between this region and other regions? Are your local employees capable of managing the local social customers, across all touchpoints? Do you have weaknesses (i.e., retail, compliance, supply chain)?
4. **Competitive landscape.** Where does your brand stand, in position against social noncustomers in this region?

Economies. How do local economic factors affect your brand's approach to social noncustomers? Keeping these five factors in mind, plus all of the regional differences we've accounted for in this chapter, you'll be in much better stead pursuing the international social customer.

CONCLUSION

About a week after I began writing *The Social Customer*, I realized that this is the kind of book that's going to need to be rewritten every couple of years, simply because the technology involved in Social CRM is moving so fast, and because, with, every passing year, we're going to see more consumer and B2B brands having robust success building relationships with the social customer.

Throughout this text I have demonstrated the value to your customers of your brand executing on the social Web, on a large scale. We've been talking about doing it with a team of 20 or 30 or 40 people, spending about a few million dollars (or more)—including creative and soft costs—and discussed coming back with ROI that will allow you to do it again. And checking the metrics and dashboards every step of the way to provide value at every stage of execution.

Notice, we haven't mentioned anything about a "Social CRM department." Even the most recent international surveys and studies don't indicate that it's a best practice (or commonly done) to have a single-function team that handles Social CRM or social business. It's *everybody's* job.

We've looked at how C-level executives must delegate and craft assessable strategies for the consumer brands that they run. Just remember, while the tools and tactics discussed in this book may need to be revisited every year (which is equivalent to a decade on the social Web), the guiding strategic principles are hundreds, if not thousands, of years old. Only the tools are new.

Most of the research done for this book actually used Social Customer Relationship Management. For instance, I needed an example for Chapter 2 about how major consumer media brands like MTV were doing Social Event Management for consumer brands. Lisa Hausman, former VP of Marketing at Gigya, now at Rocket Fuel, Inc., (whom I'd previously spoken with by phone and e-mail) saw a tweet that I sent to her company and replied with a link. The CRM I was using at the time, Salesforce Enterprise, grabbed her tweet, and I appended it to her profile and then printed out an article on this exact subject, written by her company's CEO, in early 2010. All in less than the time it took to send an e-mail.

The Social CRM strategies discussed in this book are guided by the principles of the learning organization, with the goal that the strategy's stakeholders, the brand team itself, will iterate the strategy. Note I use the phrase "brand team," not "marketing team." As discussed, all too frequently initiatives that deal with a brand becoming "social" are relegated to a marketing team—usually about 55 percent of the time. Remember that for Social CRM strategy to truly become successful it must be cross-functional and distributed across as many departmental teams as possible. The buy-in and participation by teams routinely derided as "back office" (HR, Operations, etc.) is required. Key executive sponsorship is mandatory, not optional, if you want your enterprise to be successful with the social customer.

It would be inaccurate to say that any of the clients I've worked with, or any of the case studies mentioned in this book, are completely "done." Social CRM is an evolution, and these brands are evolving with their customers. Think of the evolution of "brand as social object" as a progression that goes uphill for a while, then plateaus, then goes up again, then plateaus again, and so on.

My goal in writing *The Social Customer* was *not* to prove that I was the authoritative voice on Social CRM. No one is. There are a lot of really good thought leaders, vendors, and consultants working in the field, and every one of them brings a different valuable piece to the table. I simply set out to break it all down into an understandable format so you can apply the best practices to your customers, and get right back to the work of running your business. I hope I've made all this information clear and understandable, and that it will help you figure out what you'll get out of it, before you get into it. Now you have the blueprint—you have to get in to get out.

I want to thank you for taking the time not only to read this book, but to truly interact with it, popping the little codes into the MetzBox, printing out white papers and presentations, and trusting me enough to bring me into your conference rooms and boardrooms. I look forward to getting the chance to work with some of you in the future, or speak for your company, or maybe just eat lunch with you while you tell me about your success in Social CRM.

I'm not going to just let you out at the curb here, either. We have a great afterword, from sales leader Rich Blakeman, from Miller Heiman.

You can ring my bell at adam@metz-consulting.com—thanks for taking this time to learn about the social customer with me. If nothing else, I hope you figured out how to get the people who kind of, sort of, love you (your social noncustomers) to love you a little more.

AFTERWORD

Rich Blakeman
Sales Vice President, Miller Heiman

I'm a self-professed and career-proven revenue junkie.

What else would you call someone who has spent 34 working years measured solely by revenue and its derivatives? For me, "monetizing" and "customer" (social or otherwise) are redundant: a customer exchanges money for results. You can't have a customer without money. Our firm has thrived for over 30 years helping many of the world's best companies improve sales performance and increase value as perceived by their customers: measured by revenue. It's like golf—there's no room on the scorecard for a description, just write down the number. Nothing hypothetical about revenue.

The common thread through this book connects two key dots in the customer equation: knowing why your customers uniquely do business with you, and taking actions that cause them to repeat that choice more frequently. The fact that they do business with you makes them customers, but an understanding of the *unique* "why" is more critical than ever when making social infrastructure investments.

But there is a catch: while you can't argue about revenue at the end of the day, people love to argue about "data."

In *The Social Customer*, this catch becomes even more challenging because there is less and less empirical data available when the data is *user-generated*. Whether the source is LinkedIn or Facebook or Twitter, all of the "data" has been generated by users. The value available to be created from social data becomes quickly useless without a framework or a context to place it in (a formal Social CRM). User-generated data has a potential for riches that can only be mined with the sharpest of tools and the most sophisticated of analytics.

I'm reminded of a story about an industry-leading sales executive (the CSO, or "Chief Sales Officer") who was confronted in an executive staff meeting by his CFO, who wanted to represent "what customers are saying." He was certain of his perspective, enhanced by his bravado. There was only one question, asked by the CSO: which customers have you talked to? Which ones specifically, and when?

It's easy to speak as if you know...until someone asks you to prove it. There are a dozen cases where this is true when viewed through this lens and rereading *The Social Customer*. Anecdotes without data and context are a thousand times more dangerous in the social realm than any other. In social customer data analysis, it could never be more important to make two critical tests: *So what?* followed by *Prove it!*

For those who get it right, I'll get out my wallet. Nothing hypothetical about revenue.

NOTES

Introduction

1. If you want to get a feel for the impact that Black Flag had on America, be sure to watch the film *American Hardcore*. The 2006 documentary is a fascinating picture of how hardcore punk changed American and global culture from 1978 to 1986. I also suggest reading Michael Azzerad's *Our Band Could Be Your Life*, examining the influence on DIY and the independent music culture of Black Flag and 12 other bands.

2. If you're looking for a book that teaches you or your team how to tactically use social media tools, Tamar Weinberg's *The New Community Rules* will do just fine, *but* it's not going to teach you brand strategy built around the social customer.

3. If you're a consultant and don't own a copy of this book, it's priceless. Just go to www.adammetz.com and type MILLION in the MetzBox to grab a copy. You'll see references throughout this book referring you to the MetzBox for additional content related to the material and other social CRM information.

4. Ronald D. Michman, Edward M. Mazze, Alan James Greco, *Lifestyle Marketing: Reaching the New American Consumer* (Santa Barbara: Praeger, 2003).

5. B.L. Ochman, Self-Proclaimed Social Media Gurus on Twitter Multiplying Like Rabbits, http://www.whatsnextblog.com/2009/12/self-proclaimed_social_media_gurus_on_twitter_multiplying_like_rabbits/.

6. "Low Power Radio: Lost Opportunity of Success on the Dial?" Leadership Conference on Civil and Human Rights, April 2009, http://www.civilrights.org/publications/low-power/consolidation.html.

7. His company is responsible for Mafia Wars and Farmville, and most of the wildly successful games on Facebook. In little over three years, Zynga has gone from nothing to $600 million in revenue. These guys are a threat to the biggest video game brands out there.

8. To get a ticket or more information on FAILcon, go to www.adammetz.com and enter FAIL in the MetzBox.

Chapter 1

1. To grab a copy of the best-ever book on brand personality, Rohit Bhargava's *Personality Not Included,* enter PNI in the MetzBox at www.adammetz.com.

2. I specifically remember the Apple LCII computer (40MB hard drive, color

monitor, modem port) that I purchased with my Bar Mitzvah money in 1990 as a technological milestone, as it was the first computer that allowed me to use the Internet.

3. Charlene Li and Josh Bernoff, *Groundswell: Winning In A World Transformed by Social Technologies* (Cambridge, Massachusetts: Harvard Business Press, 2008).

4. To pick up a copy of the seminal social media/social business book *Groundswell*, enter GROUNDSWELL into the MetzBox.

5. McEwen, William J., *Married to the Brand: Why Consumers Bond with Some Brands for Life* (: Gallup Press, 2005).

6. Dan McDougall "Child Labor in the Garment Industry: Uncovering the Truth," Global March Against Child Labour, 2011 http://www.globalmarch.org/gap/the_GAP_story.php.

7. "Melamine Pet Food Recall of 2007," U.S. Food and Drug Administration, March 2007, http://www.fda.gov/AnimalVeterinary/SafetyHealth/RecallsWithdrawals/ucm129575.htm.

8. To use the awesome Groundswell Social Profile Data, type GROUNDPROFILE in the MetzBox.

9. I know, I know. This stuff is 1980s technology. We've come a long way since demographic targeting.

10. The Forrester social technographic tool: http://forrester.com/empowered/tool_consumer.html. Josh Bernoff, *Empowered: Unleash Your Employees, Energize Your Customers, and Transform Your Business* (Cambridge, Massachusetts: Harvard Business Press, 2010).

11. CRM and the Enterprise Value Chain, Paul Greenberg/BPT Partners 2006–09, Slideshare.

12. If value chains are your thing, read Porter's *Competitive Advantage: Creating and Sustaining Superior Performance.*

13. As of this writing, few people under the age of 27 have a memory of a world without the Internet.

14. To grab a copy of Alex Wippurfurth's punky *Brand Hijack*, enter HIJACK in the MetzBox.

15. We're speaking, here, of clothing phenom (and Oracle Retail customer) Wet Seal, a clothing brand aimed at young women. They also integrated Contempo Casuals into their brand a few years ago.

Chapter 2

1. All of the data for the "percentage of companies using this model" comes from the Altimeter Group's white paper on the role of the community manager.

2. This is a hotel or restaurant chain that has multiple brands (i.e., WCG Hotels manages properties for Marriott, Embassy Suites, and a host of others).

3. If you don't know anything about customer experience management, and want to get a quick 60-second preview, type CEM into the MetzBox to watch a fun and easy video.

4. At this point you probably want to see what the "before and after" picture looks like for a brand that's done the whole "social customer" thing. Type HOLLYWOODPARK into the MetzBox to download a little eBook that I wrote on what happened to our client, Hollywood Park Racetrack, between December 2008 and April 2011, in the two-plus years they spent working with us.

5. Say what you will about Wal-mart, but the social customer shops there, and every single one of our CPG clients has sought to have a relationship with that customer. If you want the five-minute version of Walton's way, check out the two-dollar eBook.

6. To learn more about emotional intelligence, especially in organizations, check out www.eiconsortium.org. I also learned a ton about it studying under Annabelle Jensen, the president of 6seconds.org, a pioneering EQ trainer, who has trained over 10,000 teachers on EQ.

7. While researching this book I found an interesting blog post, *The 6 P's to Apple's Brand Loyalty* from Real Focus Media, Inc.: http://www.pitchengine.com/realfocusmediainc/the-6-ps-to-apples-brand-loyalty/72611/.

8. Businesses that have gone at least partly Mac include Home Depot, Oracle, Google, and the White House.

9. And Steve, if you're reading this, I wanted to apologize for yelling "Somebody get this kid away from the computer" at your son, Reed, on an April night in 1995. He was three years old and banging on the computer next to mine as I was racing against a deadline, trying to lay out the high school newspaper. That was pretty lame of me.

Chapter 3

1. To grab this one—the only book that I'll pretty much *insist* that my readers pick up—put CRMSPEED in the MetzBox. This book is so good (and is in such a fast-moving space) that it's been revised four times in under a decade.

2. Lauren Vargas, Radian6, "Are You Ready to Add the Social Layer to Your CRMStrategy?" August 3, 2010. http://www.radian6.com/blog/2010/08/are-you-ready-to-add-the-social-layer-to-your-crm-strategy/.

3. These "commandments" are heavily influenced by Vargas's blog post, as well as posts by CRM experts Wim Rampen and Paul Greenberg.

4. Another Weissism: many, many teams confuse strategy with planning on the social Web, and strategy with planning, period.

5. Bob Parsons, bobparsons.me, "16 Rules for Success in Business and Life in General," 2011. http://www.bobparsons.me/bp_16_rules.php?ci=21453.

6. If at this point you haven't read Tony Hsieh's (Zappos CEO) hilarious book, *Delivering Happiness,* type ZAPPOS into the MetzBox to add a copy to your wish list. If you want an "after" picture of what the social business looks like, this is it.

7. To use the Wayback Machine to check out your brand's Web site (or any brand, as it looked in the past), go to http://www.archive.org/web/web.php.

8. The *New York Times* write-up, containing the full breakdown of the Tropicana fiasco is here: http://www.nytimes.com/2009/02/23/business/media/23adcol.html?pagewanted=all. It's a must-read if you're looking for lessons on how *not* to relaunch a brand with the social customer.

9. New Coke lived for 77 days, and eventually prompted the brand to introduce Coca-Cola Classic.

10. If you need a good list of social Web contest brands, type SOCIALCONTEST in the MetzBox.

11. The original Ad Age blog headline read: "Tropicana Redesign Met with Serving of Haterade." Ouch.

12. To grab a copy of this influential marketing book, type PUNKM into the MetzBox. Seriously, if the Clash's Joe Strummer wrote a marketing book, this would be it. Great stuff.

13. You can follow Jacob's social business Tweets on Twitter, http://twitter.com/jacobm, and pick up a copy of his Twitter book, *Twittfaced,* by putting MORGAN in the MetzBox.

14. You can get your special registration code for that by putting SOCIALCUSTOMER in the MetzBox, where you'll be able to download tons more videos and documents on Social Customer Management.

15. If you want to know more about getting statistically significant samples in your social customer research, you're going to need a copy of K.D. Paine's *Measuring Public Relations.* Just type MEASURE in the MetzBox.

16. It's a pretty big business, for consumers—the mobile phone market finally started growing again in Q4 2009 and Q1 2010, per IDC. http://www.idc.com/getdoc.jsp?containerId=prUS22322210.

17. For a full list of solid listening tools for your brand to use, with or without a CRM system, type LISTENINGTOOL into the MetzBox.

18. To check out a demo of Radian6 for your company, type RADIAN6 in the MetzBox.

19. Radian6 also wrote a great white paper on how to categorize all of those Data Inputs, called "The Monitoring & Engagement Playbook." You can download it by putting R6WHITEPAPER in the MetzBox.

20. Wim Rampen developed this thoroughly in his excellent blog post, "Social CRM: What Relationships Should You Care For and Why?" http://wimrampen.com/2010/02/02/social-crm-what-relationships-should-you-care-for-and-why/.

Chapter 4

1. To download a copy of the whole original white paper, type 18USECASES into the MetzBox.

2. If you don't have this one on your iPod or iPhone, you're walking around without a copy of "Satisfaction" and "The Last Time." Fix this by putting OUTOFOURHEADS in the MetzBox.

3. You're probably wondering how I was able to take another consulting firm's white paper and mash it up so hard that it became an entire chapter of my book. Ray and Jeremiah were cool enough to do what is called Open Research, using an Attribution-Noncommerical-Share Alike 3.0 license. I'm also going to excerpt this chapter through Chapter 10 under that same license, as a free white paper, to push the research in Social CRM forward.

4. To link to a solid list of monitoring brands, just put MONITORING in the MetzBox.

5. I know, I know. "Automagically" isn't standard English. But it's pretty darn cool how these monitoring solutions work. Kind of reminds us of the first time we used Google, 13 years ago!

6. To watch a 60-second demo of how Faceforce works, type FACEFORCE into the MetzBox.

7. Before you go saying that Salesforce is mentioned too many times in this book, consider that something like 15 percent of the entire CRM market today is—you guessed it—Salesforce. I'm not saying this because I work for a company that sells their software (as well as a number of their competitors). I'm saying this to call attention to the fact that a majority of companies under $100 million end up going with their product. That's why you'll see their name a lot, because many of my clients have chosen them over the years.

8. If you're unfamiliar with Net Promoter, it's a pretty heavily used metric by large consumer brands that seek to understand the likelihood of whether a customer is going to say something positive about their brand or recommend the brand to a friend. For a quick and thorough explanation, type NETPROMOTER in the MetzBox.

Chapter 5

1. It is completely possible to partly outsource social marketing functions; I favor a blended approach.

2. I'll leave it to the PR firms and ad agencies to try to impress their clients with what are, in my opinion, meaningless twentieth century metrics like "fans" and "followers." I don't care how many there are, I just care what the business outcome of their "fandom" is. I'd rather have 10 fans who buy $100 worth of my product each than 1,000 fans who buy 90 cents each. Any blog post that

tells you the value of a fan is $6 or any given price without stating vertical market, churn, or a number of other buy-cycle factors is erroneous.

3. You would be shocked at how many brands use free services like SocialMention, HootSuite, or even (gasp!) Google Alerts, that *don't* connect to other company systems, wasting thousands of worker-hours per year of cutting and pasting. Seriously, spending an extra $1,000 on software might save you $18,000 in labor, plus the opportunity cost of whatever that employee could be doing besides cutting-and-pasting.

4. Another great Jeremiah Owyang blog post: Jeremiah Owyang, *Web Strategy*, "A Chronology of Brands that Got Punk'd by Social Media," May 2, 2008, http://www.web-strategist.com/blog/2008/05/02/a-chonology-of-brands-that-got-punkd-by-social-media/.

5. You can read more about this defining moment in consumer-brand Internet history in Keith Ferrazzi's *Never Eat Alone*, one of my favorite books, by typing NEA in the MetzBox.

6. A quick heads-up on pharmaceutical brands: any time a pharmaceutical brand is doing anything around Social Event Management, it's a huge sign that whatever use case they are engaging in has become a "mainstream" use case. On any kind of voice-of-the-customer or customer-facing technology, pharma is usually the last industry to "get on the boat," due to regulatory compliance issues.

Chapter 6

1. To get a good idea of how the study works and what the recent conclusions are, watch this video:http://www.youtube.com/watch?v=wHfr1w5YO8E&feature=player_embedded.

2. A lot of times certain Social CRM platforms work especially well with other pieces of software, like monitoring systems. That's why I refer to the combination of Oracle and Buzzient as a "cocktail"—the combination is endorsed by both vendors.

3. Dianna Dilworth, *Direct Marketing News*, "Direct Sales Through Social Clicks," May 17, 2010. http://www.dmnews.com/direct-sales-through-social-clicks/article/171758/.

4. Molly Prior, "Meet Mark Selling Products on Facebook," *Women's Wear Daily*, December, 11, 2009.

5. You almost have to look at Wal-mart to really understand consumer RFID. Miguel Bustillo, *Wall Street Journal*, "Wal-Mart Radio Tags to Track Clothing," July 23, 2010, http://online.wsj.com/article/SB10001424052748704421304575383213061198090.html?mod=WSJ_hpp_LEFTTopStories

6. For a link to Inbound Marketing University's 16-hour course on social media tactics for you or your team, type INBOUND into the MetzBox.

Chapter 7

1. To grab a copy, type CXI into the MetzBox.
2. http://www.youtube.com/watch?v=5YGc4zOqozo.
3. http://www.youtube.com/watch?v=6kQRFB-8cEs&feature=related.

Chapter 8

1. If you've ever wondered what SAP stood for, it's *Systemanalyse und Programmentwicklung*. In English, that's "System Application & Product Development in Data Processing."
2. Footwear analysts predict that the toning/shaping shoe brand market should grow from $375 million to about $1.2 billion-plus in 2011; MBT and Skechers, combined, are set to own nearly half of that market.
3. To reduce the Edsel's failure to an overreliance on customer demand is an oversimplification; poor positioning, design flaws, and a brutal economy also played into the legendary failure of that car model.
4. The Swiffer is well known as a product that was acquired by Unilever from what is called an ideagora—it's a marketplace of ideas for products that individuals put up for acquisition or codevelopment by big companies who have the resources to do it.
5. The Kotex article is here: http://www.destinationcrm.com/Articles/Columns-Departments/Insight/What-Is-Going-On-Down-There-67419.aspx.

Chapter 9

1. This company has come up as a case-study example for a social business earlier in the book. Part of the reason is that Southwest has been very forward about evangelizing their success in this area. Perhaps other brands are as successful or more successful, but they just have not put this volume of case studies out there.
2. Microsoft has realized that Google's a pretty big competitive threat to their long popular Microsoft Office package, because it lacks Enterprise Collaboration features, so they launched Microsoft Office Live (Office Web Apps on Skydrive), which is similar to Google's Google Apps offering.
3. Very few people know this, but Lotus did actually invent the first fully integrated social software suite, the not-so-successful Lotus Connections in 2007. That's a Paul Greenberg fact.

Chapter 10

1. Type CXI into the MetzBox to grab a copy. It's only six pages long, and there are plenty of useful charts.
2. To grab a copy of this book, type SAUCE into the MetzBox.
3. Anthony Alsop, "Which Geolocation Platform is Best for Sports Marketers?"

UK Sports Network, September 3, 2010, http://www.theuksportsnetwork. com/which-geolocation-platform-is-best-for-sports-marketers.

4. This is all total conjecture, but keep in mind that these location-based companies are tiny, and the technology is still emerging.

5. Yup, just type 23USECASES into the MetzBox to print the pdf.

Chapter 11

1. The best blog post I've ever read on SMMS is Jeremiah Owyang's "List of Social Media Management Systems (SMMS)" in *Web Strategy*, March 19, 2010. http://www.web-strategist.com/blog/2010/03/19/list-of-social-media-management-systems-smms/.

2. Former client of mine from the LaunchSquad days—they support social customers inside some big companies like Kodak, JetBlue, and McDonald's.

3. If you want to figure out how to manage all of your social networks in one daily e-mail, type 1SOCIALEMAIL in the MetzBox.

4. Andrew Hailey's "Web Analytics Is Dead: Long Live Web Analytics" in *Direct Marketing News*, August 15, 2006, is a great breakdown of the evolution of Web analytics: http://www.dmnews.com/web-analytics-is-dead-long-live-web-analytics/article/92341/.

5. Mind, these are predictions about what the next five years will look like in this space.

Chapter 12

1. Charlene Li and Josh Bernoff, *Groundswell: Winning in a World Transformed by Social Technologies* (Cambridge, Massachusetts: Harvard Business School Press, 2008).

2. Strategy is the part that makes people go out and buy a copy of Sun Tzu's *The Art of War*. In fact, you don't even need to *buy* the *Art of War* anymore, because it's free on almost any electronic bookstore. The excuses for not knowing the most basic business strategy are pretty much nonexistent.

3. Sources here include "Facebook hits 500M User Milestone," BBC News, July 21, 2010: http://www.bbc.co.uk/news/technology-10713199; Michael Arrington, "Facebook Now Nearly Twice the Size of Myspace Worldwide," *TechCrunch*, January 22, 2009, http://techcrunch.com/2009/01/22/facebook-now-nearly-twice-the-size-of-myspace-worldwide/; Wikipedia, "Friendster," http://en.wikipedia.org/wiki/Friendster; "Friendster Dying? More Like Growing," *Mind of Bitbot*, June 29, 2008, http://bitbot.wordpress.com/2008/06/29/friendster/

Chapter 13

1. This white paper is crucial reading for any person under the age of 40 who is in a hands-on role with social customers, if you want to avoid having to work at the social media help desk (i.e., the social media salt mines) for the rest of your career. Type CAREERPATH into the MetzBox to get this. Seniority level is typically Manager, Director, or Strategist for this type of employee.
2. Granted, you need to keep in mind that this study cuts across small, medium, and large businesses, so that could explain the slant of the budgets.
3. You can also check out their amazing Web site, www.blueoceanstrategy.com, one of the finest business book Web sites I've ever seen.
4. This is where I think the whole supply-chain piece really comes into play. Remember what Wet Seal did with the your-friends-picks?
5. Josiah Mackenzie, "Why Jim Zito of the Morgans Hotel Group Is Keeping Social Media Local," Hotel Marketing Strategies, April 23, 2010, http://www.hotelmarketingstrategies.com/jim-zito-morgans-hotels-social-media/.
6. Right about now you're probably thinking that social demand generation use case was a pretty good idea, huh?
7. If you want to use Blue Ocean's Createware software to do this, type CREATEWARE into the MetzBox. They'll hook you up with a three-day trial.
8. If you want to see how Gillette did it, just type GILLETTE into the MetzBox.
9. Mike Veseth, "[Yellow Tail] Tales," *The Wine Economist,* February 26, 2008, http://wineeconomist.com/2008/02/26/the-yellow-tail-tale/.

Chapter 14

1. Francis Buttle, *Customer Relationship Management* (Oxford: Butterworth-Heinemann, 2003).
2. This is another one of those chestnuts that I've adapted from Buttle's *Customer Relationship Management.*
3. I think I became a serious Fugazi fan around 1994 or '95, and still listen to them weekly, to this day.
4. Krigsman's "Five Tips to Learn from Failure" is a classic blog post from October 14, 2010, on ZDnet.com: http://www.zdnet.com/blog/projectfailures/five-tips-to-learn-from-failure/11187?tag=content;search-results-rivers.
5. This is where I.T. guys go to kick back and relax; it's basically the ESPN SportsCenter for enterprise software and CRM geeks.

Chapter 15

1. You can grab this one at http://tinyurl.com/lithiumCH.
2. If you want a slightly deeper dive here, the first chapter of Robert Handfield and Ernest Nichols's *Supply Chain Redesign*'s is great: Robert Handfield

and Ernest Nichols, *Supply Chain Redesign: Transforming Supply Chains into Integrated Value Systems* (Upper Saddle River, New Jersey: FT Press, 2002).
3. A *macher* is Yiddish for someone who gets things done—a big shot, a mover.

Chapter 16

1. Net Promoter, NPS, and Net Promoter Score are trademarks of Satmetrix Systems, Inc., Bain & Company, Inc., and Fred Reichheld.
2. NPS is calculated as the percentage of promoters minus the percentage of detractors. This is also a carefully tested loyalty metric; Satmetrix and Bain have used the approach with hundreds of companies, showing that customers with a higher NPS drive more revenue and results.
3. Marsden, Samson, and Upton, "Advocacy Drives Growth." London School of Economics, 2005. http://eprints.lse.ac.uk/21889/.
4. Cymfony press release, "Social Media Listening Platform from Cymfony Enables Faster, Easier Access to Metrics." September 15, 2010, http://www.cymfony.com/press-details/Social-Media-Listening-Platform-from-Cymfony-Enables-Faster-Easier-Access-to-Metrics/11.
5. Satmetrix, "Net Promoter Economics: Exploring the Relationship Between Net Promoter and Word of Mouth in the Computer Hardware Industry," http://www.satmetrix.com/research/wom_hardware.

Chapter 17

1. That said, if you want to download it, type R6PLAYBOOK in the MetzBox.

Chapter 18

1. Miguel Bustillo and Ann Zimmerman, "Phone-Wielding Shoppers Strike Fear into Retailers," *Wall Street Journal*, December 15, 2010, http://online.wsj.com/article/SB10001424052748704694004576019691769574496.html?mod=WSJ_hp_mostpop_read.
2. That, by the way, is called generecide, and you'll learn about it later, in the legal chapter.
3. Tim Green, "Cisco Predicts Mobile Will Be 'Fourth Channel' for Retail," Mobile Entertainment, 2008.
4. It shouldn't be a big surprise to you, at this point, that the Apple Stores also run on Oracle Retail.
5. To see a cool cartoon video of how QR codes work, type QRCODE in the MetzBox.

Chapter 19

1. Yup, you can download this awesome pdf by putting TRADEMARK into the MetzBox.
2. http://en.wikipedia.org/wiki/Category:Computer_law
3. To download the pdf, type MANISHIN in the MetzBox. This presentation is priceless. You can also access it here: http://manishin.com/law/presentations/SocialStrat_93010/SocialStrat_Manishin_9-30-10.htm
4. Glenn B. Manishin, "The Law of Social Media," LexDigerati. http://manishin.com/law/?p=1031.
5. Curtis Smolar, "Who Owns User-Generated Content?" *Venturebeat*, July 12, 2010, http://venturebeat.com/2010/07/12/who-owns-user-generated-content/.
6. http://manishin.com/law/?p=1806 and http://manishin.com/law/?p=1719
7. "Controversial Media-Law Changes Approved in Venezuela," CNN, December 22, 2010, http://edition.cnn.com/2010/WORLD/americas/12/21/venezuela.media.laws/?hpt=T2.
8. "FTC Receives Largest COPPA Civil Penalties to Date in Settlements with Mrs. Fields Cookies and Hershey Foods," FTC, February 27, 2003, http://www.ftc.gov/opa/2003/02/hersheyfield.shtm.
9. "Xanga.com to Pay $1 Million for Violating Children's Online Privacy Protection Rule," FTC, September 7, 2006, http://www.ftc.gov/opa/2006/09/xanga.shtm.
10. "Children's Online Privacy Protection Rule; Final Rule," FTC, November 3, 1999, http://www.ftc.gov/os/1999/10/64fr59888.pdf
11. Lloyd J. Jassin, "Fair Use in a Nutshell: A Practical Guide to Fair Use," Law Offices of Lloyd J. Jassin, Copylaw.com, 2010. http://www.copylaw.com/new_articles/fairuse.html.
12. http://en.wikipedia.org/wiki/Section_230#Legislation_in_other_countries
13. By highlighting finer points like this, the legal team will know that you really have your information together.
14. Dallas Lawrence, "Social Media and the FTC: What Businesses Need to Know," Mashable, December 16, 2009, http://mashable.com/2009/12/16/ftc-social-media/.
15. Yes, this means that the lawyers might want to use the Social CRM software.
16. These are people attempting to steal your Web domain or maybe even your brand's identity on the social Web.
17. Steve Stecklow amd Paul Sonne, "Shunned Profiling Method on the Verge of Comeback," *Wall Street Journal*, November 24, 2010.
18. Emile Steel, "A Web Pioneer Profiles Users by Name," *Wall Street Journal*, October 25, 2010, http://online.wsj.com/article/SB10001424052702304410504575560243259416072.html.

19. Adrianne Jeffries, "FDA Asserted Authority Not Only Over Social Media, but Metadata, too," ReadWriteWeb, August 18, 2010, http://www.readwriteweb. com/archives/fda_asserted_authority_not_only_over_social_media.php.

20. Steven Greenhouse, "Company Accused of Firing Over Facebook Post," *New York Times*, November 8, 2010, http://www.nytimes.com/2010/11/09/ business/09facebook.html?_r=4&adxnnl=1&adxnnlx=1289358911- EgmLbp7IeocXnExZ5bY4yw.

21. *Stegnart* v. *Loving Care Agency, INC., LCA*, Supreme Court of New Jersey, Findlaw.com, http://caselaw.findlaw.com/nj-supreme-court/1522648.html.

Chapter 20

1. "Public Relations Firm to Settle FTC Charges that It Advertised Clients' Gaming Apps Through Misleading Online Endorsements," FTC, August 26, 2010, http://www.ftc.gov/opa/2010/08/reverb.shtm

2. Preston's two books are probably the best on the subject, and you can get them by typing PUFFERY into the MetzBox. Great armchair reading, if you're into advertising and marketing.

3. http://www.socialmedia.org/disclosure/.

4. http://www.damniwish.com/2009/10/how-to-stay-in-compliance-under- new-ftc-social-media-regulations.html.

5. National Public Radio, "Social Media Guidelines," October 15, 2009, http:// www.npr.org/about/aboutnpr/ethics/social_media_guidelines.html.

Chapter 21

1. Issie Lapowsky, "10 Steps to Starting a Business in China," Inc., July 12, 2010, http://www.inc.com/guides/2010/07/how-to-start-a-business-in-china.html.

2. BBC, "SuperPower: Visualising the Internet," 2008, http://news.bbc.co.uk/2/ hi/technology/8552410.stm.

3. Mike Froggat, *Canada Social Media Marketing*, November 2010, available from http://www.emarketer.com/Report.aspx?code=emarketer_2000734.

4. This is the tool I generally use to get a thumbnail sketch of any given country's technographic adaptation to social technologies. The numbers are from 2009, and I anticipate they'll be revised sometime soon. http://www.forrester.com/ empowered/tool_consumer.html.

5. http://en.wikipedia.org/wiki/List_of_sovereign_states_in_Europe_by_ number_of_Internet_users.

6. Harrington Curve, "Mobile Media Trends: Who's Most Sociable and Where," PCWorld, October 10, 2010, http://www.pcworld.com/article/207341/ mobile_media_trends_whos_most_sociable_and_where.html.

7. Jennifer Van Grove, "Foursquare Goes Global with Launch in 50 New Cities," Mashable, 2009, http://mashable.com/2009/11/19/foursquare-50-more-cities/.

8. http://www.slideshare.net/akankshagoel/social-media-marketing-in-the-middle-east-handbook .

9. For a little perspective, Ma Huateng, the man who runs the service, has a net worth nearly equal to Facebook's Mark Zuckerberg.

10. The December 2010 12-page special in *The Economist* on the future of the U.S.-China relationship may be a helpful resource if your company is U.S.-based.

11. Charlie White, "China Launches Communist Version of Twitter," Mashable, December 15, 2010, http://mashable.com/2010/12/15/chinas-communist-twitter.

12. Ari Sharp, "Conroy Savages Facebook 'privacy,'" *The Age*, May 25, 2010, http://www.theage.com.au/technology/conroy-savages-facebook-privacy-20100525-w8bt.html.

13. "IndiaSocial Summit 2010—Insights and Learnings," India Social, December 21, 2010, http://www.indiasocial.in/indiasocial-summit-2010-insights-and-learnings/.

14. Mashable, October 14, 2009,. Twitter Adds 110M Potential New Users with SMS Deal in India.

15. Twitter Blog, October 2010

16. Jolie O'Dell, "WikiLeaks Cables Show a China Obsessed with, Afraid of the Internet," Mashable, December 4, 2010, http://mashable.com/2010/12/04/wikileaks-china/.

17. Greg Ferenstein, "How Mobile Technology is a Game Changer for Developing Africa," Mashable, July 19, 2010, http://mashable.com/2010/07/19/mobile-africa/.

18. Frank Jacobs, "170—A Map of the Internet's Black Holes," Big Think, August 31, 2007, http://bigthink.com/ideas/21222.

19. Eshaam Rabaney, *Thinking About Social Media In South Africa*, Slideshare, 2010, http://www.slideshare.net/eshaam.rabaney/thinking-about-social-media-in-south-africa-2953846.

INDEX

ABOUT THE AUTHOR

Adam Metz is the VP of Business Development at Metz Consulting, a social customer management-consulting firm, based in Oakland, California. Metz has consulted with companies since 2006 on how to acquire, manage, monetize and retain customers from the social Web. Metz's customer community, at http://metz.customerhub.net has nearly 500 members, and offers a no-cost 10-hour training course on social customer relationship management.

He is the first consultant in the space to devise a holistic social Web analytics model for clients, and his first book, *There Is No Secret Sauce,* has sold or downloaded over 3000 copies, and is currently in its third printing.

Metz specializes in social media marketing and social customer relationship management (social CRM) for consumer brands and loves lifestyle, travel, apparel and consumer-packaged goods (CPG) companies.

Adam Metz has consulted with over 73 consumer and tech brands, including Hershey's Chocolate, Waggin' Train Pet Food, Wente Vineyards, Pirate's Booty, MBT Shoes, Maestroconference, Obama Girl (Barely Political), Lynda.com, Passport Resorts, Hollywood Park Racetrack, The San Francisco Convention and Visitor's Bureau, Mighty Leaf Tea, Timbuk2 bags, and others. He also worked on the first social media program for Pulitzer Prize–winning author Thomas Friedman.

Metz has lectured at the University of California, Berkeley, the University of Washington, and University of California, Santa Cruz and has given keynote talks at numerous conferences and associations including the California and Minnesota Chapters of the American Marketing Association.

Adam lives in Oakland, California, with his fiancée Susan and dog Teddy.